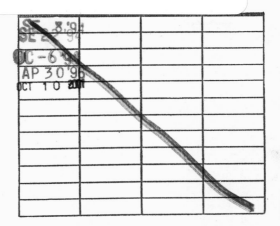

Environmental Change

Environmental Change

Federal Courts and the EPA

Rosemary O'Leary

Temple University Press
Philadelphia

Temple University Press, Philadelphia 19122
Copyright © 1993 by Temple University. All rights reserved.
Published 1993
Printed in the United States of America

The paper used in this publication meets the minimum requirements of
American National Standard for Information Sciences—Permanence of Paper
for Printed Library Materials, ANSI Z39.48-1984 ⊚

Library of Congress Cataloging-in-Publication Data
O'Leary, Rosemary, 1955–
   Environmental change : federal courts and the EPA / Rosemary O'Leary.
     p. cm.
   Includes bibliographical references and index.
   ISBN 1-56639-095-8 (cloth : alk. paper)
   1. Environmental law—United States.   2. Judicial review of administrative
acts—United States.   3. United States. Environmental Protection Agency.
I. Title.
KF3775.045   1993
344.73'046—dc20
[347.30446]   93-6637

For my parents,
Mary Jane Kelly
and
Franklin Hayes O'Leary

Contents

Figures and Tables

Preface

This book presents the findings of a four-year study of the impact of federal court decisions on the policies and administration of the U.S. Environmental Protection Agency (EPA) in all seven of its major statutory areas: clean air, clean water, hazardous waste cleanup, controlled pesticide use, resource conservation and recovery, safe drinking water, and control of toxic substances. I used the Lexis and Westlaw legal data bases to generate a list of all cases in which the EPA was either a plaintiff or a defendant in each of the agency's seven major statutory areas.[1] I verified these data and at times supplemented them with EPA records and with environmental reporters published by the Bureau of National Affairs and the Environmental Law Institute. I derived settlement agreements from the EPA, the Department of Justice, and the courts.

To begin this study, I read over 2,000 federal court decisions, examining nine key components of each case: (1) the laws involved, (2) the plaintiffs, (3) the defendants, (4) the subject matter, (5) the outcome of the case, (6) judicial actions, (7) the court orders, (8) the response of the EPA, and (9) follow-up actions by the court and the parties to the suit. Out of that group of cases, I targeted 1,400 for further review, based on indications of possible impact on the policies and administration of the EPA. (For a complete list of the 1,400 cases, write to me at the Department of Public Administration, Maxwell School of Citizenship and Public Affairs, Syracuse University, Syracuse, NY 13244-1090.) I expanded upon these cases by interviewing members of the staff of the Office of Management and Budget and the Congressional Budget Office, members of the staff of an environmental interest group, and over forty past and present EPA officials.

I reviewed twenty years of agency memos, archival material, and court documents and perused EPA budget and personnel documents as well as policy documents derived from several sources, including Freedom of Information Act requests. The study also drew on Office of Management and Budget reports, congressional hearings and studies, General Accounting Office reports, Office of Technology Assessment reports, and Federal Register notices. Environmental newsletters and newspapers provided supplemental information.[2]

The job of data analysis and validation in this type of study is aptly described by Donald Campbell and Robert Yin as analogous to doing good detective work.[3] I used a pattern-matching process that fit multiple implications derived from explanation or theory, and I established "chains of evidence" and analyzed the credibility and logic of explanations.[4] I then pitted arguments against each other to ascertain logical inconsistencies, reviewed conclusions by major informants to ensure more than a single perspective, and used cross-case analysis to compare and contrast cases.[5]

After I collected and analyzed all the data, I wrote an essay describing and analyzing the cumulative impact of all cases on the EPA in its seven major statutory areas. That essay, which is the concluding chapter of this book, discusses patterns of court involvement with the EPA, the impact of court decisions on the agency's policies, and the impact of court decisions on the management of the EPA. Then, to aid the reader in understanding the complexity and diversity of the impact of individual court decisions on the EPA, I developed several case studies. From all the cases reviewed and analyzed, I selected examples for case studies first to demonstrate the different policy issues facing the EPA in court and then to demonstrate the array of judicial actions and the different EPA responses to such judicial actions. Finally, I divided the cases between those that were upheld and those that were reversed.

Interviews with EPA employees proved helpful in the selection of case studies. Given the diverse political, economic, and social inputs in an organization's environment, the impact of court decisions on any organization is probabilistic, with causality difficult to ascertain. Therefore, only the cases with the strongest chains of evidence linking EPA organizational changes with court decisions are presented in Chapters Two through Six. To be selected for inclusion as a case study, a change in policies, procedures, rules, regulations, or budget had to be evidenced and strongly linked with a court decision.

This book is designed to be easily accessible to a broad variety of readers, both academic and nonacademic. It is intended for public administrators, students, attorneys, environmentalists, conservationists, and the general public alike.

Many people have commented on earlier papers or draft copies of this volume, and I deeply appreciate their frank and helpful critiques. David Rosenbloom (American University) provided early encouragement and unflinching faith in my abilities, as well as inspirational critiques of what were often very rough drafts. Other readers of the complete manuscript include Phillip J. Cooper (University of Kansas), Patricia Ingraham (Maxwell School, Syracuse University), Harry Lambright (Maxwell School, Syracuse University), Marie Provine (Maxwell School, Syracuse University), Lettie Wenner (Northern Illinois University), Paul J.

Culhane (Northern Illinois University), Richard Schwartz (Syracuse University College of Law), and Charles Wise (Indiana University).

Readers of individual chapters, usually in the form of conference papers, include A. James Barnes (former deputy administrator and general counsel of the EPA, currently dean of the School of Public and Environmental Affairs [SPEA] at Indiana University, and my official mentor at SPEA), Dick Bauer (deputy regional administrator of the EPA's Chicago Regional Office, formerly deputy regional administrator of the EPA's Seattle Regional Office, and a first-rate colleague at SPEA), Daniel Fiorino (senior EPA policy advisor and deputy director of the EPA Office of Policy, Planning and Evaluation), Richard Miller (chief of the Planning and Analysis staff, Office of Surface Mining, Department of the Interior), and Jim Perry (professor, Indiana University).

Lynton K. Caldwell, who served as my informal mentor as a colleague at Indiana University, deserves thanks for offering invaluable advice on publishing. Kevin Wood and Kelly Johnson, my able graduate assistants at Indiana University, deserve thanks for their research assistance, as do four helpful graduate assistants at the Maxwell School: Heidi Koenig, Robin Lamott, Jennifer Burrell, and Chris Bates. I thank Santa Falcone-Grannis and Bruce Riddle for their help with graphics and Esther Gray, Karen Bernal, Rhonda Allen, Kathi Clark, and Pat Grimsley for typing several drafts. I thank my editors at Temple University Press, Doris Braendel and Joan Vidal, for their professional treatment of my work and Sally Bennett for her expert copy editing. A special note of appreciation goes to my husband, Larry Schroeder, as well as to my closest scholar-friends: Casey Cleary-Hammerstedt, Rita Hilton, Phil Joyce, and Dan Mullins. Their laughter and friendship helped relieve pressures on many occasions.

Finally, I owe many thanks to the women and men of the

EPA who were the subject of my research. I began this study, quite frankly, with a negative view of the bureaucrats who run our nation's most important public environmental organization. I ended my research a few years after the EPA's twentieth anniversary with an immense amount of respect and awe for those same public servants. Given the propensity of businesses and environmental groups to sue the EPA, and the propensity of Congress to encourage such suits through sometimes irrational statutory provisions, it is amazing that the EPA is able to accomplish anything. To have done so much with so little is a terrific service to our country.

Abbreviations

AEA	Atomic Energy Act
AFL-CIO	American Federation of Labor and Congress of Industrial Organizations
ALJ	Administrative Law Judge
AO	Administrative Order
APA	Administrative Procedure Act
APHA	American Public Health Association
ANPR	Advance Notice of Proposed Rulemaking
BAT	best available technology
CAA	Clean Air Act
CEQ	Council on Environmental Quality
CERCLA	Comprehensive Environmental Response, Compensation and Liability Act (or Superfund)
CFR	Code of Federal Regulations
CMA	Chemical Manufacturers' Association
CWA	Clean Water Act
D	Democrat
DDT	dichloro-diphenyl-trichloroethane
DOE	United States Department of Energy
EDF	Environmental Defense Fund
EIS	Environmental Impact Statement
EO	Executive Order
EPA	United States Environmental Protection Agency
FIFRA	Federal Insecticide, Fungicide and Rodenticide Act

FOIA	Freedom of Information Act
FWPCA	Federal Water Pollution Control Act (also known as the Clean Water Act)
GAO	United States General Accounting Office
GOCO	government-owned, contractor-operated facilities
HEW	United States Department of Health, Education and Welfare
ITC	Interagency Testing Committee
LEAF	Legal Environmental Assistance Foundation
MOU	Memorandum of Understanding
mrem/y	millirems per year
NCP	National Contingency Plan
NEPA	National Environmental Policy Act
NMP	National Municipal Policy
NRC	Nuclear Regulatory Commission
NRDC	Natural Resources Defense Council
OMB	Office of Management and Budget
PCB	polychlorinated biphenyl
PL	Public Law
POTW	publicly owned treatment work
ppm	parts per million
R	Republican
RCRA	Resource Conservation and Recovery Act
SAB	Science Advisory Board
SARA	Superfund Amendments and Reauthorization Act
SDWA	Safe Drinking Water Act
TSCA	Toxic Substances Control Act

Environmental Change

Setting the Stage

Chapter One

You get two days in the sun at the EPA. Once when you come and once when you leave. Every day in between it rains on you.
—WILLIAM D. RUCKELSHAUS

In 1966, in one of her frequent trips to a family cabin in rural upstate New York, Carol Yannacone was shocked to find hundreds of dead fish floating on the surface of Yaphank Lake, where she had spent her summers as a child. After discovering that the county had sprayed the foliage surrounding the lake with DDT to kill mosquitos immediately prior to the fish kill, Yannacone persuaded her lawyer husband to file suit on her behalf against the county mosquito control commission. The suit requested an injunction to halt the spraying of pesticides containing DDT around the lake.[1]

Although the Yannacones initially were able to win only a temporary one-year injunction, they set into motion a chain of judicial events that would permanently affect the policies of the then-nonexistent U.S. Environmental Protection Agency (EPA). For it was through this lawsuit that a group of environmentalists and scientists formed the Environmental Defense Fund, a not-for-profit group dedicated to promoting environmental quality through legal action. After eight years of protracted litigation, the Environmental Defense Fund won a court battle against the EPA that Judge David Bazelon heralded as the beginning of "a new era in the . . . long and fruitful collaboration of administrative agencies and reviewing courts."[2] That judicial decision triggered a permanent suspension of the registration of pesticides containing DDT in the United States.

The Yannacone case is only one of several hundred court cases that have affected our nation's most important environmental agency since its inception in 1970. This book is about the impact of federal court decisions on the policies and administration of the EPA in all seven of its major statutory areas from 1970 through October 1, 1991. It is important for several reasons. A large public agency with a staff of over 17,500 and a budget of more than $6.94 billion, the EPA is responsible for implementing most federal laws designed to protect the environment. The EPA has jurisdiction over the air we breathe, the water we drink, and the food we eat. Its far-reaching regulations penetrate every level of our society. With each lawsuit filed in federal court concerning the EPA there is the possibility of change, both positive and negative, in important policies and regulations that affect our collective health and the environment.

Moreover, environmental policy and environmental administration are growing daily as important areas of study. In 1990 the EPA concluded that the United States devoted 2 percent of its gross national product to controlling pollution and to cleaning up the environment.[3] As new sources of pollution are discovered and the full impact of old and new sources of pollution becomes more fully understood, the delayed effects on our ecosystem become increasingly apparent and the percentage of the gross national product that is devoted to pollution cleanup is expected to rise. The policy questions and administrative challenges inherent in environmental issues are of interest to academics and nonacademics, public managers, environmentalists, conservationists, and members of the general public alike. In 1991, for example, a Gallup poll reported that 78 percent of U.S. citizens think of themselves as environmentalists.[4] That study also reported that 71 percent of U.S. citizens favor protecting the environment even at the risk of curbing economic growth. Two-thirds of the respondents expressed concern about contamination of drinking water and pollution of lakes, rivers, soil, air, and beaches. More than one-half (57 percent) said they would choose immediate, drastic action to save the environment.

At the same time, several authors maintain that judges are becoming increasingly active in their oversight of administrative agencies.[5] Judges in many instances are no longer passive reviewers of agency actions but are full participants, shaping litigation and its outcomes.[6] Some say a new relationship, a "partnership" between the courts and public agencies, has been forged,[7] and administrators and scholars are hotly debating the nature of the effects of the new judiciary-agency partnership.

This "critical case study"[8] of the courts and the EPA challenges much of the conventional wisdom about judicial influence on agency policy making and administration espoused by modern authors and other contemporary thinkers, both conservative and liberal. This challenge is accomplished through the analysis of both a range of changes in EPA policies and procedures across statutory areas and a range of reactions evidenced by EPA administrators to court decisions. By providing a broad window into the world of the interaction of the EPA and federal courts, this case study yields a more complete understanding of the impact of court decisions on public agencies.[9]

Setting the Stage: The U.S. Environmental Protection Agency

When President Richard M. Nixon called for a major reshuffling of federal agencies to create the Environmental Protection Agency in July of 1970, he did so apparently less out of an interest in cleaning up the environment than out of concern for his own political career. Two months earlier, on Earth Day—April 22, 1970—millions marched to demonstrate their commitment to a less polluted earth. Public opinion polls showed that U.S. citizens ranked pollution second only to crime in their list of the most serious domestic problems.[10] Nixon had been in office for two and a half years, and his most visible challenger in the next presidential election was Senator Edmund Muskie (D-Maine) who had preempted the environmental policy field on the national level. Nixon apparently wanted to take the spotlight off of Muskie and other Democratic environmental legislators and shine it on himself.

Initially the EPA was given no new functions or powers by Congress or by the president. When the agency opened its doors on December 2, 1970, it began operation for fiscal year 1971 with 5,650 employees and a budget of $1.4 billion, combined from several different federal programs and departments (see Table 1). The largest organizational components were taken from the National Air Pollution Control Administration, housed in the Department of Health, Education and Welfare (HEW), and the Federal Water Quality Administration, housed in the Department of the Interior (see Figure 1).

The reorganization was bitterly opposed by Walter J. Hickel, then secretary of the interior, who had proposed that all environmental programs be shifted to his department and that the name be changed to the Department of the Environment. (Hickel was

Table 1
The EPA "Inheritance"

Inherited Subunit	"Donor"	Number of Personnel	Fiscal Year 1971 Budget ($ millions)
Federal Water Quality Administration	Interior	2,670	1,000.0
Bureau of Water Hygiene	HEW	160	2.3
National Pollution Control Administration	HEW	1,100	110.0
Bureau of Solid Waste Management	HEW	180	15.0
Pesticides Regulation Division	Agriculture	425	5.1
Office of Pesticides Research	HEW	275	10.7
Research on Effects of Pesticides on Wildlife and Fish	Interior	9	0.2
Bureau of Radiological Health	HEW	350	9.0
Federal Radiation Council	Intra-agency	4	0.1
Division of Radiation Protection Standards	Atomic Energy Commission	3	0.1

Source: Kennedy School of Government, *William Ruckelshaus and the Environmental Protection Agency,* Case #C16-74-0270.

dismissed by the president a few months later for taking too harsh a stand against perpetrators of oil spills.) Clifford M. Hardin, Nixon's secretary of agriculture, and Robert H. Finch, Nixon's secretary of HEW, also vigorously opposed the creation of the EPA, apparently fearing a loss of programs and power. Although the plan was accepted by Congress generally, it was

Figure 1
EPA Organization Chart, December 2, 1970

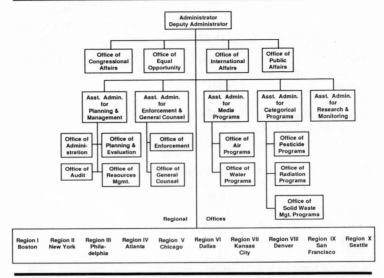

Source: Council on Environmental Quality, *Second Annual Report of the Council on Environmental Quality* (Washington, D.C.: Government Printing Office, August, 1971).

criticized by many congressional committee chairpersons who were afraid that the reorganization would lessen their power over particular departments and agencies.

The creation of the EPA was initially supported by many industry officials, who wanted one federal regulator, not several, establishing pollution control standards. A 1970 *Fortune* magazine poll concluded, for example, that 53 percent of the executives surveyed approved of having a single federal agency to implement pollution control programs. Moreover, the same survey showed that 57 percent of the executives supported increased environmental regulation. Eighty percent of the respondents said that they favored environmental protection even if it would inhibit new products, cause production to become stagnant, and reduce profits.[11] The new agency was also supported by conservationists who believed that no organization charged with promoting the development of a natural resource (such as minerals, oil, or forests) should be charged with protecting the environment against the potentially negative effects of this development. Joining the conservationists were those who delighted in the smashing of long-held bureaucratic strongholds. For example, the new agency was heralded in a *New York Times* editorial as "the triumph of imagination over the politics of special interest."[12]

The early months of the agency were tumultuous. On his first day as administrator of the agency, William Doyle Ruckelshaus pledged to "go after the polluters," adding that antipollution enforcement must be "as forceful as the laws provide." Urging the "development of an environmental ethic," Ruckelshaus said that the United States could no longer afford the unbridled progress symbolized by "industrial smokestacks belching their poisons into the air."[13] In return, the new EPA director was immediately confronted with an administrative proposal to withdraw the tax-exempt status of public interest groups that file environmental lawsuits and a presidential proposal to relax regulations concerning oil spills.

In other areas, the EPA has been caught between the White House, which generally has expressed concerns about the potential negative impact on the economy that pollution control laws may have, and Congress, which generally has sought to push the EPA toward rapid pollution cleanup. A prime example is the 1970 Clean Air Act. The EPA estimated that $320 million would be needed in fiscal year 1973 to implement the law. President Nixon officially requested only $171.6 million: $148.4 million less than the EPA's estimated need. Congress eventually upped the ante, authorizing $300 million for that year, and the Clean Air Act was shepherded through Congress by Senator Muskie. When the president held a ceremony to sign the act, however, Senator Muskie was excluded from the invitation list.

The Nixon administration's lukewarm treatment of the agency also was reflected in the continual lack of support exhibited by other federal agencies. When the EPA proposed guidelines to aid states in drawing up plans for implementing the Clean Air Act, for example, it asked other federal agencies for comments. The Federal Power Commission (now the Federal Energy Regulatory Commission) objected to the EPA's preference for the use of low-sulfur fuels in power plants, citing the need for more electricity. The Commerce Department objected to the economic infeasibility of the plan, citing the lack of opportunity for states to take into consideration the ability of individual plants to meet the Clean Air Act regulations. And the Department of Defense objected to the fact that military installations and major defense contractors were not exempted from the antipollution plans.

These battles over political turf between the EPA and other federal organizations continue today, exacerbated by an increasingly complex political and economic environment. The EPA of the 1990s is continually caught between competing interests— the president, Congress, the public, environmental groups, and industry. As soon as they feel the cost of regulation, industry groups complain, and politicians wince, putting pressure on the agency to back off. An example is the statement by Senator Jake Garn (R-Utah) that if the EPA failed to "clean up its act," then as chairperson of a congressional budget committee he would "do anything he . . . [could] to gut . . . [the agency's] budget."[14]

Nevertheless, since the days of EPA Administrator Anne M. Gorsuch, when "sweetheart deals" with polluting industries were reported, politicians have become even more demanding of the agency and much more confrontational.[15] Accordingly, Congress's function in overseeing the agency has grown in a topsy-turvy fashion. The EPA originally had only a handful of congressional committees to deal with, and these were generally friendly (with the exception of Representative Jamie Whitten's Agricultural Committee, discussed in Chapter Three). Today over one hundred congressional committees and subcommittees are responsible for overseeing the EPA.

Organizational Structure

The EPA is organized in what Bruce Ackerman and William Hassler call a new approach to regulation.[16] Unlike most regulatory agencies, the EPA has one administrator, rather than a board or commission. The EPA administrator is appointed by the president and confirmed by the Senate, without the protection of the fixed term that is usually granted to heads of regulatory agencies.

By design the agency is not a member of the president's cabinet, but this may change in the 1990s. Several bills were introduced in Congress to elevate the EPA to cabinet status, but none was successfully endorsed by both the House of Representatives and the Senate as of July, 1993.[17] In November, 1992, William J. Clinton was elected president of the United States. One of Bill Clinton's campaign promises was that he would elevate the EPA to cabinet-level status. Senator John Glenn (D-Ohio), at the request of President Clinton, introduced a bill soon after the inauguration that would elevate the EPA to the cabinet. On February 24, 1993, however, the White House asked the Senate to halt consideration of the bill temporarily.[18] Congresspersons and environmentalists had expressed concern about President Clinton's announced plan to eliminate the Council on Environmental Quality (CEQ) and to transfer CEQ functions to the new Office of

Environmental Policy at the White House. Further, draft bills were circulating that would give all CEQ responsibilities not to the White House but to the EPA, and jurisdictional conflicts were emerging among congressional committees. As of the writing of this chapter, Senator Glenn and President Clinton were attempting to address these controversies before proceeding with the

Figure 2
EPA Organization Chart, 1992

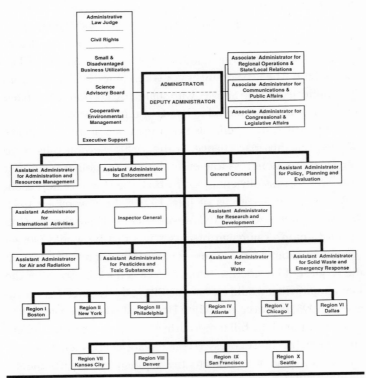

Source: U.S. Environmental Protection Agency Office of Public Affairs.

elevation of the EPA to cabinet status. At the same time, Carol Browner, the new EPA administrator, was participating fully in the president's cabinet and was fostering discussion among cabinet members concerning the coordination of environmental policy among federal organizations.

Many maintain that the additional prestige derived from cabinet-level status would be more than offset by a lack of effectiveness prompted by increased pressures to support presidential programs regardless of their effect on the environment. Moreover, because environmental problems cut across so many jurisdictions and the EPA is forced to work with a myriad of federal agencies, many believe that the independence of the agency is essential.

The EPA comprises a headquarters with eleven core offices located in Washington, D.C., and ten regional offices. Although the agency was originally conceived as an organization molded around "functional" administrative offices (such as research and monitoring, planning and management, and standards and compliance), it has evolved into a combination of functional and programmatic units (see Figure 2).

EPA regional directors and assistant administrators are a mix of those who have made their careers in antipollution work and those who received their appointments primarily because of political connections. In the first year of the agency, Ruckelshaus became involved in a fight concerning these appointments. In July of 1971, one environmental newsletter wrote:

> The scramble for EPA regional directorships . . . [is]
> nothing short of ghoulish. Apart from the wrecked
> careers of some dedicated civil servants now acting
> as regional directors, *Air and Water News* sees a
> heightened potential for chaos in antipollution en-

forcement. We urge the White House to stop paying off political debts with our environmental heritage.[19]

At that time, Ruckelshaus was able to control seven of the ten regional appointments and most of the assistant administrator appointments. In Atlanta, however, a man with twenty-seven years of experience in environmental work and a reputation for strict enforcement of pollution laws was replaced by an individual whose only claim to the job, by all accounts, was an eleven-month appointment as the administrative assistant to Senator Strom Thurmond of South Carolina.[20] Similar politically motivated appointments were made in Denver and Boston that year, to the dismay of many supporters of the new agency.[21] This tension between political and career employees continues today and has exacerbated policy differences between diverse factions both inside and outside the agency.

EPA's Programs and Functions

Although all of the EPA's organizational units share its goal "to protect and enhance our environment today and for future generations to the fullest extent possible under the laws enacted by Congress,"[22] the agency derives its authority from a patchwork of statutes with different legal foundations. Adding to the air and water statutes inherited from the Department of the Interior and HEW, Congress passed legislation in 1970 to increase the agency's authority to regulate solid waste and in 1972 to increase the agency's authority to regulate pesticides. In 1974 Congress created a new drinking water program, and in 1976 both a toxic substances program and a hazardous waste program were born. In 1980 Congress enhanced the agency's capacity for cleaning up hazardous wastes by creating the national Superfund program.

Seven major environmental laws enacted by Congress are implemented by the EPA:

1. Clean Air Act (CAA)
2. Comprehensive Environmental Response, Compensation and Liability Act (CERCLA or Superfund) as amended by the Superfund Amendments and Reauthorization Act (SARA)
3. Federal Insecticide, Fungicide and Rodenticide Act (FIFRA)
4. Federal Water Pollution Control Act (FWPCA or the Clean Water Act [CWA])
5. Resource Conservation and Recovery Act (RCRA)
6. Safe Drinking Water Act (SDWA)
7. Toxic Substances Control Act (TSCA)

The EPA also has some responsibility to implement other statutes, including the following:

Asbestos School Hazard Abatement Act
Coastal Management Act
Deep Water Ports Act
Energy Policy and Conservation Act
Emergency Planning and Community Right to Know Act
Environmental Research, Development and Demonstration Authorization Act
Federal Food, Drug and Cosmetic Act
Marine Protection, Research and Sanctuaries Act
National Environmental Policy Act
Noise Control Act
Nuclear Regulatory Act
Nuclear Waste Policy Act
Ocean Dumping Act

Outer Continental Shelf Lands Act
Quiet Communities Act
Rivers and Harbors Act (Refuse Act)
Surface Mining Control and Reclamation Act
Uranium Mill Tailings Radiation Control Act
Used Oil Recycling Act

The six major programs and functions controlled by the EPA are pesticides, air protection, water protection, radiation, toxic substances, and hazardous waste.[23]

Pesticides.   The major objectives of the pesticide program are to protect the public from unreasonable pesticide risks and to permit the use of necessary techniques for controlling pests. The EPA reviews new and existing pesticide products, while developing techniques for the proper application of pesticides. It undertakes research to develop up-to-date information on pesticide products, and it enforces pesticide laws through the administrative and judicial process.

Air Protection.   The EPA coordinates a nationwide program of air pollution research, regulation, and enforcement comprising several activities. The agency oversees state and local governments, which have primary responsibility for the prevention and control of air pollution, and takes action where states do not fulfill their responsibilities. The agency also determines and enforces standards for air quality, emissions control, and the regulation of hazardous air pollutants. The air research and development program attempts to identify, and if possible quantify, the adverse effects of exposure to air pollutants on human health and to develop new technologies for preventing and controlling air pollution.

Water Protection.   The EPA's water quality program is multifaceted. The agency, or a delegated state agency, issues permits for pollution discharges pursuant to National Pollutant Discharge Elimination System guidelines. A pretreatment program for industrial sources that discharge pollution into municipal wastewater treatment facilities also is administered by the EPA or delegated to the states. The construction grants office oversees state and U.S. Army Corps of Engineers activities in the construction of wastewater treatment plants, but funds for such activities are rapidly diminishing.

EPA officials work with state administrators to train operators of municipal wastewater treatment facilities. The agency also implements a program to regulate ocean disposal of pollutants and oversees the monitoring and analysis of national water quality by the states and the U.S. Geological Survey under a grant program.

The EPA's drinking water program is primarily an effort to protect public health. The agency supervises public drinking water systems to ensure that utilities comply with appropriate standards. In addition, the agency implements a program to protect present and future sources of drinking water from contamination by underground injection. All of these responsibilities can be delegated to the states.

Radiation.   The radiation program spans all media regulated by the EPA. A substantial effort to identify and characterize the problem of indoor radon was initiated in 1980 and continues today. The radiation research and development subunit identifies and evaluates the health effects of exposure to radiation. The abatement and control activities concentrate primarily on the establishment of specific criteria and standards for environmental radiation protection programs.

Toxic Substances. The EPA's toxic substances program centers on two main functions. The first function entails the development of adequate data on the effects of chemical substances on health and the environment. The second function concerns the regulation of chemicals that present an unreasonable risk of injury to health or the environment. The program also responds to toxic emergencies through either legal or administrative proceedings.

Hazardous Waste. The main purpose of the EPA's hazardous waste program is to protect public health and the environment from damages caused by improper waste management. The agency regulates the generation, transportation, storage, treatment, and disposal of hazardous wastes. Where states have primary responsibility over hazardous wastes, the EPA oversees their programs. In states that have not assumed primary responsibility for hazardous waste management, enforcement centers on administrative and public hearing requirements for issuing permits and monitoring compliance.

Under the Superfund program, the EPA undertakes a number of responsibilities. The agency responds to emergencies involving hazardous substance spills and emergencies caused by uncontrolled and abandoned hazardous waste sites that may present an imminent danger to public health. EPA staff members and contractors take long-term remedial and containment actions at sites where responsible parties cannot be identified or refuse to take appropriate action.

The EPA takes responsibility for continually updating and revising the National Contingency Plan for hazardous waste, which contains definitive guidelines on methods of site discovery, evaluations, and alternative remedial actions. The agency also conducts enforcement activities designed to identify parties responsible for hazardous waste sites and spills. Once a potentially responsible party is designated, the agency uses enforcement actions to induce the party to undertake acceptable remedial actions. Finally, the agency uses enforcement actions against liable parties to recover costs incurred by the EPA for cleanup actions at sites and spills.

The EPA in Court: The Players

The enforcement strategy of the EPA was developed by the agency's first administrator in the early 1970s. Formerly an attorney with the Justice Department, Ruckelshaus brought with him a preference for aggressive enforcement of environmental laws through the courts. The agency attorneys were initially on the offensive and deliberately sought to win court victories to send a message to polluters and to the general public. At first industry officials were reluctant to challenge the EPA at every turn, fearing that they might generate a negative public image. As the agency has matured and the financial stakes involved in pollution control have increased, however, the EPA has found its actions challenged more frequently by industry officials who maintain that the agency oversteps its bounds and environmental groups that maintain that the agency is not being aggressive enough. Congress sided with environmental groups by strengthening their position in court through the enactment of citizen suit provisions in six of the EPA's seven major statutes (although industry, state, and profit-motivated attorneys in private practice also have filed suit under such provisions). These laws give "citizen groups" the right to sue and often reward successful anti-EPA plaintiffs with attorneys' fees and litigation expenses. EPA Administrator William K. Reilly once estimated that 80 percent of his decisions were appealed to the courts.[24]

Several kinds of groups regularly engage with the EPA in

court. Most can be categorized as "repeat players":[25] organizations that frequently interact with the agency over extended
periods of time. First and foremost is the Justice Department,
which approves and files the majority of EPA lawsuits. Attorneys
for the EPA often grumble about the time and effort they put into
the preparation of a lawsuit only to be upstaged by a Justice
Department attorney who may take the lead in court. Justice
Department attorneys are also consulted about the EPA's implementation of court decisions.

The major foes of the EPA in court are generally at opposite
ends of the spectrum of pollution control policy.[26] Large companies whose products are regulated by the EPA (such as Monsanto, Dow Chemical, Shell Oil, and Union Carbide) and trade
associations that represent groups of companies (such as the
National Coal Association or the National Solid Wastes Management Association) often appeal EPA administrative decisions and
rules to courts. They usually complain that the EPA regulations
cost jobs, restrict economic growth, and are unnecessarily costly
and cumbersome to comply with.

On the other end of the spectrum are the not-for-profit environmental groups. These organizations range from the hundred-
year-old Sierra Club to the newer organizations founded in the
late 1960s and early 1970s, such as the Environmental Defense
Fund, the Natural Resources Defense Council, and Citizens for a
Better Environment. The largest of the litigious not-for-profit environmental groups is the National Wildlife Federation, with a
membership of approximately 4.5 million. Most environmental
groups are funded by grants, membership fees, donations, and
court-awarded attorneys' fees. When in court, representatives of
these environmental groups usually maintain that EPA antipollution measures are not stringent enough to protect the environment and human health adequately.

Other individuals and groups interact with the EPA in court

on a much less frequent basis. These include other federal government organizations such as the Department of Energy (see Chapter Six) and the Department of Defense, whose facilities have had environmental problems. Although the general rule in the past has been that the EPA will not fine another federal agency, that is changing. In October, 1992, President George Bush signed into law the Federal Facilities Compliance Act that gives the EPA and states the authority to levy fines and penalties against federal facilities that violate the Resource Conservation and Recovery Act (see Chapter Six). Critics of this approach point out that these EPA-levied fines merely transfer funds from, and then back to, the U.S. Treasury. Supporters of the fines think it may be the only way the EPA can show that it is serious about cleaning up polluting federal facilities. Matters concerning other federal organizations typically are handled out of court, but that may change in the future. The Office of Management and Budget has been cited as a defendant in a suit filed by environmental groups that charged that the office unduly interfered with the EPA's process of promulgating regulations (see Chapter Six). State attorneys general, state environmental agencies, local governments, and affected citizens have gone to court with the EPA, both as plaintiffs and as defendants.

The EPA in Court: The Process

A dispute involving the EPA can get to court in several ways. In situations where the EPA proposes to assess a civil penalty against a party violating a statute or regulation, or where the agency proposes to deny, modify, or revoke a license or permit, most environmental statutes require that it first grant the party a hearing on the matter.[27] Most of these hearings are governed by the Consolidated Rules of Practice[28] and are presided over by one of the EPA's administrative law judges.[29] The administrative law judge issues an opinion, which may be appealed to the agency

Figure 3
District Court Cases Filed by the EPA, 1970–June, 1992

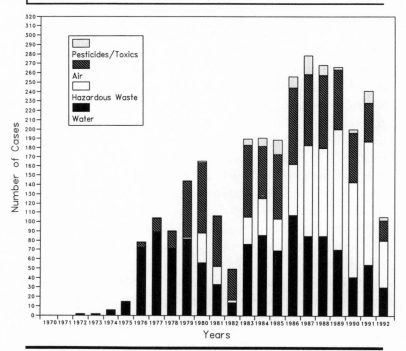

Note: Over 50 percent of these cases were settled, withdrawn, or dismissed.

head.[30] The decision may then be appealed to federal district court.

Rule making at the EPA is guided by the Administrative Procedure Act. The Administrative Procedure Act requires agencies to provide notice and an opportunity for participation in the rule-making process. The EPA's general policy is to provide a hearing on regulations upon written request. Challenges to EPA

Figure 4
Appeals of EPA Administrative Decisions to U.S. Courts of Appeals, June, 1976–June, 1992

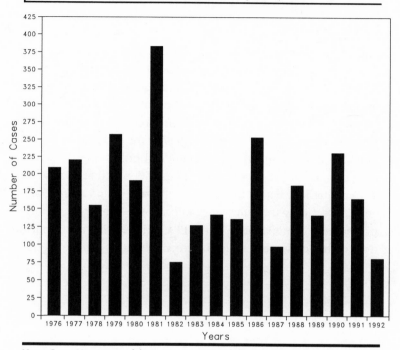

Note: Over 50 percent of these cases were settled, withdrawn, or dismissed.

rules, as well as alleged violations of the Administrative Procedure Act, are appealed to the courts of appeals.

Most of the EPA's statutes contain specific provisions for direct judicial review of other agency actions either in district courts (see Figure 3) or in courts of appeals (see Figure 4). Unless an issue falls within a category specifically set aside for review in a court of appeals, however, the proper forum is a district court. Industry groups and environmental groups are becoming increasingly sophisticated in "forum shopping," in which they search for the court most sympathetic to their side of a case.

Conclusion

The unique setting of the EPA provides an opportunity to examine the impact of federal court decisions on an entire federal agency. Viewing the varying impacts from an agencywide perspective is important because it serves to widen and balance our understanding of the implications of court-EPA interactions. This book presents several intricate case studies of the judicial-EPA "partnership" in the important environmental policy areas of water pollution, hazardous waste, toxics, pesticides, and air pollution. The concluding chapter moves out of the sample and into the universe, describing the cumulative effects of federal courts on the policies and administration of the EPA and assessing the implications of the "new partnership" between the courts and the agency.

In Search of Clean Water

Chapter Two

Any judicial decision compelling agency action infringes to some degree on an agency's discretion.
—JUDGE THOMAS A. FLANNERY
in Toxics Consent Decree case

Today the United States enjoys relatively clean water. The amount of pollution discharged to waterways annually is less than one-fifth the amount of pollution discharged into the air. The Clean Water Act has drastically curbed the amount of toxics pumped into our rivers and lakes. But this has not always been the case.

In 1976, when Judge Thomas A. Flannery modified and approved a settlement agreement concerning the Clean Water Act between environmental groups and the EPA, he could not have known the sweeping changes in U.S. water policy that were set in motion. The so-called Flannery Decision mandated that the EPA promulgate regulations to control sixty-five toxic pollutants for twenty-one industrial groups. It was reopened fourteen times in ten years and was the subject of intense disputes among industry groups, environmentalists, Congress, and the agency. Most important, however, the Flannery Decision shaped the EPA's water policy as it exists today.

The Flannery Decision Challenge

In response to previous failures to control water pollution, in 1972 Congress passed amendments to the Federal Water Pollution Control Act (FWPCA), later renamed the Clean Water Act (CWA),[1] with explicit requirements, goals, and deadlines for the EPA to follow. Included in the amendments were provisions for the control of toxic water pollutants.[2] Regulation under the toxic pollutant section was specifically mandated to proceed on a pollutant-by-pollutant basis, rather than on the industry-by-industry basis that was required by most other sections of the act.

Section 307(a) of the new act ordered the EPA to develop a list of toxic pollutants within 90 days of the passage of the amended FWPCA.[3] The EPA also was mandated to propose an effluent standard for each of the listed pollutants within 180 days of the standard being placed on the list.[4] Final standards were to be promulgated within 180 days of the proposed standards.[5] The regulations were to become effective within one year of promulgation.[6]

By June, 1973, however, the EPA had missed fourteen deadlines under the FWPCA (see Table 2).[7] In response to a suit filed by the Natural Resources Defense Council (NRDC) to force the EPA to fulfill its statutory mandates, the agency entered into a consent decree that established a new deadline for promulgation of the list of toxics, as well as other requirements.[8] When the new deadline arrived and the list was published, however, it contained only nine substances: mercury, cadmium, cyanide, benzidine, polychlorinated biphenyls, and four pesticides (DDT, aldrin/dieldrin, toxaphene, and endrin).[9]

An unrelenting NRDC sued again, alleging, among other things, that a greater number of toxics should have been listed. Moreover, the environmental group challenged the criteria used

Table 2
Toxics Consent Decree: Chronology of Events

Year	Events
1973	EPA missed FWPCA deadlines; NRDC sued; settled
1974	EPA listed only nine pollutants; NRDC sued; dismissed; dismissal reversed; settled by 1976 consent decree
1975	EPA withdrew proposed regulations for nine pollutants; three environmental groups sued; settled by 1976 consent decree
1976	EPA failed to promulgate final pretreatment standards; NRDC sued; settled by 1976 consent decree
1976	consent decree approved; intervention denied
1977	court of appeals remanded intervention decision
1977	Congress adopted provisions of decree in 1977 CWA
1978	district court awarded NRDC $100,976.14 in costs from EPA
1979	EPA missed consent decree deadlines; show cause order pending; consent decree modified
1979	industry groups moved to have decree vacated; denied; appealed
1980	court of appeals held that 1976 consent decree not superseded by 1977 FWPCA amendments; remanded discretion question
1982	district court held that discretion not infringed upon; appealed
1982	district court denied EPA motion to modify decree; appealed
1983	court of appeals affirmed both 1982 decisions of district court
1983	consent decree modified
1984	consent decree modified twice
1984	Supreme Court refused to hear appeal of industry groups
1984	Court awarded NRDC additional $24,161.15 in costs from EPA; fees requested from industry groups denied
1985	consent decree modified
1986	court of appeals upheld attorneys' fee decision
1986	consent decree modified
1987	consent decree modified
1987	last 1976 consent decree regulation promulgated; appealed
1993	regulations being revised

by the EPA in selecting the toxics to list, since those criteria included factors not mentioned in the statute, such as the availability of other remedies and the existence of data for establishing the standards. Finally, the NRDC charged that information outside of the record had been improperly considered in developing the list.[10]

In response to the lawsuit the EPA agreed to add more substances to the list of toxics; the district court then dismissed the suit.[11] The NRDC appealed the decision to dismiss to the U.S. Court of Appeals for the District of Columbia. The appellate court responded by remanding the case back to the district court based on a finding that the EPA had not submitted all pertinent records to the lower court.[12]

While this litigation was pending, the EPA proposed standards for the nine listed pollutants. In public hearings on the effluent standards, however, the EPA was blasted by industry groups who maintained that the regulations were too strict, not scientifically justifiable, and economically infeasible. At the same time, environmentalists criticized the agency for proposing standards that were not strict enough and did not meet the requirements of the FWPCA.[13] The EPA responded by abandoning the proposed standards, stating that "the hearing record, though voluminous, did not contain sufficient evidence upon which defensible standards could be promulgated. The proposed standards could not be defended on the record, and no specific modification could be 'justified based on a preponderance of evidence adduced at the hearings.'"[14]

In February, 1975, outraged that the EPA had failed to promulgate final regulations for the nine toxic substances, the NRDC, together with the Environmental Defense Fund, filed a third lawsuit. The environmental groups alleged that EPA Administrator Russell Train had failed to perform the nondiscretionary duty of promulgating final toxic effluent standards within 180 days of those toxics having been listed.[15] In addition, the NRDC filed a fourth suit in August, 1975, alleging that the administrator had failed to perform another nondiscretionary act by not promulgating final pretreatment standards for a number of industrial categories.[16]

Settlement Agreement Proposal

With several lawsuits pending against it, and the possibility of multiple judicial orders forcing the agency to take actions with which it did not agree, the EPA approached the plaintiffs with a proposed settlement agreement.[17] After hours of negotiations, a revised document that consolidated all three cases was presented to Judge Thomas A. Flannery for approval. Judge Flannery, however, refused to sign the agreement.

Flannery objected specifically to a provision in the agreement that would have allowed the court to arbitrate any dispute over exclusions of point source categories or pollutants from regulation. (A point source is a discrete source of pollution, such as outfall from a pipe, as opposed to other more diffuse, nonpoint sources of pollution, such as storm water runoff.)[18] The requested judicial control, Flannery maintained, would improperly involve the court in supervising the EPA's discretionary authority under the act. The judge also objected to a provision that would have allowed the cases to remain before the court until the EPA completed all the duties specified under the agreement. Flannery suggested that the cases be closed, with the provision that the parties return to the court should a dispute arise. Moreover, while prohibiting the intervention of industry groups, the judge directed the parties to respond to the "broad attack" by industry on the court's jurisdiction "to approve any agreement at all." Flannery gave the parties one month to file a modified decree.[19]

On May 26, 1976, after a modified settlement was filed with the court, Judge Flannery sent a letter to all parties articulating exactly how he would interpret the terms. Saying that the agreement as modified was "open to an interpretation which would result in an acceptable role for the court," Flannery said he would construe the consent decree to mean that the EPA, upon completion of the rule-making procedures, "may, in its discretion, decide not to issue a regulation for a specific pollutant or point source covered by the agreement."[20] Flannery told the parties that "the court's role in enforcing the Decree . . . [would] be limited to ordering compliance with the various deadlines set out therein, ruling on requests by the EPA for modification of deadlines, and ordering the EPA to supply written justifications for deletion of pollutants or point sources. At no time," the judge closed, "will the court rule on the wisdom of including or excluding a pollutant or point source from regulation."[21]

In response to Flannery's letter, the parties further modified the agreement. In addition, the EPA sent Flannery a letter stating that the judge's interpretation limiting the role of the court was consistent with its own interpretation. The environmental groups also sent the judge a letter saying that they "fully appreciate[d], and intend[ed] to respect, the court's reluctance to review the Administrator's decisions when this review would require the court to evaluate scientific and technical data." The NRDC, however, emphasized the need for plaintiffs to be able to seek judicial review of EPA actions "when necessary to ensure good faith compliance" with the agreement.[22]

The Toxics Consent Decree Signing
On June 9, 1976, against the wishes of industry groups who "vehemently oppose[d]" the settlement, Judge Flannery signed an order implementing the settlement agreement. Calling it a

"classic agreement," the judge acknowledged that even the modified decree would "require a substantial investment of judicial resources."[23] The court then retained jurisdiction to effect compliance with the terms and conditions of the decree.

Under the terms of the Toxics Consent Decree, the EPA agreed to change its policies and administrative operations drastically, shifting from regulating individual toxic pollutants to regulating them on an industry-by-industry basis. The agency agreed to initiate studies and to promulgate regulations to control sixty-five toxic pollutants discharged from twenty-one industrial categories. Industry groups appealed Flannery's decision to prohibit their intervention in the proceedings involved in implementing and overseeing the settlement agreement. On June 15, 1977, the Court of Appeals for the District of Columbia Circuit reversed and remanded the case to the district court to allow intervention. The court found that the special and distinct interests of the various industry groups justified their admission as parties to the suit.[24] The EPA agreed to

1. Regulate sixty-five toxic pollutants in twenty-one industry groups
2. Regulate toxic substances on an industry-by-industry basis
3. Set effluent limitations for categories of existing sources, requiring the use of the "best available technology economically achievable" by mid-1983 (pursuant to sections 301(b)(2)(A) and 304(b)(2)(A) of the FWPCA)
4. Set performance standards for categories of new sources (pursuant to section 306 of the FWPCA)
5. Set pretreatment standards for sources that discharge into publicly owned treatment works (POTWs) (pursuant to section 307(b) of the FWPCA)
6. Regulate pollutants that are not susceptible to treatment by

POTWs, or that interfere with, pass through, or are otherwise incompatible with POTW systems

7. Proceed with promulgating regulations for six of the nine
substances previously listed by the EPA by mid-1976 (pursuant to section 307(a) of the FWPCA)

8. Contract with consultants by specific dates

9. Provide quarterly oral briefings to all parties with evidence
of progress

Congress's Amendment of the FWPCA

Six months later, on December 28, 1977, Congress amended the
FWPCA.[25] Congress accepted the new water policies by endors-
ing the consent decree's approach to the control of toxic pollutants and writing several parts of the decree into the act. In
debating the bill, Senator Muskie told the Senate:

> Another, and possibly more important, reason for
> maintaining the BAT [best available technology] re-
> quirements is that the Agency currently has a major
> program underway of using BAT to control toxics.
> Technology-based effluent limitations are being de-
> veloped which will place limits on toxic pollutants
> which pose or are likely to pose human health and
> ecological hazards.
>
> *The conference agreement was specifically de-
> signed to codify the so-called "Flannery-decision,"
> which set forth 65 families of pollutants which are to
> be regulated by BAT, and EPA has been implement-
> ing this Decree.* To take a different course for deal-
> ing with toxics at this point would require a major
> reprogramming of EPA resources. Such a delay . . .
> would only cause confusion and add still more de-

lay in efforts to solve the toxics problem. . . . Because EPA is already embarked upon a program to
control toxics using a proven mechanism . . . and
because of the urgency to control toxics, prudent
public policy demands that this policy be maintained. [Emphasis added][26]

The list of the sixty-five pollutants became law,[27] and the
EPA was given clear authority to regulate toxic pollutants on an
industry-by-industry basis, with technology-based effluent limitations.[28] A deadline for promulgating regulations was established
as July 1, 1980.[29] In addition, the deadline for industry compliance with the BAT regulations for priority pollutants was extended by one year to July 1, 1984.[30]

NRDC Reimbursement and Charges of Contempt

On August 16, 1978, the NRDC was awarded $100,976.14 by the
court to be paid out of the EPA budget in reimbursement for its
attorneys' fees and expenses incurred in developing the Toxics
Consent Decree.[31] Ironically, one month later, on September 26,
1978, the environmental group instituted a contempt of court
action against the EPA administrator for failing to comply with the
deadlines set out in the 1976 consent agreement. One month
after that, industry groups filed a motion to vacate the 1976
consent decree on the ground that the 1977 amendments to the
FWPCA made the continuation of the decree inappropriate.

In filing the contempt of court action, the NRDC noted that
the EPA had not met any of its deadlines under the decree. The
EPA responded with a motion to amend the agreement to extend
the deadlines for promulgating regulations, to allow the agency
additional discretion to exclude certain pollutants and industry
categories from regulation, and to extend the deadline for indus-

try compliance with the guidelines by a year. On November 28, 1978, after hours of heated negotiation, the EPA and the NRDC announced to industry representatives that they had agreed to modify the consent decree. The industry representatives were given a chance to comment on the proposed modification, and some of their suggested changes were written into the document.[32]

Modification of the Toxics Consent Decree

On December 15, 1978, the NRDC and the EPA filed a joint motion with the district court to modify the settlement agreement. At the same time, both parties withdrew their previous motions and pleadings. The angry industry groups, however, refused to withdraw their motion to vacate the decree because of the 1977 amendments. The industry groups also maintained that the district court had no power to approve the provisions of the modified agreement directing the EPA to take actions not expressly required by the statute, that the modification of the decree violated public notice and comment requirements, and that it violated constitutional requirements of due process.[33]

On March 9, 1979, the district court issued an order, denying the industry representatives' motion to vacate the settlement agreement and granting the NRDC and EPA's motion to modify the agreement.[34] The modification of the Toxics Consent Decree consisted of nine parts. The most significant change was the extension of time granted to the EPA to issue effluent guidelines, new source performance standards, and pretreatment standards. The deadlines were extended to 1980.[35]

Industry groups again appealed the decision. On September 16, 1980, the Court of Appeals for the District of Columbia Circuit issued a decision upholding the lower court's order in part. The appellate court reasoned that the amended FWPCA "amounted [to] little more than an attempt to conform the statute to the reality of the program." If Congress wanted to supplant the decree, the court reasoned, "it would have said so." The case was remanded to the district court, however, to consider whether the modified settlement agreement impermissibly infringed on the EPA administrator's discretion by preventing the administrator from taking action otherwise open to him or her under the act.[36]

On remand, the district court found that the decree did, in fact, encroach upon the discretion of the EPA, but the court determined that this infringement was not "impermissible." Maintaining that "any judicial decision compelling agency action infringes to some degree on an agency's discretion," Judge Flannery said that there was "no doubt" that the consent decree infringed "to some degree" on the EPA administrator's discretion. The decree in question, however, did not impermissibly infringe upon the EPA since it was oriented toward procedures rather than specific results, it was formulated with the participation of the parties, it was open to modification by the court should circumstances change, and it was approved by Congress in the 1977 FWPCA amendments.[37]

The Decision of the Court of Appeals

On appeal, the Court of Appeals for the District of Columbia Circuit upheld Flannery's decision.[38] Judge Malcolm R. Wilkey, however, strongly dissented and urged that the decree be modified to "restore the agency's discretion." Wilkey wrote: "The Consent Decree at issue in this case is a judicial act. It is not a contractual settlement agreement or a tentative projection of agency policy. The court shaped it, scrutinizing and even altering its terms. The court will be called upon to enforce it, should the agency have a change of heart."[39]

Moreover, Wilkey maintained, case law "makes it perfectly clear" that "the sort of judicial relief in question here[,] . . .

commanding the Executive Branch to exercise its administrative discretion in a particular way," exceeded the reach of the federal court.[40] Calling the decree a violation of the separation of powers, the judge said that the court was in fact affecting substantive agency policy in the guise of "procedure" and "process."[41] Quoting the EPA's testimony earlier in the proceeding, the court commented that "extra obligations not required by statute necessarily infringe on EPA's ability to allocate its limited resources in the way it finds best."[42] The court, Wilkey concluded, was acting as an administrator without any statutory or constitutional mandate.[43]

Wilkey also decried the fact that the decree allowed one EPA administrator to bind future EPA administrators "who may vehemently oppose it," something "American courts have never allowed." The proper action, Wilkey maintained, would have been for the agency to issue the substance of the Toxics Consent Decree as regulations.[44] The judge concluded that "government by Consent Decree" improperly "freezes" the regulatory process of representative democracy. It not only makes it harder for citizens to participate in regulatory affairs, but also inhibits congressional influence on agency policy because the agency is no longer free to respond to congressional concerns. Moreover, the control of the executive branch over agency policy is hindered because of the consent decree, since approval of the court must be achieved before policy changes can be made. Conversely, "the Consent Decree provides the executive with a vehicle for avoiding responsibility for its programs," Wilkey wrote. The only winners are "those special interest groups" who are party to the decree, who stand "enshrine[d] at the center," and so are likely to enjoy material influence on proposed changes in agency policy.[45]

Based on Wilkey's dissent, the industry intervenors appealed the decision to the Supreme Court. On May 29, 1984, the Supreme Court declined to hear the case.[46] The court of appeals decision stood firm.

Congressional Hearings

Even with the extended deadlines, the task of promulgating the regulations for toxics proved to be more than the EPA could handle. One environmental newspaper wrote that the "EPA found itself with a monumental task that went beyond its available resources. It had neither the technical expertise, the money, nor the time to put together the complicated control mechanism."[47] Robert B. Medz, chair of the EPA Test Method Development Work Group, said that to implement the consent decree

> the agency first had to develop reliable methods for analyzing pollutant levels. . . . Following the settlement EPA started to research analytical methods, which led the agency to propose new test procedures in 1979. . . . However, EPA could not promulgate the promised methods until they had been validated by a number of laboratories.[48]

Further insights into the administrative and technical problems encountered in implementing the decree can be found in this statement by Douglas Costle, who was then the EPA administrator, to a congressional subcommittee:

> Development of [the] . . . limitations for toxics has proven to be a complex process. For many industrial categories which had no previous regulatory base, we did not have either the technical or eco-

nomic history from which to develop a standard. Where such background data were available, we lacked analytical techniques of sufficient sophistication to quantify levels of toxics in discharges; this prevented evaluation of the removal capabilities of a given technology. Most importantly we had no long term performance data available to establish defensible limits.[49]

The EPA's Request for a Second Extension

These challenges were among the reasons why the EPA missed even more deadlines imposed by the Toxics Consent Decree. Consequently, in August, 1981, the agency petitioned the court to modify the decree, first, to extend the deadlines, and second, to release the agency from obligations that "in the absence of the Decree, would lie within the Agency's discretion under the Clean Water Act."[50] The agency argued that the combined circumstances of new statutory responsibilities, scarce resources, and the appointment of a new EPA administrator (Gorsuch) by a new president (Reagan) created the need for greater administrative flexibility and was reason to grant relief from the decree.[51] The agency later amended its pleading, admitting that funding for the effluent program had in fact increased.[52]

The NRDC argued vigorously against the EPA's motion. The environmental group—fueled by internal EPA documents found through discovery and reports that Administrator Anne Gorsuch, out to cripple the agency, was slashing the EPA budget by 30 to 40 percent—maintained that the agency had "manufactured most of their 'changed circumstances' through proposed budget cuts, internal resource allocations, and decisions to pursue extraneous processes that are neither sanctioned by law nor necessary for sound rulemaking practices. Plaintiffs believe EPA *planned* to delay and diminish the Consent Decree program, and then set about to do so outside this litigation."[53]

Judge Flannery's Order

In a strongly worded order, Judge Flannery refused the extension, noting that the agency was nearly ten years late in promulgating the rules that had originally been mandated by the FWPCA in 1972.[54] Also noting that the July 1, 1984, deadline for industry compliance was "rapidly approaching," Flannery said that "the EPA must be pushed to work harder."[55] Hoping that his ruling would "serve like adrenalin to heighten the response and to stimulate the fullest use of [EPA] resources,"[56] Judge Flannery ordered the agency to promulgate, within 180 days, all of the regulations previously proposed; to propose, within 180 days, all remaining regulations; and to promulgate final rules within 180 days of the proposed rules.[57]

Further, Flannery directed the agency to submit to the court, within six weeks, a schedule for proposing and promulgating the guidelines. "The schedule," he ordered, "shall contain not time" for review by the Office of Management and Budget pursuant to Executive Order 12291 or "any delays to prepare impact assessments" under the same. In addition, the schedule was not to contain more than ninety days for EPA internal agency review.[58]

In an apparent softening of his 1976 policy of not interfering with the inner workings of the agency, Flannery ordered the agency to report on "all possible internal and external agency actions" taken to minimize or eliminate "all funding and personnel constraints" that might serve as barriers to compliance with the Toxics Consent Decree.[59] In addition, the judge wrote that the

schedule must reflect the EPA's "best efforts to resolve all out-
standing technical and methodological problems that might ma-
terially delay" compliance with the decree.[60] Flannery closed by
stating that the schedule shall "include no time to resolve presently unanticipated issues or problems, or to avoid clustering
regulatory actions [in response to a presidential directive]."[61]

On May 7, 1982, industry groups, angry that the EPA was still
locked into the consent decree, appealed Flannery's rejection of
the EPA modification proposal to the Court of Appeals of the
District of Columbia Circuit. The appellate court affirmed the
order.[62] Environmental groups, by contrast, were encouraged by
the decision, citing it as a way of breaking up the "logjam" at the
EPA and anticipating that the agency would "now proceed with
the program."[63] Six weeks later, the EPA returned to court and
filed a motion for partial relief asking that it not be ordered to
propose regulations for two industrial categories within 180 days.
The first category comprised nonferrous metals, while the second category comprised organic chemicals, plastics, and synthetic fibers. The agency also requested that it be granted more
than 180 days to promulgate regulations for ten industry groups
following the proposal of the regulations.[64]

In the affidavit, the EPA assured the court that by November 2, 1982, it would be able to promulgate all previously
proposed rules and to propose all other regulations under development. The agency also filed several affidavits justifying the
exclusion of certain substances from regulation, as required by
the consent decree. As required by the court, the EPA explained
in detail the steps it had taken to streamline the implementation
process for the consent decree "to an even greater degree than
the Agency previously thought was feasible." The administrative
actions taken by the EPA included shortening review time within
the agency to less than ninety days and deleting provisions for

further time to assess the financial impact of regulations, to prepare regulatory impact analyses, to submit regulations to OMB for review, and to resolve unanticipated issues. Finally, resources within the EPA were "reprogrammed" as funds were shifted from other areas of the agency to the Effluent Guidelines Division to support the development of the consent decree regulations.[65]

Modification of EPA Deadlines

On August 25, 1982, Judge Flannery ruled that the EPA was making "substantial, good faith efforts towards fulfilling its duties under the May 7th order" and that the EPA had "established a sufficient likelihood of the future occurrence of substantial problems in the promulgation of the regulations at issue" to warrant the court's granting the requested relief.[66] On October 26, 1982, Judge Flannery entered an order that relaxed some of the deadlines for regulations.[67] Subsequently, the "logjam" at the EPA was at least partially broken the following November, when, in direct response to the court order, the agency proposed six effluent guidelines and promulgated six final regulations. Noting that regulations for twelve of the twenty-one industry groups were finally completed, EPA Administrator Anne M. Gorsuch said the EPA intended to stay on schedule with the court mandate and called the rule making "a breakthrough in implementing the Clean Water Act."[68]

Soon after this time, the NRDC was awarded an additional $24,161.15 in attorneys' fees and expenses by the court to be paid out of the EPA budget for the environmental group's actions in enforcing the consent decree.[69] The NRDC's request for fees for fighting industry representatives was denied, however. That decision was upheld in 1986 by the Court of Appeals for the District of Columbia Circuit.[70]

Implementation of the Toxics Consent Decree

From 1983 through 1987, the consent decree was modified six more times.[71] On November 5, 1987, the EPA promulgated regulations for organic chemicals, synthetic fibers, and plastics, the last of the consent decree requirements.[72] It had taken over ten years to implement a decree that, when approved by Flannery in 1976, was estimated to take three years to complete. Moreover, many of the regulations issued in response to the consent decree (such as the pesticides regulations) have been challenged and are still the subject of litigation at the beginning of the EPA's third decade.

Advantages of the Toxics Consent Decree

In interviews with members of the EPA staff, several positive attributes of the Toxics Consent Decree were mentioned.[73] First, instead of regulating toxics on a pollutant-by-pollutant basis, entire industry groups were regulated at once, avoiding what EPA staff members called "the [piecemeal] pollutant of the month approach."[74] Second, far more substances were regulated under the decree than could have been regulated under the old approach.[75] Third, where the EPA had originally interpreted section 307(a) of the FWPCA as mandating a public hearing prior to setting a final standard, the decree eliminated that requirement. Instead, interested parties were given an opportunity to comment in writing.[76] Fourth, under the consent decree, industries were given more time to comply with new best available technology standards.[77] Fifth, the decree allowed the EPA to consider cost and technology in its decision making.[78] Finally, the new program was easier to administer.[79]

The consent decree had a dramatic effect on both the budget and the staffing level of the EPA's Effluent Guidelines Division (see Figures 5 and 6). During the fiscal year following

Figure 5
Budget, EPA Effluent Guidelines Division, 1973–1987

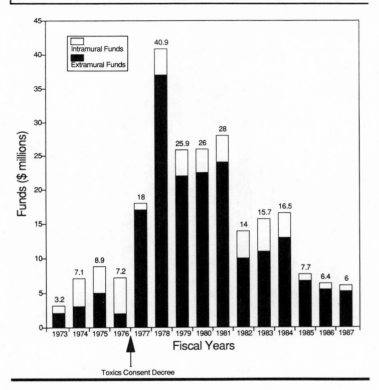

the consent decree, the size of the staff increased from fifty-eight positions to eighty-six positions, a 33 percent increase, while the total budget for the division more than doubled as it rose from $7.2 million to $18 million. According to representatives of the EPA budget staff, the Congressional Budget Office, and the Office of Management and Budget, this increased funding may be at-

Figure 6
Staff, EPA Effluent Guidelines Division, 1973–1987

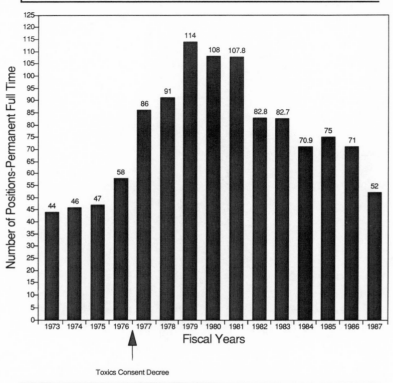

tributed both to increased resources from Congress and to "re-programming," in which funds from other areas of the agency were moved to the water division.

By fiscal year 1978 and fiscal year 1979, the peak years in implementation of the consent decree, the staff and budget of the Effluent Guidelines Division were also at their peak. By fiscal year 1978, the division's budget was at $40.9 million, a 460 percent increase over fiscal year 1976. Of this $40.9 million, 93 percent went to outside consultants. By fiscal year 1979, the staff of the division had grown to 114, nearly a 200 percent increase over fiscal year 1976. Although other projects, court decisions, and statutory mandates were certainly competing within the Effluent Guidelines Division for these funds, according to EPA staff members, 75 to 80 percent of the budget and personnel at that time were devoted to implementing the Toxics Consent Decree on a full-time basis. In addition, other staff members in the Office of General Counsel as well as the Office of Statistics worked on implementing the court order.

By fiscal year 1982, after the bulk of the mandated regulations had been promulgated, the division's budget dropped to $14 million, a 65 percent decrease from fiscal year 1978. That same year, the staffing level was lowered to eighty-three permanent full-time positions, a 27 percent decrease. By fiscal year 1987, the year that the last consent decree regulation was promulgated, the division's staffing level was down to fifty-two permanent full-time positions, while the budget was approximately $6 million.

Despite the legal, political, and technical challenges involved in carrying out the decree, members of the EPA water staff pointed to the period of implementing the Toxics Consent Decree as their "glory days" in terms of resource acquisition and productivity. The turning point was the consent decree itself, they maintained, which served as a catalyst for congressional support. By sparking positive interest in Congress, the consent decree was seen by EPA staff members as an opportunity that made it easier to acquire funds to establish data bases, hire staff, and contract with consultants. Moreover, the consent decree was heralded as a way to "focus on getting something done." With the pressure and resources brought by the consent decree, "people were motivated better." Consequently, the "final product was better."[80]

Moreover, in implementing the consent decree, the EPA staff became aggressive and accomplished technical feats that have helped in other regulatory areas within the agency's jurisdiction. For example, the list of toxic substances developed in response to the consent decree has been used as a benchmark when starting up new programs, such as those concerning hazardous wastes. Instead of starting from scratch, the agency used the list of toxic substances from the consent decree and applied it to the new area. The negative side of the Toxics Consent Decree, according to EPA staff members, is that now that the push is over, "everyone has assumed that the problems have gone away."[81] Accordingly, in recent years, it has been more difficult for the Effluent Guidelines Division to acquire funds. Staff members expressed frustration at this turn of events, since new problems, such as dioxin found in wastewater discharged from paper and pulp mills, are arising daily and are not, in their opinion, being addressed adequately.[82]

Conclusion

The implementation of the CWA Flannery Decision presents a number of issues that have been faced by other administrative agencies around the nation. Confronted by statutory mandates it was unable or unwilling to fulfill and hoping to avoid potentially conflicting judicial decisions, the agency settled out of court with the plaintiffs. What is particularly significant about this case, however, is the extensive judicial involvement, the overreaching breadth of the final agreement, the subsequent amendment of the CWA by Congress to comply with the decree, and the years of divisiveness surrounding the changes.

Additional examples of the use of courts to force change in the EPA can be found under other water statutes, too. In the case of *National Wildlife Federation v. EPA,* concerned with statutory deadlines under the Safe Drinking Water Act, for example, the agency was forced to take responsibility in 1984 for directly administering thirty-three state programs to control the underground injection of substances that may pollute drinking water. Because of the lawsuit, for the first time in the history of the agency, the EPA provided "nationwide wall-to-wall coverage of underground injection operations" under the Safe Drinking Water Act.[83]

What is not apparent in these cases is the fact that the EPA itself is a heavy "user" of courts in its enforcement efforts. Perhaps the best example is the EPA's National Municipal Policy. Alarmed that publicly owned treatment works were lagging "substantially behind" major industrial dischargers in pollution control,[84] the EPA in 1984 began to enforce municipal wastewater laws "aggressively."[85] To do so, the agency consciously used the courts as leverage to force municipalities into compliance.[86] In fact, according to one report from the General Accounting Office, prior to such court-ordered mandates, there had been little municipal compliance with CWA regulations.[87]

EPA's strategy for the National Municipal Policy has included a greater emphasis on litigation and a diminishing use of administrative orders. An internal EPA memorandum providing guidance for regional offices in carrying out the National Municipal Policy, for example, emphasized that the

> EPA and the States should not use administrative orders (AOs) for major POTWs [publicly owned treatment works] with [compliance] schedules that extend beyond July 1, 1988; all such schedules should be contained in *judicial orders.* EPA should also consider *judicial action* for minor POTWs;

where available resources preclude *judicial action,*
EPA and the States should use AOs with penalties.
[Emphasis added][88]

In discussing these National Municipal Policy cases in an
internal agency memo, one EPA official wrote, "The court[s] . . .
implicitly affirmed the National Municipal Policy as an appropriate enforcement response by the EPA. The order[s] should be of
great value in future litigated cases and settlement discussions."
The same staff member concluded, "Case law, which establishes
the appropriateness of compliance without [federal] funding,
therefore becomes strong support for implementation of the
Policy."[89] The National Municipal Policy is being vigorously enforced at the end of the EPA's second decade. On October 4, 1989,
for example, the EPA filed suit against several cities, including El
Paso, Texas, to force compliance with the National Municipal
Policy.[90] El Paso paid a $395,000 civil penalty and agreed to
modify its pretreatment program to better meet its obligations
under the Clean Water Act.[91]

Controlling
Pesticides

Chapter Three

*We stand on the threshold of a new era in the
history of the long and fruitful collaboration of
administrative agencies and reviewing courts.*
—JUDGE BAZELON
in decision concerning DDT

During the twentieth century, the use of pesticides to stop the
spread of weeds and to reduce crop damage caused by insects
and animals has become increasingly important for agricultural
productivity. Although immensely beneficial, these pesticides
have also been shown to present health and environmental hazards. Some have been proven to be carcinogenic, while others
have been linked with the precipitous decline of certain species.
Numerous court decisions have affected the EPA's policies concerning the regulation of such pesticides, as well as the administration of our federal pesticide law.[1]

The first two lawsuits examined here were filed by private
businesses challenging the constitutionality of the Federal Insecticide, Fungicide and Rodenticide Act (FIFRA)[2] and seeking to
halt the disclosure of the ingredients constituting their companies' products. The second set of lawsuits examined here were
filed by an environmental group seeking a halt to the use of the
carcinogenic pesticides DDT, aldrin, and dieldrin. The lawsuits
prompted by business interests affected the policies and admin-

istration of the EPA for six years. The lawsuits filed by the environmental group, however, changed the pesticide policies of our nation forever.

The Trade Secrets Challenge

The Federal Insecticide, Fungicide and Rodenticide Act requires registration of all pesticides with the administrator of the EPA. The act also provides, generally, that trade secrets (concerning the ingredients of pesticides) may not be released by the EPA under most circumstances. At the same time, however, the act encourages public access to nonsecret pesticide data gathered by the EPA.

In 1979, Monsanto, a chemical company, filed suit against the EPA in the U.S. District Court for the Eastern District of Missouri alleging, among other things, that the provisions of the Federal Insecticide, Fungicide and Rodenticide Act, which allow public access to data submitted to the EPA by firms applying for pesticide registration, amounted to an unconstitutional taking of the company's property without just compensation.[3] Monsanto asserted that these data were trade secrets, worth millions of dollars to both Monsanto and its competitors. The release of such data by the EPA, the firm maintained, served no public purpose and was in violation of the Fifth Amendment of the Constitution. (The Fifth Amendment of the Constitution provides that private property shall not be taken for public use, without just compensation.)

Soon after the filing of the suit, the judge assigned to the case issued a pretrial order requiring the EPA to give Monsanto sixty days' notice, rather than the statutorily mandated thirty days, before releasing any of the firm's confidential data. Before the case came to trial, however, a staff member in the Office of Pesticide Programs at the EPA responded to a Freedom of Information Act request from a law firm in Washington, D.C.,[4] by releasing an agency review of "glyphosate" data. The agency review contained confidential Monsanto data that should have been purged from the file. For example, confidential names of inert ingredients in Monsanto's pesticide Roundup were revealed. (Inerts are chemicals lacking active properties.)

FIFRA prohibits disclosure of deliberately added inerts.[5] In addition, the statute bars disclosure of data unless the requesting party certifies that it is not seeking the data on behalf of a foreign or multinational pesticide firm.[6] Such certification was neither requested nor received in the case at hand.

Monsanto asked for and was granted a court order on May 25, 1982, requiring EPA Administrator Anne Gorsuch to show why she should not be held in contempt of court for failing to give Monsanto sixty days' notice of the release of the confidential data. The EPA maintained that the requirement for sixty days' notice did not apply to the case at hand since agency documents, rather than "raw" Monsanto data, were released. After hours of negotiation, however, Monsanto and the EPA filed a joint motion on August 31 with the court requesting a court order that would incorporate new agency procedures to address such situations.

Under the court-approved agreement, any similar future requests were to be submitted to the EPA's scientific advisory panel for advice as to whether the document contained confidential Monsanto data.[7] The agreement also required the EPA to give Monsanto time to comment and to take appropriate court action prior to the future release of Monsanto data. In exchange, the contempt of court proceeding was dismissed.

The Monsanto *Decision*
The *Monsanto* case went to trial. On April 19, 1983, Judge H. Kenneth Wangelin issued a decision finding FIFRA unconstitutional. Congress, the court said, "exceeded its regulatory authority and

violated the Fifth Amendment" when it enacted provisions allowing public access to data submitted to the EPA by firms applying
for pesticide registration.[8] The judge issued a permanent injunction barring the EPA from carrying out "in any manner, directly or
indirectly" the provisions of section 3(c)(1)(D) concerning the
EPA's use of data filed by firms, section 3(c)(2)(A) concerning
standards for data requirements, and sections 10(b) and 10(d)
concerning the use of trade secrets. In addition, Judge Wangelin
specifically enjoined the EPA from using certain data submitted
by Monsanto before 1970 to support registration applications
from other firms. Last, the court ordered that no Monsanto data
be released to a third party by the EPA without written permission
from the company.[9]

The EPA responded to the court order first by asking the
district court for a stay of the decision. The agency then asked the
court to clarify how the decision affected other pesticide registration activities not specifically enjoined. Next, the EPA temporarily
halted its entire pesticide registration program, effective April 18,
1983.[10] The agency then appealed the decision to the Supreme
Court, arguing first that the case was incorrectly decided and
second that if the decision were upheld, it would require drastic
changes in the EPA's rules governing data submission.[11] (Direct
appeal to the Supreme Court was possible because of the constitutional question involved in the case.) The agency had already
rewritten its FIFRA rules in response to another court decision
issued the previous year and had extended the period for public
comments at that time after a third district court had invalidated
still other provisions of the act in January, 1983.[12] Edward Gray,
the EPA's assistant general counsel for pesticides, said that the
Monsanto decisions left "unclear whether anybody can register
pesticides under the act."[13]

Monsanto simultaneously asked the district court to clarify
that the EPA should continue to grant pesticide registrations to

firms submitting their own complete sets of data.[14] The company asserted that the agency had incorrectly interpreted the decision as forbidding pesticide registration unless the company seeking registration is the only company submitting data on the product. With five of its pesticide registrations pending, Monsanto was distraught that the agency was committing "bureaucratic blackmail" by refusing to process its applications.

In May of 1983, Judge Wangelin denied the EPA request for a stay of his decision pending appeal. In addition, he issued a clarification of his order. In that clarification the judge stated that the EPA may approve pesticide registrations if a firm has all its own data or the permission to use the data of other firms in support of its application.

The Agency's Response

Seven weeks later, the frenzied agency requested another stay, this time from the Supreme Court. In addition, Stanley H. Abramson, the EPA's associate general counsel for pesticides and toxic substances, responded to the judge's new order by drafting a legal memorandum to Edwin L. Johnson, director of the Office of Pesticide Programs, changing his previous interpretation of the *Monsanto* decision.[15] According to the memorandum, earlier Abramson had advised EPA staff members that they could approve end-use pesticide registrations if the applicant had the permission of all the "below-the-line" or end-product data owners. Judge Wangelin's clarification, Abramson said, made it necessary to get the approval of the "above-the-line" or active ingredient data owners too, greatly complicating the EPA regulatory process.

On July 26, 1983, the EPA issued a final rule prescribing conditional procedures for registering pesticides.[16] In announcing the new rule, the agency said that the changes reflected two recent court decisions, one of which was the *Monsanto* case.[17]

The EPA clarified that the two court decisions led it to distinguish between the data an applicant must furnish to support a registration and the data that must be available for the EPA to make a determination of risks and benefits.

The following day, July 27, 1983, Supreme Court Justice Harry A. Blackmun denied the EPA's request for a stay of the district court's decision. Blackmun said there was no evidence that the decision would cause irreparable harm pending appeal. Blackmun also commented that the EPA's seven-week delay in seeking the stay refuted the agency's claims that immediate action was necessary. Rather, Blackmun noted, Monsanto might be harmed because trade secrets, once disclosed, cannot be made secrets again.[18]

As the EPA struggled to keep its head above water, on October 11, 1983, the Supreme Court decided to review the *Monsanto* case. In its brief to the Court, as well as in oral arguments before the Court, the EPA maintained that trade secrets do not fall under the definition of property[19] and that "when Monsanto chose to reveal the data to the EPA in exchange for commercially valuable pesticide registrations, the firm accepted the conditions attendant upon issuance of the registrations."[20] Monsanto, by contrast, argued that companies that develop expensive test data to obtain pesticide registration from the EPA might as well "conduct research in the sunshine" if FIFRA were interpreted as allowing disclosure of such data.[21] Monsanto considered such data as property, the company's attorneys argued, because "if it's released to the world, Monsanto can hardly sell it."

The Supreme Court's Decision

On June 26, 1984, the Supreme Court reversed the district court and upheld the constitutionality of the data provisions of FIFRA by a vote of 8 to 0.[22] In doing so, the Court said a company has no concrete guarantee of secrecy from the government with regard to pesticide registration data. In addition, the Court maintained that it was in the public interest for the EPA to disclose certain health and safety information because it "allows members of the public to determine the likelihood of individualized risks peculiar to their use of the product."[23] Moreover, Blackmun wrote that "as long as Monsanto is aware of the conditions under which the data are submitted, and the conditions are rationally related to a legitimate government interest, a voluntary submission of data by an applicant in exchange for the economic advantages of a registration can hardly be called a taking."[24]

Despite its victory in court, the EPA took measures to streamline the process of data registration under FIFRA. On August 1, 1984, for example, the EPA proposed a new rule providing two options for citing data to support an application for pesticide registration. "The rule," the agency said, "permits applicants to demonstrate that they have met the [data] requirements by any method which . . . [FIFRA] allows—generating their own new data, citing their own previously submitted data, citing data previously submitted by others, relying on public literature, seeking a 'waiver' or showing the existence of a 'data gap.' "[25]

Under the first option, an applicant could cite all relevant data in the possession of the EPA, called the "cite-all" method. If this option was chosen, according to the new rule, the applicant must either make an offer to pay the original registrant for the data or obtain permission from the registrant to use the data. Under the second option, an applicant could identify one or more studies to satisfy individual data requirements, called the "selective method." If this option was chosen, the applicant had a variety of alternatives, including submitting its own new study and citing "all pertinent" studies in the possession of the EPA.[26]

The *Monsanto* case disrupted the administration of the

FIFRA program for nearly five years, yet it is not the only instance in which the act was challenged as unconstitutional in a lawsuit that affected the policies and administration of the EPA's FIFRA program. A two-year court battle concerning the constitutionality of the binding arbitration provision of FIFRA also dealt a blow to the FIFRA pesticide registration program and totally halted its implementation.[27]

The Binding Arbitration Challenge

As indicated previously, FIFRA allows firms applying for pesticide registration to cite data already submitted to the EPA in a previous application by another company. When the firms cannot agree on how much the original applicant should be paid for the use of the information, either party can initiate binding arbitration. In such an instance, an arbitrator makes a final decision concerning the proper compensation to the firm that developed the data. Pursuant to FIFRA, such a decision is not reviewable by a court, "except for fraud, misrepresentation, or other misconduct."[28]

In 1983, Union Carbide brought suit against the EPA, asserting, among other things, that the binding arbitration provision of FIFRA was unconstitutional for two reasons. First, the company alleged that it was an unlawfully overbroad delegation because it contained no standards for decision making, failed to set forth a system through which standards could be developed, and restricted sufficient access to judicial or administrative review. Second, Union Carbide alleged that the provision impermissibly intruded on areas of decision making that were constitutionally entrusted to the judiciary.

Judge Richard Owen of the U.S. District Court for the Southern District of New York agreed with Union Carbide, ruling that the binding arbitration section of FIFRA was unconstitutional because it "utterly deprive[d] the federal courts of any meaningful role in ensuring the provision of fair compensation to data submitters."[29] The role left to the courts, according to Owen's interpretation of the act, was a powerless one. Such a great delegation of authority to arbitrators, the judge said, could not be sustained constitutionally.

On November 29, 1983, Judge Owen permanently enjoined the EPA from using binding arbitration to establish a firm's compensation for data.[30] The court's order virtually halted the registration of pesticides, except in cases where a firm had its own data to support its application or where two firms agreed to share data.[31] One month later, on December 21, 1983, the EPA issued a notice that it would appeal the *Union Carbide* case to the Supreme Court.

On March 20, 1984, attorneys for the EPA filed a jurisdictional statement with the Supreme Court. In addition to arguing that the provision in question was constitutional, the attorneys explained the effect of the decision on agency administration of the pesticide registration program. The number of pesticide registrations handled by the EPA had been severely reduced, the attorneys wrote, because "the judgment prevent[ed] . . . [the] EPA from granting registrations based on previously submitted data without the permission of the firm that submitted the data."[32]

On July 2, 1984, the Supreme Court struck down Judge Owen's injunction and sent the case back to the district court for reconsideration in light of another decision it had just issued. In that case, *Ruckelshaus v. Monsanto,* which is discussed above, the Supreme Court upheld the constitutionality of the EPA's right to consider, and at times disclose, data the pesticide companies termed "trade secrets."[33] In addition, another district court had considered a case concerning the same issues and had ruled that a firm that benefits from the pesticide data-sharing provisions of

FIFRA cannot challenge the constitutionality of the law to avoid its requirements.[34]

But Judge Owen was not persuaded by the Supreme Court's actions. On August 7, 1984, Owen boldly issued his third order. Refusing to follow the lead of the Supreme Court, Owen astonished all parties to the case by concluding "that there is no basis for changing the views earlier expressed herein." Owen then re-entered his decision that the binding arbitration section of FIFRA was unconstitutional. Further, he again permanently enjoined the EPA from implementing that section of the act in blatant disregard of the Supreme Court.[35] The EPA's FIFRA program had been shut down.

The EPA immediately filed a motion with the Supreme Court seeking a stay of the second injunction pending a second appeal to the Court. In that document, the attorneys again described the effect of the decision on EPA operations. The district court's order, they wrote, "prevent[ed] not only the registration of many new products but the amendment of registrations for new uses." Describing great harm to the EPA and to the public, the attorneys asked for immediate relief.[36] Such relief was granted by Justice Thurgood Marshall on October 9, 1984, without comment.[37]

On November 26, 1984, the Supreme Court agreed to hear the full *Union Carbide* case,[38] and on July 1, 1985, the Court unanimously overruled Judge Owen, upholding the constitutionality of the FIFRA binding arbitration provision. Writing on behalf of the Court, Justice Sandra Day O'Connor said that the arbitration scheme was necessary as a "pragmatic solution to the difficult problem of spreading the costs of generating adequate information regarding the safety, health, and environmental impact of a potentially dangerous product." Moreover, O'Connor wrote that the lack of opportunity for judicial review did not "threaten the independent role of the judiciary."[39]

The court, however, left undecided the question of whether the statute was "so vague as to be an unconstitutional delegation of legislative powers"[40] and remanded the issue to the district court for consideration. One agency official prophetically predicted that the EPA would return to the Supreme Court a third time to settle that issue. The July 1 decision, the staff member said, "just protects us from injunctions in the meantime."[41]

Indeed, the EPA did return to the Supreme Court a third time, as Judge Owen again, in blatant disregard for the Court, reinstated his previous judgment when the case was remanded to his court.[42] But the Supreme Court was unwavering. On July 1, 1985, Justice O'Connor, writing for the Court, again upheld the constitutionality of the FIFRA binding arbitration provisions. "To hold otherwise," O'Connor wrote, "would be to erect a rigid and formalistic restraint on the ability of Congress to adopt innovative measures . . . [for a] regulatory scheme."[43]

The two cases concerning the constitutionality of FIFRA are important for two reasons. First, they are realistic examples of aggressive, uncompromising judges who ignored statutory mandates in one case and Supreme Court rulings in another. Second, they are lucid examples of the effect of such judicial personalities on the policies and administration of a huge bureaucracy: in both instances, major parts of the EPA's FIFRA program were forced to come to a screeching halt.

As interesting as these two cases are, however, they are not the only important cases that have affected the policies and administration of the FIFRA program. Among the most significant court decisions in the history of the EPA are those that prompted a nationwide banning of the pesticides DDT, aldrin, and dieldrin.

The DDT Challenge

On December 13, 1973, the Court of Appeals for the District of Columbia upheld the decision of EPA Administrator William D. Ruckelshaus to ban the use of pesticides containing DDT.[44] Yet it was not this court decision, but the five judicial decisions concerning DDT that preceded it, that served as catalysts for national regulatory change in the United States.[45] Indeed, the DDT case is an excellent example of how environmental interest groups have used the federal courts to force the EPA to alter its policies.

The DDT issue gained public prominence in 1963 with the publication of Rachel Carson's *Silent Spring.*[46] "The central problem of our age," Carson wrote, is the contamination of human beings, animals, and the environment with chemical pesticides. These substances, she charged, disrupt the ecosystem and "even penetrate the germ cells to shatter or alter the very material of heredity upon which the shape of the future depends." Carson then presented evidence that the pesticide DDT might be carcinogenic and mutagenic.

Three years later, the issue of DDT contamination was first litigated in a state court in New York when Carol Yannacone thought DDT was killing the fish in Yaphank Lake, where she had grown up. As mentioned earlier, Yannacone persuaded her lawyer husband to file suit on her behalf against the Suffolk County Mosquito Control Commission, seeking an injunction to prohibit the use of pesticides containing DDT.[47] It was through this lawsuit that the Environmental Defense Fund (EDF) was formed. Although the plaintiffs were able to get only a temporary injunction for one year, their success sent a signal around the nation that the courts could serve as catalysts for bureaucratic change in the area of environmental policy.[48]

Federal Action

Federal action began in 1969, when the EDF failed to convince the secretary of agriculture to suspend all DDT registrations.[49] In addition, the EDF failed that same year in its petition to the secretary of health, education, and welfare to reduce to zero the levels of DDT in food.[50] The EDF appealed the secretary of agriculture's decision, and the court of appeals remanded the case to the secretary for a "fresh determination of the question of suspension."[51] In response to the remand, the secretary surprised many by merely reissuing his original decision. Angry and frustrated, the EDF again appealed. This time, however, since the EPA had just been created and responsibility for FIFRA had been shifted to the new environmental agency, the defendant was William D. Ruckelshaus, the first administrator of the EPA.[52]

In a classic decision, Judge Bazelon, writing for the court, remanded the case to the EPA. "An important beginning has been made," Bazelon wrote, but the government had not gone far enough. "We stand on the threshold of a new era in the history of the long and fruitful collaboration of administrative agencies and reviewing courts," Bazelon continued. "For many years courts have treated administrative policy decisions with great deference, confining judicial attention primarily to matters of procedure."[53]

It had become necessary, however, "to insist on strict judicial scrutiny of administrative action," Bazelon said. "Courts should require administrative officers to articulate the standards and principles that govern their discretionary decisions in as much detail as possible."[54] Judge Robert Robb dissented, asserting that the court was substituting its judgment for the judgment of the secretary or administrator.

In March, 1971, Ruckelshaus announced that he was immediately initiating the administrative procedures that would be necessary before making a decision on canceling the registration of DDT and four other pesticides: 2,4,5-T, aldrin, dieldrin, and mirex. The procedures for DDT and 2,4,5-T were started in response to court orders. The initial aldrin, dieldrin, and mirex procedures were begun by the EPA administrator himself, although court orders were pending on the issue of whether the agency should ban the pesticides. In announcing his actions, Ruckelshaus said that he was not immediately suspending all uses of these pesticides before the conclusion of the administrative process because he did not see an "imminent hazard" to public health, which was required by law for suspension. Ruckelshaus also expressed a fear that a precipitous suspension might lead some farmers to substitute the much more toxic pesticide parathion for DDT.

In August, 1971, in response to Bazelon's decision, the EPA issued cancellation notices (which initiated administrative proceedings) for the registrations of pesticides containing DDT. A month later an advisory committee, appointed at the request of users and producers of DDT,[55] issued a report confirming the dangers of the chemical and urging a suspension or immediate decrease in its use. At the same time, the EPA refused to suspend, or immediately ban, the use of DDT, pending the outcome of the hearings. The EDF returned to the court of appeals.

This time the court directed the administrator to reconsider his decision not to suspend the use of DDT on an interim basis. Ruckelshaus reconsidered but did not change his mind. The court later gave EPA a deadline of April 15, 1972, before which to conduct "meaningful administrative proceedings."[56] After seven months of hearings on the cancellation issue, the hearing examiner recommended that the use of DDT be permitted and that all cancellations be withdrawn, with the exception of nonmilitary mothproofing and fruit spraying.[57]

Review of the Hearing Examiner's Decision

Ruckelshaus, in one of his last actions as the administrator of the EPA, took the unusual step of personally reviewing the hearing examiner's decision. On June 14, 1972, after further oral argument and written briefs, the EPA administrator surprised most of the parties involved and overruled the examiner. The examiner's decision, Ruckelshaus said, was not based on relevant testimony or a good assessment of the credibility of the witnesses. The evidence "compellingly demonstrate[d] the adverse impact . . . [of DDT] on fish and wildlife," Ruckelshaus wrote. Moreover, as to the pesticide's effect on humans, he continued, DDT "should be considered a potential carcinogen." The administrator ordered the cancellation of all remaining DDT registrations, with a few exceptions allowed.[58]

The EDF appealed the decision, unhappy that the EPA's order had not gone far enough by allowing a few uses of DDT to remain. At the same time, the chemical industry appealed the decision, complaining that the order had gone too far in banning most uses of DDT. The chemical industry also asserted that the administrator had erred in not filing an environmental impact statement, since the EPA's action would have a significant effect on the environment.[59]

The court of appeals, in a decision written by Judge Malcolm R. Wilkey, found that the EPA's decision was supported by substantial evidence found in the record.[60] Further, the court said that the EPA had provided the "functional equivalent" of an environmental impact statement under the National Environmental Policy Act. The EPA administrator's decision stood. Thus, the DDT issue represents the first time a citizen's group succeeded in halting a government-sanctioned, environmentally damaging activity of nationwide scope through litigation upheld by a federal court of appeals.[61]

The final cancellation of DDT registrations by the EPA jolted the agricultural sector of the country and terrified many who feared the demise of agricultural productivity in the United States. This fear prompted an intense lobbying effort in Congress to reintroduce the use of DDT during times of unusual insect infestations. Later, the lobbying concentrated on promoting the use of other pesticides, especially aldrin and dieldrin. Enormous political pressure was placed on the EPA to allow the registration of these pesticides.[62]

The Aldrin and Dieldrin Challenge

On December 3, 1970, the Environmental Defense Fund petitioned the EPA for immediate suspension of all registered uses of aldrin and dieldrin.[63] The pesticides had been used primarily in the Midwest to kill parasites and were known to cling to plant and air particles, then concentrate themselves in animal fats. They had been shown to cause significant increases in cancerous tumors in mice and rats, even at low dietary levels. In 1974, measurable aldrin and dieldrin residues were found to be present in 96 percent of meat, fish, and poultry; 88 percent of all garden fruits; and 83 percent of all dairy products sampled.[64]

On March 18, 1971, before a court decision was issued in the EDF's aldrin and dieldrin case, EPA Administrator Ruckelshaus announced the issuance of "notices of cancellation" for the two pesticides. The basis of the cancellation decision was "a substantial question as to the safety of the registered products which ha[d] not been effectively countered by the registrant," Shell Oil.[65] The administrator, however, did not order an interim suspension pending the outcome of administrative hearings.

The Environmental Defense Fund appealed the administrator's decision not to suspend immediately aldrin and dieldrin to the U.S. Court of Appeals for the Seventh Circuit. In May, 1972, the court remanded the case to the agency for a fuller explanation of the rationale for the decision not to suspend, as well as an examination of new findings that had been filed with the agency after the close of the hearings.[66] Despite this prompting by the court, in August, 1972, Ruckelshaus reaffirmed his original decision but stated that he was reconsidering whether to ban certain uses of aldrin and dieldrin. In the end, however, the administrator stood firm. After reconsidering his decision, he issued a final decision not to ban the pesticides in December, 1972.

From October, 1973, to March, 1974, after several attempts to convince Shell Oil to voluntarily suspend use of the pesticides failed, the EPA presented its case against the substances to an administrative law judge.[67] In late March, just as the EPA had concluded its case, 7,600,000 chickens were ordered to be destroyed in Mississippi because they were found to contain more than fifteen times the allowable levels of aldrin and dieldrin. The EPA had been asked by the Department of Agriculture to increase the allowable tolerance of aldrin and dieldrin to save the birds and thus lessen the economic impact on Mississippi farmers. The EPA refused.[68]

As Shell Oil was about to present its evidence in support of the pesticides at the agency hearing, EPA Assistant Administrator for Enforcement and General Counsel Alan Kirk notified the company that, based on the case presented by EPA attorneys during the preceding months, the agency was considering issuing an interim ban on aldrin and dieldrin. Representative Jamie Whitten (D-Mississippi), considered the pesticide industry's "firmest friend" in Congress, immediately wrote a letter to the EPA recommending against the proposed action. The EPA budget for fiscal year 1975 had not yet been approved by the committee Whitten chaired—the Agriculture, Environmental, and Consumer Protec-

tion Subcommittee of the House Appropriations Committee—
and Whitten would not hesitate to use his power to smash the
agency.[69]

Under intense political pressure, the EPA decided not to
ban the pesticides, but again asked Shell Oil to take them off the
market voluntarily. Representative Whitten's committee recommendation then was forwarded to the House: the EPA had received more money than it had requested. Much of the additional
funds was earmarked for future testing of DDT to determine
whether the 1972 ban of the chemical should be reversed.

In a letter dated April 16, 1974, Shell Oil attorney William D.
Rogers angrily rejected the EPA's request for a voluntary ban.
Rogers wrote:

> There are only 545,000 non-skin cancer cases each
> year in the entire United States, from all causes. . . .
> Does your Agency . . . really mean to suggest it can
> halve the non-skin cancer cases in the United States
> by the simple expedient of banning [aldrin and]
> dieldrin? Does it mean to say that [aldrin and]
> dieldrin is really a more serious cancer threat than
> cigarettes . . . ? Does it mean to tell the American
> people that the fight against cancer is so easy and
> inexpensive? . . . [A] suspension order at this time
> would be a legally fruitless gesture which could
> serve no purpose but to greatly damage and preju-
> dice Shell in terms of both public relations and [the]
> pending cancellation proceeding.[70]

On July 29, 1974, the *Washington Post* published an
abridged version of an article written by the Environmental Law
Institute blasting the EPA for its failure to suspend aldrin and

dieldrin immediately.[71] The EPA was smothered with letters and telephone calls from angry citizens. Five days later, on August 2, 1974, EPA Administrator Russell Train suspended at once further manufacture of the pesticides on the grounds that they posed an "imminent hazard" to public health.[72] The administrator, however, allowed the continued sale of existing supplies of the pesticides.[73] The decision came one month before the end of the agency's hearings on the matter and two months prior to the administrative law judge's decision.[74]

Shell Oil denounced the EPA's action as "blatantly unfair, a fundamental violation of basic due process, and an insult to the integrity of EPA's own administrative process."[75] The company immediately filed suit, alleging that the administrator's actions were arbitrary and capricious. Shell Oil was joined by Florida Citrus Mutual and Earl Butz, the secretary of agriculture. The EDF and the National Audubon Society sued the EPA because of its decision to allow the sale of any of the already manufactured stock of aldrin and dieldrin.[76] On April 4, 1975, the U.S. Court of Appeals for the District of Columbia issued its decision. The court affirmed the EPA administrator's decision to suspend the registrations and prohibit the manufacture and sale of the pesticides aldrin and dieldrin.[77]

Conclusion

The case studies in this chapter illustrate that whether a public organization wins or loses a legal battle in the end, there are immense opportunities along the way for the courts to affect the policies and administration of that organization. In the first set of cases concerning the constitutionality of FIFRA, major parts of the agency's pesticide program were shut down completely over a six-year period. This halting of agency operations affected not only the two companies bringing the suits, Monsanto and Union Carbide, but hundreds of other companies regulated by the EPA. Moreover, EPA officials interviewed for this study reported having been shifted among FIFRA subprograms pending the outcome of these cases, making it "difficult to get anything done" within certain areas.[78] Although the EPA was victorious in the end, the cases left an indelible mark on the agency.

The second set of cases concerning the banning of pesticides are examples, in varying degrees, of the intertwining of courts, economic influences, political influences, and the media to affect the policies and administration of a large bureaucracy. While the upshot was a path-breaking banning of the pesticides, EPA staff members interviewed for this study indicated that the daily administration of the agency had not been massively affected. The rapid development of new pesticides produced, almost immediately, new substitutes for DDT, aldrin, and dieldrin, which demanded the attention of the EPA pesticide registration program staff. For example, in 1976, the EPA banned the pesticides heptachlor and chlordane, in 1979 it banned the herbicides 2,4,5-T and silvex, in 1983 it banned the use of ethylene dibromide in most agricultural uses, and in 1986 the agency banned the sale of the pesticide dinoseb.[79] In September, 1991, the EPA limited the use of products containing the pesticide ethyl parathion, which has poisoned over 650 farm workers, and as of this writing the agency was considering additional limits.[80] Additionally, in January, 1993, as one of his last actions as EPA administrator, William Reilly signed a proposed rule that would phase out the production and importation of the ozone-depleting pesticide methyl bromide by the year 2000.[81]

The EPA's pesticide regulation policy remained a controversial subject at the end of the agency's second decade. In September, 1989, for example, a U.S. Senate committee issued a report citing, among other things, concerns over the effects of pesticides on children.[82] The EPA responded by proposing amendments to FIFRA to strengthen regulatory provisions of the act, but such changes have been vigorously opposed by the Department of Agriculture, which remains fearful of the effect of stiffer pesticide laws on U.S. farmers.[83]

On July 8, 1992, the U.S. Court of Appeals for the Ninth Circuit issued a decision overturning an EPA order permitting the use of four pesticides as food additives. Although all four pesticides (benomyl, mancozeb, phosmet, and trifluralin) had been found to induce cancer, the EPA concluded that the risk was minimal and allowed the use of the pesticides. The court set aside the EPA's order because an examination of the history and purpose of a special provision of the Federal Food, Drug, and Cosmetic Act, known as the Delaney clause, revealed that Congress intended the EPA to prohibit all additives that are carcinogenic, regardless of the degree of risk involved.[84] The Supreme Court denied the petition of agricultural groups requesting a review of the decision.[85] As of this writing, the EPA was studying alternative methods of regulating pesticides, and some congresspersons were drafting legislation to attempt to overturn the court decision.

Regulating Toxic Substances

Chapter Four

*Our entire program was wiped out. We had to
start over at ground zero.*
—MEMBER OF THE EPA STAFF
(commenting on effect of court decision)
Natural Resources Defense Council v. Ruckelshaus

Over 60,000 chemical substances are manufactured or pro-
cessed for commercial use in the United States annually, and an
estimated 1,000 additional chemicals are expected to be introduced into the market each year. Because many commonly used
and widely dispersed chemicals have been found to be toxic
(both the National Cancer Institute and the World Health Organization maintain that 60 to 90 percent of cancers are environmentally induced), the Toxic Substances Control Act (TSCA) au-
thorizes the EPA to require the testing of chemical substances
entering the environment and to regulate them.

In 1980, Judge Lawrence Pierce of the U.S. District Court for
the Southern District of New York ordered the EPA to initiate
rule-making proceedings for the testing of certain chemicals
or explain why it would not do so, triggering an avalanche of
changes in the EPA's policies and administrative practices.[1] The
Natural Resources Defense Council (NRDC) had filed suit against
the agency to compel the administrator to act within a statutorily
mandated twelve-month period on chemicals designated by an

interagency testing committee as possibly causing or contributing to cancer, gene mutations, or birth defects.[2] By law the head
of the EPA was required either to initiate a rule-making proceeding for such chemicals or to publish in the Federal Register the
administrator's reason for not initiating such a proceeding.[3] The
EPA had done neither.[4]

That same year, the Environmental Defense Fund also sued
the EPA in the U.S. Court of Appeals for the District of Columbia,
challenging the agency's regulation of the toxic chemicals called
polychlorinated biphenyls, or PCBs. The court's decree, which
invalidated all of the EPA's PCB regulations, had many unanticipated effects, including making the use of almost all electrical
equipment in the United States a violation of law.

The Toxic Chemicals Testing Challenge, Part One

In 1978 the federal Interagency Testing Committee, comprising
representatives from the EPA, the Department of Labor, the Council on Environmental Quality, the National Institute of Environmental Health Services, the National Institute for Occupational
Safety and Health, the National Cancer Institute, the National
Science Foundation, and the Department of Commerce, designated eighteen chemicals and categories of chemicals for EPA
consideration as mandated by TSCA. Instead of concluding the
rule making, or deciding conclusively not to pursue rule making
as directed by law, however, the EPA issued statements to the
effect that it had not yet completed a full evaluation of the chemicals. The agency then removed the chemicals from their priority
designation. The NRDC filed suit, alleging that the agency was not
fulfilling its statutory mandates.

In response to the NRDC lawsuit, the EPA issued a letter

explaining its actions.[5] The letter emphasized the difficulties the EPA was experiencing, including a shortage in trained personnel and office space. Further, upon oral argument, the attorney for the EPA discussed the agency's funding problems but, when questioned by the judge, was unable to provide evidence that EPA administrators had sought additional funds from Congress to enable the agency to carry out its new responsibilities.[6]

The court, unpersuaded by the EPA's arguments of "administrative impossibility of performance," issued a judgment finding the agency in violation of TSCA. The court ordered the EPA to submit a plan for complying with its statutory mandates. The agency returned with an expedited schedule for testing the priority chemicals (see Table 3), which the court incorporated into a second order.[7]

In the second order, Judge Pierce mandated that the EPA file with the court twice a year for three years written reports on the progress of the agency in meeting the Interagency Testing Committee's list of backlogged chemicals and the tentative dates of action. The court also ordered the EPA to file a statement indicating whether the agency expected to be able to comply with the court-ordered schedule for the year in which the report would be filed and, if not, a detailed statement why such compliance would not be made. Further, should the EPA fail to meet any year-end goal, the court ordered the agency to file "a detailed explanation as to the reasons for the failure to meet the schedule along with a statement as to when the required action . . . [would be] taken."[8]

In addition, the judge took the unusual action of ordering the plaintiff, NRDC, to act as the agency's watchdog and enforce his order by "commencing a new action" should the EPA not comply with the court mandate. In this regard, the judge overstepped statutory bounds and held that the TSCA-mandated re-

Table 3
Court-Ordered Compliance Schedule:
Natural Resources Defense Council v. Costle

Deadline for Action	No. of Single Chemicals or Categories	Action Ordered	Chemicals
5/81	3	Proposed rules and/or decisions not to test	Nitrobenzene Dichloromethane 1,1,1-trichloroethane
1981	8	Proposed rules and/or decisions not to test	Eight of the following chemicals: Acetonitrile Alkyl phthalates Antimony Antimony trioxide Antimony sulfide Aryl phosphates Benzidine dyes Chloroparaffins Chloronaphthalenes Cresols Dianisidine dyes Hexachlorobutadiene Methylenedianiline O-tolidine dyes Phenylenediamines Polychlorinated terphenyls
1982	13	Proposed test rules and/or decisions not to test	1. The eight remaining chemicals on the 1981 list 2. Five of the following chemicals: Alkyl epoxides Acrylimide (Environmental) Anilines

Table 3. Court-Ordered Compliance Schedule:
Natural Resources Defense Council v. Costle (continued)

Deadline for Action	No. of Single Chemicals or Categories	Action Ordered	Chemicals
			Chlorobenzenes (environmental) Cyclohexanon 1,2-dichloropropane Haloalkyl epoxides Pyridine Toluene Xylenes
1983	13	Proposed rules and/or decisions not to test	1. The five remaining chemicals on the 1982 list 2. The following eight chemicals: Glycidol group Hexachlorocyclopentadiene Hydroquinone Isopherone Mesityl oxide Methyl ethyl ketone Methyl isobutyl ketone Quinone

quirement of sixty days' notice to the agency prior to filing a suit[9] would be waived for the environmental interest group.

The Agency's Response

The EPA's initial response to the court decision was swift and immediate. Members of the EPA staff responsible for TSCA directed all of their efforts to complying with the court order.[10] In 1981 eleven test rule decisions were issued, exactly as the court had mandated.[11] On December 31, 1981, the agency submitted an affidavit to the court signed by EPA Deputy Administrator John W. Hernandez. The document reported the success of the agency in meeting its 1981 goal and promised thirteen test rule decisions in 1982 (six by the end of June and seven by the end of December).[12]

Four months later, EPA issued its "Semi-Annual Regulatory Agenda,"[13] in which it pledged to comply with the court-ordered schedule. In addition, that same document reported that the EPA would announce in April whether testing would be required on hexachloroethane, diethylenetriamine, and chlorotoluene as recommended by the Interagency Testing Committee. Plans to issue other test rule decisions were also included in the agenda.

Sometime between April 12 and June 12 of 1982 the EPA changed its strategy, however, as agency officials announced that no test rule decisions would be issued. Instead, voluntary testing agreements would be negotiated with industry groups on most of the chemicals.[14] Under the voluntary testing agreement policy, the EPA would negotiate compacts with industry groups concerning the testing of certain chemicals. In such cases, the agency would be able to issue a decision not to require testing by rule because testing was already being done.

In explaining its change in policy and procedure, the EPA cited a stronger effort to meet the court-ordered deadlines.[15] While many outside the agency assumed that the new administrator, Anne M. Gorsuch (who was charged with streamlining and weakening environmental regulations), had created the voluntary testing agreements, they were incorrect. The new policy had been under consideration by the agency since the late 1970s.[16] The intensity of complying with the NRDC decision left members of the EPA staff charged with administering the TSCA with no time or resources to devote to other statutorily mandated responsibilities. Something had to change, and voluntary testing agreements seemed to be the answer both administratively and politically.[17]

One environmental newsletter called the new policy a "short-cut method for obtaining test data without having to go through the two-year rulemaking procedure."[18] Ironically, however, the EPA later had to concede that it had not issued any test rule decisions in the first half of 1982 because the newly initiated negotiations with industry groups took too long, delaying the agency's efforts in this regard.[19] The start-up costs of the new voluntary testing agreement policy proved to be enormous in terms of staff resources and time.

The EPA's Affidavit

On June 30, 1982, the EPA filed its required affidavit with the court and explained that the agency had failed to meet its June deadline for issuing test rule decisions because it had chosen "to pursue negotiations with the affected companies in an effort to secure testing agreements in lieu of rulemaking. . . . We believe that these negotiations are in the public interest," the EPA reported, "because testing agreements will result in a more expeditious initiation of testing than could be achieved under any test rule."[20]

The document also stated that the agency planned to make six test rule decisions in the third quarter of 1982 and seven decisions in the fourth quarter.[21] The agency added a caveat concerning three chemicals: acetonitrile, cresols, and acrylimide. Test rule decisions on those groups, the EPA wrote, would be issued in the third quarter only if manufacturers of each chemical would form testing groups or "delegations of signatory authority" under which voluntary testing could be conducted. If the agency was unable to negotiate voluntary testing on the chemicals, however, the test rule decisions would be delayed until the fourth quarter.[22]

In December, EPA Administrator Gorsuch announced voluntary testing agreements on eight chemicals and a decision not to require testing on three other substances, thus meeting the court's deadline for 1982.[23] In addition, the agency responded to new 1981 recommendations from the Interagency Testing Committee by announcing one more voluntary testing agreement, six more decisions not to test, and one proposed test rule. On December 18, 1982, EPA Deputy Administrator Hernandez signed another affidavit filed with the court stating that test rule decisions would be issued during 1983 on the last thirteen chemicals or chemical categories discussed in the 1981 court order.[24]

The EPA's Policy and Administrative Changes
The EPA commitment to meeting the court-ordered schedule through its new voluntary testing agreement policy was reflected in many of the agency's official documents. First, the EPA's *Fiscal Year 1984 Budget Summary,* released January 31, 1983, cited compliance with the court's order as a priority and described a resulting shift in agency resources. Specifically, the *Budget Summary* explained:

> In early 1984, the toxic substances program will complete the court-mandated schedule for responding to the backlog of ITC [Interagency Testing Committee] recommendations by negotiating agreements, proposing test rules, or publishing its reasons for not requiring testing. In addition, the program will continue to respond to all new designations within the statutory time limit. We will also shift resources from the test guidelines program to the test rule/agreement development area as a result of completing the bulk of the test guidelines work.[25]

Second, the actual EPA budget approved by President Ronald Reagan that same year proposed lowering the funding for the toxic substances program to $66.7 million for fiscal year 1984, from about $69.9 million estimated in fiscal year 1983 and $74.9 million in fiscal year 1982. According to the budget document, the proposed funding and personnel cuts in implementing TSCA were possible partly because of the "elimination of the backlog of chemicals recommended for additional testing by the ITC. Under a court order," the document indicated, "the agency has until the end of 1983 to decide whether to require additional testing of those chemicals. After that time, EPA only need answer the testing recommendations issued by ITC twice a year."[26]

Members of the EPA staff interviewed for this book reported that this sort of budget reduction in response to the fulfillment of a court order was not unusual in the Gorsuch administration. In fact, in her efforts to slash the EPA budget by 30 to 40 percent, Gorsuch cited compliance with court decisions as her highest priority. Statutory mandates came second, and "everything else dropped to the bottom," fair game for budget cuts.[27]

Third, the *TSCA Annual Report to Congress* for fiscal year 1982, which called that year "a dynamic period of TSCA implementation," provided an update on the review of chemicals recommended by the Interagency Testing Committee. "The use of negotiated testing agreements with industry was emphasized," the report said, "in deciding whether new testing was needed on chemicals designated by the committee." The EPA document also reported that during the year, "the agency met TSCA's one-year deadline for answering 1981 ITC recommendations and a court-imposed schedule for handling backlogged ITC chemicals."[28]

Last, the "List of 1982 Accomplishments" issued in January, 1983, by John A. Todhunter, EPA assistant administrator for pesticides and toxic substances, discussed the program's success in meeting Judge Pierce's order. Specifically, the memo from Todhunter to EPA Administrator Gorsuch listed compliance with "statutory and court-ordered schedules for deciding whether to issue TSCA test rule decisions" as a significant accomplishment.[29]

Ruckelshaus's Completion of the Court-Ordered Action

The year 1983 was a tumultuous one for the EPA. Administrator Gorsuch resigned from her position under a cloud of controversy. Gorsuch had slashed the EPA budget, had destroyed morale at the agency, and had alienated Congress by refusing to provide an investigating committee documents concerning the agency's controversial Superfund program. William D. Ruckelshaus, the first administrator of the EPA, was called upon to replace Gorsuch in an effort to save the ailing agency.

On June 30, 1983, Ruckelshaus filed an affidavit with the court stating that the agency had issued three test rule decisions in the first half of 1983[30] and would issue another ten by the end of the year. In late December of the same year, the ten remaining decisions were issued.[31] EPA officials breathed a sigh of relief. Ironically, however, just as the agency had completed its court-ordered three-year, thirty-nine-chemical test program, an unanticipated consequence of the implementation of the court decision reared its ugly head. A new NRDC lawsuit challenging the legality of negotiated testing agreements was filed in court.

The Toxic Chemicals Testing Challenge, Part Two

The NRDC had criticized the use of voluntary testing agreements from the start. NRDC attorney Jacqueline M. Warren faulted the policy, calling it a "back room process which lacks the public participation opportunities of a formal rulemaking process."[32] The environmental group described other flaws in the policy: no court review, the inability of citizens to file suit against those violating a rule, the lack of enforceable deadlines, minimum publicity, and the failure to trigger other parts of TSCA that are affected by the test rules. The not-for-profit group also said it feared that the EPA would accept an inferior testing program from chemical companies in an attempt to obtain voluntary testing.[33]

In November, 1982, the Senate Environment and Public Works Subcommittee on Toxic Substances and Environmental Oversight had asked the General Accounting Office to investigate the legality of the negotiated testing agreements.[34] The General Accounting Office, persuaded by EPA arguments that the negotiated agreements produced testing data on a chemical within one year, while issuing a traditional test rule could result in a two-year delay (which might further slow EPA compliance with the court order), found nothing improper about the new EPA policy.[35] Despite this stamp of approval from the General Accounting Office, on February 9, 1983, the NRDC sent a letter to the EPA threatening legal action.[36] One year later, in January of 1984, the NRDC, this time coupled with the Industrial Union Department of the American Federation of Labor and Congress of Industrial Organizations (AFL-CIO), filed suit again in the U.S. District Court for the Southern District of New York[37] alleging that the EPA violated TSCA in four instances.

First, the EPA violated the law by entering into voluntary testing agreements with industry groups instead of promulgating test rules. Such voluntary testing agreements were not authorized by TSCA, the NRDC and AFL-CIO argued, and circumvented "key statutory provisions which are triggered only with the issuance of final test rules." Second, the EPA violated the law by issuing an "advance notice of proposed rulemaking" on the chemical substances known as fluoroalkenes, because a notice that suggests testing may be necessary does not "initiate rulemaking" within the meaning of TSCA. Third, the EPA violated the law by proposing a "two-phase rulemaking process" that delayed some rules by as many as seven years. Fourth, the EPA violated the law by delaying the promulgation of final rules on five chemicals recommended for testing in 1977 and 1978. The plaintiffs asked the court to find the EPA in violation of TSCA in all four instances and to establish a "prompt" schedule for the agency to comply with the act.[38]

The Court-Ordered Schedule

On August 23, 1984, the court found in favor of the NRDC and AFL-CIO on two of the four counts. First, Judge Kevin T. Duffy ruled that the use of voluntary testing agreements in lieu of issuing formal rules to require evaluation of chemicals under TSCA was invalid. The court gave the EPA thirty days to meet with the NRDC and the AFL-CIO to develop a compliance schedule. Second, Judge Duffy ruled that the EPA had unlawfully delayed promulgation of final test rules on five chemicals on which proposed rules had been completed. Although the EPA had argued that TSCA does not set deadlines by which final rules must be issued and that the agency was lacking the necessary resources to implement the program, the judge imposed his own time limitation of "reasonableness" on the EPA's actions.[39]

Nearly three weeks after Duffy's decision, the NRDC and the EPA jointly requested an additional thirty days to develop the court-ordered timetable. The request was denied. Judge Duffy wanted immediate action. The EPA and the NRDC filed a timetable ten days later.[40]

On October 5, 1984, Senator David Durenberger (R-Minnesota) introduced a bill to amend TSCA. Senate Bill 3075 would have overturned Duffy's court order by allowing the EPA to negotiate testing agreements with industry groups when the EPA deter-

Table 4
Court-Ordered Compliance Schedule:
Natural Resources Defense Council v. Ruckelshaus

Chemical	Action	Deadline
Benzyl butyl phthalate	Program review of data to yield notice of proposed rule making (NPRM) or decision not to test (DNT)	October, 1985
2-chlorotoluene	Program review of data to yield NPRM (single-phase) or DNT	October, 1985
4-chlorobenzotrifluoride	Program review of data to yield NPRM (single-phase) or DNT	October, 1985
Formamide	Program review of data to yield NPRM (single-phase) or DNT	March, 1986
Fluoroalkenes	Program review of data to yield NPRM (single-phase) or DNT	October, 1985
Chloromethane	Program review of data to yield withdrawal of proposed rule	June, 1985
Chlorinated benzenes	Withdrawal of portion of proposed rule	December, 1984
Health effects of chlorinated benzenes	Final rule (single-phase)	June, 1986
1,1,1-trichloroethane	Phase II NPRM Phase II final rule	July, 1985 March, 1986

mined that their use would speed development of adequate test data. The bill never became law.

Three weeks later, Duffy issued a second order that adopted the proposed timetable submitted by the EPA and the NRDC (see Table 4). Under the schedule, a final decision on whether eight chemicals should be tested under TSCA test rules was ordered by June, 1986.[41] In addition, the judge ordered the agency to submit four semiannual progress reports, due in 1985 and 1986. The reports, Duffy mandated, were to include information on whether the EPA would be complying with the schedule and detailed reasons for any delays.[42]

The Agency's Response

In commenting on the court decision, one EPA official said, "our entire program was wiped out. We had to start over at ground zero."[43] Another expressed shock that the decision had "effectively invalidated all [twenty-one] industry voluntary testing agreements."[44] One environmental newsletter wrote that "in light of the court's ruling, the agency's testing program faced very real difficulties in responding to the ITC recommendations."[45] Members of the EPA staff also expressed concern with the effect the decision might have on future industry cooperation in providing needed chemical data.[46] Another staff member complained that the court did not show a comprehensive understanding of TSCA.[47] Yet another staff member said he doubted whether the agency should appeal the case during a presidential election year since it was obviously a political hot potato.[48]

In response to this second decision, the EPA initiated several changes in its policies and procedures. First, although the use of two-phase rule making was not overturned by the court, the agency reacted by announcing the initiation of one-phase test rules, rather than the two-phase rule-making approach. In adopting the new procedure, Don R. Clay, head of the EPA's Office of Toxic Substances, said the testing program "costs more than it's been worth. I'm looking for an easier way [to speed the testing process]."[49] The change was incorporated into a rule that became effective June 16, 1984.

Next, the agency entered into negotiations with the NRDC and the Chemical Manufacturers' Association to explore alternatives to the EPA's testing program following Judge Duffy's ruling.[50] After several months of discussion, the groups agreed on two new policies. The first new policy changed the designation process conducted by the Interagency Testing Committee by creating an "intent-to-designate" category that would give the EPA six extra months to study chemical testing recommendations. The Interagency Testing Committee adopted this suggested change immediately.[51] The second new policy consisted of the initiation of "enforceable consent agreements" that would replace the voluntary testing agreements struck down by the court. Enforceable consent agreements would be used "only when the chemical makers and the public agree on the need for and scope of testing."[52] Under this new policy the EPA would limit to ten weeks the amount of time chemical companies have to devise a voluntary testing plan unless continued negotiation was likely to result in a draft agreement without four additional weeks. The enforceable consent agreements would thus require companies to meet a schedule for testing a chemical and would be enforced by the agency. If no agreement could be reached, the EPA would issue a test rule. The EPA published an interim final rule on June 30, 1986, authorizing enforceable consent testing agreements.[53]

Last, in response to the specifics of Duffy's order, the EPA began to take action on the eight priority chemicals listed in the order. For example, the EPA acted on a policy for chlorinated benzenes in December, 1984, by first withdrawing a portion of the proposed rule.[54] A final chlorinated benzene rule was issued by the EPA eighteen months later.[55] The regulation called for the testing of health effects on five chemicals within the chemical group.[56] A second environmental rule for chlorinated benzenes was issued in July of 1987. As to the other chemicals, rules were promulgated as follows: chloromethane—May, 1985; benzyl butyl phthalate—July, 1985; 4-chlorobenzotrifluoride—October, 1985; 1,1,1-trichloroethane—December, 1985; formamide—February, 1986; and fluoroalkenes—June, 1987.[57] Finally, a consent agreement was reached for 2-chlorotoluene in October of 1988.[58]

The New Policy's Lack of Success
By the end of 1986, the chemical industry was complaining that enforceable consent testing agreements had been a failure. The EPA, the Chemical Manufacturers' Association said, was unwilling to negotiate actual testing schemes and did not encourage the exploration of options to testing. The EPA held a public meeting in November, 1986, to respond to industry concerns.[59] Another public meeting was held for similar reasons in December, 1987.[60]

Members of the EPA staff indicated in November, 1989, that the enforceable consent agreement policy was being reviewed both internally and with all interested stakeholders and possibly would be revised or replaced in 1990.[61] In four years, only one consent agreement had been reached out of almost a dozen attempts.[62] The problem, according to members of the EPA staff, is that the issue of exactly what would be negotiable in the enforceable consent agreements was never explicitly discussed in post–court order talks with the NRDC and the Chemical Manufacturers' Association.[63] The chemical industry assumed everything would be negotiable, while the EPA assumed very little would be negotiable.[64] Other problems include staff turnover and the missing of some deadlines by as much as one and one-half years.[65]

"No one is happy with the present arrangement," said one EPA staff member who worked on a December, 1989, report criticizing the program. "Industry officials do not think they have enough of a say in the process. The EPA staff think the process is too cumbersome and time consuming. And NRDC has only participated in one case, dealing with isopropyl alcohol. If NRDC drops its support, the agency may drop the whole thing, go to pure rule making, or renegotiate a brand new way of responding to the 1984 court decision."[66]

In July, 1992, the EPA announced an "open season" on proposals from industry groups for chemicals to be the subject of enforceable negotiated testing agreements.[67] Two and one-half years had passed since the agency had issued a final TSCA test rule, the number of staff in the EPA TSCA testing branch had been cut in half since 1988, a General Accounting Office report had criticized the TSCA testing program, and Representative Mike Synar (D-Oklahoma) had blasted the agency for the lack of timeliness and the low quality of the chemical review process.[68] Desperate EPA staff members were searching for a creative way to deal expeditiously with the backlog of chemicals to be tested.

Out of approximately 120 industrial chemicals labeled as possible candidates for testing, the EPA received 22 testing proposals for 12 chemical substances and 4 chemical categories. As of this writing, the EPA had screened the proposals and was seeking individuals interested in participating in, or monitoring, the negotiations.[69]

The PCB Challenge

Section 6(e) of TSCA orders the administrator of the EPA to promulgate regulations concerning the disposal, marking, manufacture, processing, distribution, and use of polychlorinated biphenyls (PCBs).[70] The statute, however, allows the EPA to promulgate regulations to reduce the impact of any PCB ban. When the EPA promulgated regulations in 1979 to implement the section,[71] it excluded from the ban several categories of PCBs.

As a result, the Environmental Defense Fund (EDF) sued the EPA seeking the review of three aspects of the agency's PCB regulations.[72] First, the EDF challenged the categorization of certain commercial uses of PCBs as "totally enclosed," a designation that exempted those uses from regulation under TSCA. Second, the EDF challenged the EPA's practice of only regulating materials containing concentrations of PCBs greater than fifty parts per million (ppm). Third, the EDF challenged the decision by the EPA to authorize the continued use of eleven non–totally enclosed uses of PCBs.

On October 30, 1980, Judges Harry Edwards, Spotswood W. Robinson, III, and Howard F. Corcoran of the U.S. Court of Appeals for the District of Columbia Circuit issued a ruling agreeing with the EDF on the first and second of its challenges, finding that the EPA regulations and practices were in violation of TSCA. The court, however, upheld the EPA regulations that were the subject of EDF's third challenge. In overturning the EPA's regulations in the first and second instances, the court effectively invalidated the EPA's 50 ppm regulatory exclusion as well as its determination that the use of PCBs in electrical equipment was "totally enclosed." The court remanded these issues to the EPA for further action consistent with its opinion.[73]

Had the court's decision gone into effect immediately, it would have made the manufacture, processing, or distribution in commerce of products containing any concentration of PCBs illegal. This would have had the sweeping effect of making the use of all electrical equipment, other than railroad transformers, containing any concentration of PCBs a violation of TSCA. In effect, the decision would have made the use of most household appliances and business machines a violation of law. Citing the "severe economic hardship" that would have evolved from an immediate ban of these uses, the EPA, the EDF, and other industry intervenors asked the court to stay its mandate.[74] The court granted an eighteen-month stay and issued two different orders allowing both the "totally enclosed" classification and the 50 ppm regulatory cutoff to remain in effect during the duration of the stay.[75]

"Totally Enclosed" PCBs

Prior to the issuance of the court's stay concerning "totally enclosed" PCBs, the EPA entered into court-ordered negotiations with industry groups and the EDF and agreed on an appropriate agency response to the court's directive. The EPA agreed to conduct rule making on the use of PCBs in electrical equipment, beginning with an advance notice of proposed rule making. In the meantime, the Edison Electric Institute, through the Utility Solid Waste Activities Group, agreed to develop some of the factual material necessary for rule making. The parties agreed to interim risk-reduction measures (called "the Interim Measures Program") for transformers containing PCBs at 50 ppm or greater. The court made all of these measures a condition of the eighteen-month stay and required the EPA to promulgate a final rule within six months of receipt of the study from the solid waste group.[76]

On March 10, 1981, the text of the court's order was published in the Federal Register along with the EPA's advance notice of proposed rule making on the use of PCBs in electrical equipment.[77] Simultaneously, "an enormous effort" was launched under the direction of the EPA to gather new data on PCBs.[78] One year later, the EPA received the Report of the Utility Solid Waste Activities Group. The four-volume report boldly concluded that the EPA should, in effect, thumb its nose at the court and re-adopt the PCB rule exclusions that had been overturned by the court. The solid waste group said that data examined in the study showed that PCB exposure from electrical equipment "is far less than thought when EPA originally adopted the May, 1979, regulations or when the Court of Appeals reviewed those regulations."[79]

In the meantime, partially in response to the court decision, the EPA issued a policy statement on the compliance program, concerning, among other things, the Interim Measures Program. A. E. Conroy II, director of the Pesticides and Toxic Substances Enforcement Division, released the document, which stated that during the court's stay, the EPA would leave intact most of the provisions of the original PCB regulation but would continue working on new regulations. The policy statement also required individual companies to inspect their facilities regularly for transformer leaks.[80]

On April 22, 1982, the EPA proposed a new rule concerning the use of PCBs in electrical equipment to replace the regulation invalidated by the EDF court decision.[81] A final version of the rule was published in the Federal Register on August 25, 1982. Among other things, the rule authorized the continued use of PCB small capacitors and the use of PCB transformers, if certain conditions were met.[82] Members of the EPA staff breathed a sigh of relief and congratulated themselves on a job well done. The celebration, however, was short-lived.

Immediately after the promulgation of this rule on electrical equipment, the EDF, joined by the NRDC and three industry groups, sued the EPA again challenging the legality of the new regulation. The EPA settled with the NRDC and the EDF in October, 1983, by agreeing to minor modifications of the rule. The concerns of industry groups were settled in March, 1984, when the agency agreed to revise the PCB regulations to eliminate wording indicating that any exposure to PCBs is significant and therefore potentially harmful. The final regulation was signed by Alvin Alm, EPA deputy administrator, on July 13, 1984,[83] thus partially fulfilling the EPA's responsibility as mandated by the court.

PCBs Below 50 Ppm

In response to the portion of the court's order invalidating EPA's 50 ppm regulatory exclusion, the agency addressed low concentrations of PCBs that are produced in two categories. The first category was "closed and controlled waste manufacturing processes," while the second category was "uncontrolled" environments. In both instances, the EPA, in negotiations with environmental and industry groups, agreed to conduct new rule-making activities while industry groups agreed to initiate studies to provide information for the rule making. Once again, this agreement was made a part of the formal court order.

In its order, the court required the EPA, first, to publish two advanced notices of proposed rule making to develop rules to cover PCBs in concentrations below 50 ppm. Second, the court required the EPA to promulgate a final rule, within eighteen months from the date of the order, for PCBs generated in closed and controlled waste manufacturing processes, or to explain its reasons for not doing so. Third, the judges ordered the environmental agency to advise the court within eleven months after the date of the order of the EPA's plans and its schedule for further action on PCBs in concentrations below 50 ppm that were generated as uncontrolled PCBs. On May 20, 1981, the EPA published two advance notices of proposed rule making on the 50 ppm regulatory cutoff.[84]

Ten months later, also in direct response to the judges' order, the EPA submitted a report to the court concerning the agency's plans for further regulatory action on uncontrolled

PCBs. The EPA asked the court for an extension of its stay, arguing that the agency could not adequately define its plans concerning uncontrolled PCBs until the rule-making process on closed and controlled waste processes was completed. The court acquiesced, granting a stay of its mandate until December 1, 1982.[85]

In October, 1982, the EPA promulgated a rule concerning closed and controlled PCBs.[86] That rule was modified a year later under pressure by the NRDC, the Chemical Manufacturers' Association, and other groups. The final rule-making package changed the EPA's policies in two significant ways. First, it limited the level of inadvertently generated PCBs in most products to an annual average of 25 ppm, with a maximum concentration of 50 ppm. Second, the rule set limits on PCBs vented into the air or discharged into water and required that process wastes containing PCBs in excess of 50 ppm be disposed of in accordance with PCB disposal requirements.[87]

In late 1983, the EPA proposed a regulation concerning uncontrolled PCBs produced in small quantities. That rule closely followed a joint recommendation by the Chemical Manufacturers' Association and the NRDC that set 25 ppm as the limit for the annual average PCB concentration in most products and processes.[88] By promulgating the rule in July, 1984, the EPA fulfilled its responsibilities as ordered by the court in *EDF v. EPA.*[89] Champagne bottles were uncorked throughout the agency.

The U.S. Court of Appeals for the District of Columbia put a damper on the celebration by ordering the EPA to pay the EDF, from the EPA budget, $99,534.50 in attorneys' fees incurred in connection with the PCB lawsuit. In making the award, the court said it was doing so partially because of the "critically important and difficult issues" involved in the case.[90] TSCA allows the awarding of attorneys' fees "if the court determines such an award is appropriate."[91]

The regulation of PCBs continues to be a significant challenge for the EPA in the decade of the 1990s. A congressional committee blasted the EPA for its lax management of PCBs, urging the agency to address loopholes that still exist in its regulations.[92] Representatives criticized the agency for inadequate protection of the public and the environment from PCB contamination.[93] Moreover, legislation was introduced in the 100th and 101st congressional sessions to strengthen PCB control under TSCA. At the beginning of 1993, the EPA was developing three new PCB regulations to address some of these concerns. Clearly, the PCB problem will continue to pose great administrative, legal, economic, and political problems for the EPA both inside and outside the courtroom.

Conclusion

An examination of these TSCA case scenarios provides not only a study of the true complexities of the intended and unintended impact of court decisions on the policies and administration of an administrative agency, but also a realistic view of two ongoing, affirmative decrees. Further, in both instances, the judges took unusual steps to ensure the implementation of their orders. One judge ordered the plaintiffs to file a new suit should the EPA not comply with the order, then overstepped judicial bounds by waiving the statutorily mandated provision for sixty days' notice. Another judge later also imposed a time frame of "reasonableness" on the agency's actions even though none existed in the statute. The judge in the PCB case ordered the EPA to negotiate an implementation plan with industry and environmental groups, then incorporated that plan in his order.

In the cases studied in this chapter, the EPA responded, generally, by complying with the courts' orders directly and expeditiously. The EPA response was one of rechanneling staff and funds, with no indication of any intent to purposefully ignore statutory mandates. There have been other instances, however, especially in the early years of the Reagan administration, where EPA actions have been obvious attempts to circumvent statutory mandates for political purposes. In one example concerning formaldehyde, a chemical used in products from plywood to diapers, the mere filing of a lawsuit served as a check against such abuse.

Under the Carter administration, the EPA made a decision (based on a scientific study that found formaldehyde caused cancer in rats and thus possibly in humans), to rank the chemical as a substantial risk.[94] That decision was overturned under the Reagan administration by John A. Todhunter, administrator for pesticides and toxic substances, in what EPA career staff members called a "purely political decision."[95] Members of the EPA staff said, "A political appointee with no scientific or technical background made that decision."[96] Other sources reported that the decision was made after a series of "by invitation only" closed-door meetings with industry representatives that excluded members of the public, including environmental and public health groups.[97] EPA staff members testified before a congressional committee that Todhunter had ordered the staff formaldehyde study altered to make the chemical appear less dangerous.[98] In response to Todhunter's action, in July, 1983, the NRDC and the American Public Health Association sued, charging that the EPA had set an unreasonably high standard for meeting health hazard criteria in TSCA and that the EPA had violated its own scientific principles in assessing the chemical's carcinogenicity.[99]

Within a year, the EPA had reversed that decision. NRDC attorney Jane Bloom heralded the action as a tremendous victory. "As a result of our lawsuit the agency rescinded its previous decision and agreed to put in place a chemical risk assessment which they had abandoned," Bloom stated.[100] Later, in April, 1987, the EPA announced that it had completed a health risk assessment for formaldehyde. Based on animal and human studies, the agency confirmed formaldehyde as a probable human carcinogen. An update of the formaldehyde risk assessment was presented to the EPA's Science Advisory Board in 1990. Following a public meeting to receive comments on the study, the EPA revised the document again in 1991, still supporting its 1987 finding that formaldehyde is a probable human carcinogen. In July, 1992, the Science Advisory Board urged the EPA to further revise the risk assessment by using new "nasal DNA-protein cross-link data" that more accurately measure how much formaldehyde reaches a cell.[101] In the meantime, the EPA continued to work on rules to control the use of formaldehyde. As of this writing, the EPA was concentrating much of its efforts on studies concerning formaldehyde emissions in new homes.[102]

In Search of Clean Air

Chapter Five

The . . . [EPA] is under the misperception that it is shackled and bound by the court's decision. The agency should not roll over and play dead before the obiter dictum.

—CARL E. BAGGE
president, National Coal Association
EPA Public Hearing, January 8, 1985

The issue of regulating hazardous air pollutants is complex and technical in nature. The controversy usually begins with the question of which air pollutants should be classified as hazardous and continues as emission standards are set and regulations are promulgated. The 1990 Clean Air Act (CAA) lists 189 toxic air pollutants that must be regulated by the EPA, including benzene, chlorine, asbestos, formaldehyde, methanol, styrene, and vinyl chloride.[1] The complex process of regulating hazardous air pollutants has been exacerbated by politics, economics, scientific uncertainty, and court intervention. One case drew the agency into court seven times and put the EPA administrator in the position of choosing between credibility with the scientific community and credibility with the courts.

The Radionuclides Challenge

On November 8, 1979, the EPA (under the Carter administration), finding that radionuclides increase the risk of cancer, genetic damage, and premature death, added the radioactive substances to its List of Hazardous Air Pollutants for which emission standards would be issued.[2] Radionuclides are radioactive particles that may be released into the atmosphere from a wide range of sources, including facilities that use radioactive materials (nuclear power plants, weapons factories, hospitals) and uranium and phosphate mining operations. In urban settings, the largest source of radionuclides is usually coal-fired power plants.[3]

The pre-1990 Clean Air Act[4] provided that

within 180 days after the inclusion of any air pollutant in . . . [the List of Hazardous Air Pollutants], the . . . [EPA] shall publish proposed regulations establishing emission standards for such pollutant together with a notice of a public hearing within thirty days. Not later than 180 days after such publication, the Administrator shall prescribe an emission standard for such pollutant, unless he finds, on the basis of information presented at such hearings, that such pollutant is clearly not a hazardous pollutant.[5]

When a year and a half passed and the EPA (directed by Anne Gorsuch, appointed by newly elected President Ronald Reagan) had published neither proposed regulations nor a notice of a public hearing, the Sierra Club sued the EPA. The Sierra Club's request to the U.S. District Court for the Northern District of California was four-pronged. First, the group requested a declaration that the CAA imposed a duty on the EPA to issue proposed radionuclide regulations within 180 days of their being listed. Second, the group requested a declaration that the EPA failed to fulfill this duty. Third, the Sierra Club sought an order directing the EPA to prepare a proposed schedule for issuing draft radionuclide standards and to meet with all parties within 30 days to agree on a final compliance schedule. Finally, the environmental group asked for an order directing the parties to inform the court if they could not agree on a final schedule so that the court could then issue one.

Although the EPA defended its lack of action by citing "administrative impossibility" because of the complexity of regulating radionuclides, the court was not persuaded. The court granted the Sierra Club's motion for partial summary judgment and ordered the EPA to propose a compliance schedule within thirty days. Moreover, the court ordered all parties to the lawsuit to meet within forty-five days to determine whether they were able to agree on a schedule. Further, the court retained jurisdiction over the matter until the EPA complied with the court order.[6]

Sierra Club v. EPA: *Part Two*

In response to the court order, the EPA drafted and submitted to the court a proposal for compliance indicating that it needed nine years after the statutory 180-day deadline, or until 1989, to issue proposed regulations for radionuclides.[7] The already overburdened EPA argued that the issues were unduly complex and that the agency was constrained by budget and staff limitations. The Sierra Club, angry and shocked at the request, objected to the nine-year extension and asked the court instead to place the EPA on a 180-day compliance schedule.

The court found in favor of the Sierra Club. On September 30, 1982, noting that it had been five years since the enactment of the section of the CAA in question, nearly three years since the EPA listed radionuclides as a hazardous air pollutant, and almost two and one-half years since the expiration of the original 180-day deadline for issuance of proposed radionuclide regulations, the court chastised the agency for its ineptness. The EPA envisioned "a level of thoroughness and scientific certainty not within the contemplation of Congress," the court said.[8] The court also expressed its lack of sympathy for the EPA's claims of staff and budget constraints. The EPA was ordered to issue radio-nuclide regulations within 180 days.

Exactly 180 days after the court order, on April 6, 1983, the EPA issued a proposal to regulate five sources of radionuclides: Department of Energy (DOE) facilities, non-DOE federal facili-ties, facilities licensed by the Nuclear Regulatory Commission, underground uranium mines, and elemental phosphorus plants. The agency declined to regulate five other sources, including coal-fired utilities and industrial boilers.[9] Coal-fired utility boil-ers were not being proposed for regulation, one EPA staff mem-ber said, because the benefits derived from retrofitting existing plants did not outweigh the costs.[10] Specifically, the EPA had calculated that the maximum exposure to an individual from radionuclides emitted from a coal-fired power plant was about one millirem per person per year. (A chest x-ray is equivalent to twenty to thirty millirems. Ten millirems for one individual per day for seventy years poses a lifetime risk of cancer of one in 10,000, according to the EPA.)

Glen L. Sjoblom, director of the agency's Office of Radiation Protection, said that the agency hoped the regulations would become law the following October. Radionuclide-producing fa-cilities would then have two years to meet the proposed stan-dards.[11] Kathryn Dickson, attorney for the Sierra Club, said she would examine the regulations but was "worried about industry pressure, particularly from the mining and utility industries. The real question is whether they're regulating with an ample margin of safety in mind or with industry in mind."[12]

On June 13, 1983, Gary Baise, an attorney for FMC Corporation (which owned a phosphorus processing plant subject to the EPA's regulations), wrote a letter to Terrance McLaughlin, chief of the EPA Environmental Standards Branch in the Office of Air, Noise and Radiation, in which he protested the proposal of the radionuclide regulations without consultation with the EPA's Science Advisory Board (SAB), as urged by section 7417(c) of the CAA.[13] The same objection was echoed only days later by the Idaho Mining Association.[14] One EPA official said that such a review is usually initiated by the EPA's Office of Research and Development. In the radionuclide case, however, the regulations were handled by the Office of Radiation Protection, which had failed to initiate such a review. "There might have been a glitch," one EPA staff member said in an understatement.[15] On January 16, 1984, EPA Administrator William D. Ruckelshaus sought to remedy this situation by referring the radionuclide rules to the SAB for review of the scientific basis for the standards.[16]

One month later, the Sierra Club again filed suit against the EPA in an effort to force the agency to issue final radionuclide regulations expeditiously. "We are disappointed and frustrated at having to goad the agency into issuing the rules," Kathryn Dickson said.[17] Because the regulations were referred to the SAB, the final rules would have to be delayed until July of 1984, Dickson pointed out. The Sierra Club asked the court to order the EPA to promulgate final radionuclide regulations within thirty days. The court did nothing until the SAB issued its report.

Science Advisory Board Report

On July 19, 1984, after a seven-month review, the SAB presented an executive summary of its findings to Administrator Ruckelshaus. The Office of Radiation Protection, the SAB said, had erred grievously by not preparing risk assessment information for the proposed radionuclide regulations in a manner that provided a "scientifically adequate basis for regulatory decisions" concerning the radioactive air pollutants. The Office of Radiation Protection's handling of the radionuclide regulations was embarrassing as it included "an inter-weaving of scientific facts and interpretation, economic considerations, and social and political value judgments" that blurred the EPA's judgment, the SAB said.[18]

A stunned Ruckelshaus told the SAB that the issue of setting a standard for radionuclides was "so contentious and controversial" that more help from the board would be needed in the process of developing regulations. Additionally, Ruckelshaus said that there was no issue that "arouse[d] the emotion" as did the issue of radionuclides. The administrator said that he had been contacted by several members of Congress who were concerned about the issue. "The opposing sides are farther apart on this issue than any other [I have dealt with as EPA administrator]," Ruckelshaus said.[19]

Ruckelshaus then agreed with a recommendation by the SAB to appoint a new standing committee of the board to guide the EPA in reviewing risk assessments for the radiation standards. The formation of the standing committee, however, was opposed by some members of the EPA staff in the Office of Radiation Protection as being "duplicative and not constructive."[20] Despite these objections, EPA staff member Sjoblom said that he was not surprised with the SAB's report, since the regulations were put together in great haste while the EPA was under the 180-day court order.[21]

One week later, the District Court for the Northern District of California ordered the EPA to promulgate final radionuclide regulations within ninety days. (The order was later modified on motion of the EPA, and an alternative possible course of action was added: The administrator might find that radionuclides were "clearly not a hazardous pollutant.")[22] Sarcastically characterizing the EPA's motto as "further study always makes everything better," the court said it would allow no more EPA "footdragging." To do otherwise, the court said, would be an effective repeal of the mandate from Congress to regulate hazardous air particles.[23]

EPA Response to Court and Science Advisory Board

In early August, a new director, Sheldon Myers, was chosen to head up the EPA's Office of Radiation Protection. When the final SAB report was issued three weeks later, Myers announced that he would make every effort to respond to the report, yet would also attempt to avoid being found in contempt of court.[24] In response to the SAB report, Richard J. Guimond, Director of the Office of Radiation Protection Criteria and Standards Division, commented that the board "went a little overboard" in its criticisms of the proposed radionuclide regulations. "If you look at the details they have faulted us for, we don't think they are very significant and if we made all the changes they recommended, it would not significantly change the final risk numbers," Guimond said. In addition, the EPA staff member said that some of the SAB's recommendations, such as an analysis of uncertainty in the risk assessment process, would take years to complete. Such a task simply could not be undertaken under the court-ordered schedule, Guimond said.[25]

On August 24, 1984, in an effort to stem the mounting public criticism of the agency's inaction, the EPA announced that information being considered in formulating final radionuclide regulations was available to the public. This included transcripts of the SAB meetings and the final SAB report. Also distributed were documents containing technical information concerning the source categories for which the EPA had proposed standards.[26]

Within three weeks, the Idaho Mining Association asked the

EPA to withdraw its proposed radionuclide regulations because of the SAB findings. Such a step, the association said, was "the only course of action consistent with the Administrator's often stated philosophy that 'in agency rulemakings . . . [the] science analysis be rigorous and the quality of . . . data be high.'" By withdrawing the proposed regulations, the EPA could reassess whether any standards were necessary. If it were determined that the standards were necessary, the EPA then could prepare "a credible and sustainable basis for regulation," the association maintained.[27]

Around the same period of time, an environmental newsletter published an article that highlighted the divisions and tensions within the EPA surrounding the radionuclide issue. Ruckelshaus, it reported, was extremely concerned with the "shredding" of the agency's proposed radionuclide regulations by the SAB and was contemplating withdrawing the regulations to maintain the credibility of the agency. The same article reported an interview with an agency official indicating a concern that the risks posed by public exposure to radionuclides generally were not significant enough to require regulation for most of the facilities being examined. On the other hand, another EPA staff member was quoted as saying that new studies indicated that elemental phosphorus plants were emitting up to five times more radionuclides than had been previously reported, which could increase potential dosage to the public by a factor of twenty.[28] Rumors were rampant.

The EPA administrator was faced with one of the toughest dilemmas of his career. Should he promulgate regulations that were considered scientifically questionable to comply with a federal court order? Or should he withdraw the radionuclide regulations for further study, thus preserving the scientific credibility of the EPA—an action that was sure to yield a contempt of court citation?

Ruckelshaus's Action

Four days after the publication of the article, on the last day of the ninety-day court-ordered period, Ruckelshaus amazed the nation by withdrawing the proposed radionuclide regulations for phosphorus plants, DOE facilities, non-DOE federal facilities, and facilities licensed by the Nuclear Regulatory Commission.[29] In doing so, the EPA said that the airborne radioactive materials from these sources did not represent unreasonable risks to public health. The agency also said that it based its decision in some of the cases on the high cost of controls and the relatively low level of health benefits that would ensue.[30] Calling the move a "significant change" in policy, one agency spokesperson said, "[We will] now look at what risk is significant and what is not significant in order to regulate. In the past the agency just drove the risk down as far as possible."[31]

As to underground mining sources, the agency announced its intention to regulate them but said that the previous regulations were improper because they would only disperse radioactive emissions over a wider area, not reduce them. Accordingly, the EPA published an advance notice of proposed rule making indicating that new standards would be proposed only for underground uranium mines and uranium mills.[32]

A second environmental interest group, the Environmental Defense Fund (EDF), blew up in anger. Calling the EPA move "outrageous," the EDF reacted to the EPA announcement by immediately filing suit in the U.S. Court of Appeals for the District of Columbia to force the agency to issue all the radionuclide regulations.[33] "It is unconscionable," said EDF attorney Robert E. Yuhnke, "that the government has failed to carry out its duty to protect innocent Americans from known cancer risks over which people have no control."[34] The group's spokesperson also said that the agency was loosening the health standards of the Clean

Air Act by applying cost and other nonhealth tests to regulation. "This decision is the most dramatic example of the radical environmental policies we have seen in the last four years," Yuhnke said. The Natural Resources Defense Council (NRDC) joined the suit, also blasting the EPA action as "a radical and outrageous departure from the public health requirements of the Clean Air Act."[35] In addition, within a few days, the Sierra Club filed a motion with the U.S. District Court for the Northern District of California asking that EPA Administrator Ruckelshaus be cited for contempt of court for not issuing final regulations as the court had ordered.

On October 31, 1984, the California court held a preliminary hearing on the Sierra Club's contempt of court motion. Judge William H. Orrick said that he was "very disturbed that a person as high in the U.S. government as Mr. Ruckelshaus [would] prove to be nothing more than a scofflaw. . . . I think it's outrageous," Orrick continued, "that a responsible person in the U.S. government, a man who has been Assistant Attorney General in charge of the Civil Division . . . and then the first head of the EPA, can so cavalierly disregard an order of the United States District Court." Saying that he was "extremely irritated," the judge called for a full explanation by the EPA on November 21.[36]

On the appointed day, a tense and prolonged hearing on the matter was held. Judge Orrick began by admonishing the agency for its inaction. Referring to a document filed by the EPA with the court in which the agency pointed out that it had been given only two months to read a long and tedious technical report by the SAB, Orrick yelled, "You can read 'War and Peace' and 'The Decline and Fall of the Roman Empire' in two months!"[37] Then, referring to the fact that the EPA had not given the court any realistic estimate of the time needed to issue the radionuclide regulations, Judge Orrick said, "The difficulty in issuing workable final regulations cannot be a valid excuse for noncompliance with the order."[38]

In his defense a ruffled Ruckelshaus told the court that he was aware that withdrawing the radionuclide regulations might not "constitute compliance" with the judge's order. But his rationale, he offered, was based on new data indicating that risks from Nuclear Regulatory Commission (NRC) facilities would amount to only one cancer death every fifty years, while risks from Department of Energy facilities would amount to only one cancer death every thirteen years. Risks from elemental phosphorus plants, the administrator said, would amount merely to one cancer death every seventeen years.

"Given the inevitable burdens that regulation imposes just by its existence, and the shortage of resources to deal with real health risks both in EPA and the society at large, these risks did not appear to me to be large enough to warrant regulation," Ruckelshaus told the court.[39] Further, the EPA's Office of Policy, Planning and Evaluation also opposed the radionuclide regulations because the health risks were not significant, he said. As to the regulations for underground uranium mines, the administrator said that he and EPA staffer Guimond agreed that the sources should be regulated, but the proposed regulations needed improvement.

Confusing the situation and contradicting Ruckelshaus's testimony, Guimond filed a statement with the court indicating that the Office of Radiation Protection had recommended to Ruckelshaus that the EPA promulgate final standards for the NRC facilities, the DOE facilities, and elemental phosphorus plants, "but at a level slightly less stringent than the levels [originally] proposed." Further, Guimond said that control technology was readily available to reduce radionuclide emissions from the four sources and that developing emission standards was relatively straightforward. Guimond pointed out that the EPA had spent $7.6 million in contract funds and 150 staff work-years over a six-year period in preparing the radionuclide regulations.[40]

EPA attorneys begged the court not to hold Ruckelshaus in contempt for several reasons. First, while the district court could order the EPA to issue the radionuclide standards, it had no power to enforce its order, they maintained. Coupled with this, the court's order was not clear enough to be enforceable by a contempt finding, the attorneys argued. Next, the withdrawal of the EPA regulations was a final agency action reviewable only in the U.S. court of appeals. Again, the court had no jurisdiction. Last, the administrator's decision that the record of the case would not support a decision to regulate radionuclide emissions for the four sources was in compliance with the Clean Air Act, it was argued. The agency had a right to change its mind. As to regulations for uranium mines, the agency simply did not have time to promulgate final rules.

Judge Orrick's Action

On December 11, 1984, EPA Administrator Ruckelshaus was found in contempt of court. An angry Judge Orrick called the EPA actions "nonresponsive" and "patently meritless." Moreover, the agency's arguments were labeled "unpersuasive" and "frankly incomprehensible" by the judge.[41] Orrick then ordered the EPA either to issue regulations for NRC-licensed facilities, DOE facilities, non-DOE federal facilities, and elemental phosphorus plants within 30 days and issue regulations for uranium mines within 120 days, or to make a finding that radionuclides clearly are not a hazardous pollutant.[42]

The EPA responded to Orrick's order by requesting a stay of the decision, first from the U.S. Court of Appeals for the Ninth Circuit, and then from the U.S. Supreme Court. "We were disap-

Table 5
Comparison of EPA Radionuclides Regulations

Source	1983 Standards	1985 Standards
NRC-licensed facilities	Indirect emission Standard of 10 mrem/y to any organ	Indirect emission Standard of 25 mrem/y to entire body or 75 mrem/y to any critical organ
DOE facilities	Whole-body dose limit of 10 mrem/y; limit of 30 mrem/y to any organ	Whole body dose limit of 25 mrem/y; limit of 75 mrem/y to any critical organ
Non-DOE facilities	Indirect emission	Indirect emission

Note: mrem/y = millirems per year.

pointed [in Orrick's order]," said A. James Barnes, EPA general counsel, but are "confident that ultimately the agency's position will be upheld."[43] It was not. On January 9, 1985, one day before the deadline imposed by Judge Orrick, the U.S. Court of Appeals denied the EPA's request for a stay.[44]

Eight days later, on January 17, 1985, U.S. Supreme Court Justice William H. Rehnquist denied the agency's request for an extension of the district court's deadline. In his brief opinion, Rehnquist said that Judge Orrick's decision did not conflict with any federal appeals court or Supreme Court decisions. Further, the justice indicated that he was not sure that the Supreme Court would ultimately want to review the case.[45]

Within hours of Rehnquist's opinion, the EPA announced new regulations for facilities licensed by the NRC, DOE facilities, non-DOE federal facilities, and elemental phosphorus plants to comply with the district court's order.[46] Table 5 lists these new radionuclide regulations compared with those originally proposed by the agency in 1983. Regulations for uranium mines, the agency announced, would be issued by April 10, 1985, to comply with the second part of Orrick's order.[47]

It did not take a genius to figure out what the EPA had done: The EPA had issued sham regulations. In its announcement, the EPA amazed the environmental groups by admitting that it was issuing the regulations merely to purge the court order and that, in fact, the regulations would not require polluters to reduce emissions in the least.[48] The agency also said it was contemplating granting waivers from the regulations to DOE, NRC-licensed, and non-DOE federal facilities.[49] EPA spokesman Philip Angell said the agency continued to believe that the regulations were unnecessary and that the new regulations would eventually be withdrawn. "The standards will not require that sources [of radioactive pollution] do anything," Angell said.[50] This wording was echoed in the notice published February 6, 1985, in the Federal Register that announced the regulations.[51]

A distraught NRDC reentered the picture. Barbara Finamore, NRDC attorney, said the environmental group was "very dissatisfied with the content of the [new] standards." Further, she said, the new regulations did not comply with the Clean Air Act. Both the NRDC and the EDF were contemplating filing a sixth lawsuit to challenge the new regulations, Finamore said. At the same time Donald Scroggin, attorney for the law firm Beveridge and Diamond, representing the Ohio Mining Association, said that the EPA's behavior was "bizarre" and "a waste . . . of time."[52]

On February 22, 1985, the EPA proposed new regulations for underground uranium mines. The new standards required inactive and mined-out caverns to be sealed off to diminish radionuclide emissions. In explaining the need for the regulations, the agency said that emissions from uranium mines posed a lifetime cancer risk of between one in 100 and one in 1,000 for persons living nearby. Radionuclide emissions from uranium mines would be reduced by 10 to 60 percent with the promulgation of the new regulations, the EPA said.[53] Those regulations became final on April 17, 1985.[54]

Environmentalists' Sixth Lawsuit

On February 26, 1985, the EDF, the NRDC, and the Sierra Club jointly asked the Court of Appeals for the District of Columbia to review the EPA's final radionuclide regulations for federal facilities and elemental phosphorus plants.[55] In filing the suit, the groups said that the new standards "fail[ed] to provide an ample margin of safety to protect public health." In addition, the plaintiffs maintained that once the agency made a threshold determination that radionuclides were hazardous, it did not have the authority to look further into the significance of the hazard. The complaint also challenged the EPA's review of the costs of regulating hazardous pollutants.

On December 19, 1985, EPA attorney Christopher Herman filed a brief with the appeals court on behalf of the agency. Taking all factors into account, Herman wrote, including the orders of the district court, the agency had acted reasonably. Further, the agency's analysis of costs and risks were allowed under the CAA, the agency maintained.[56]

One month later, the Idaho Mining Association, worried about the economic implications of the regulations, filed a legal memorandum with the court defending the EPA's actions. Pointing out that a $250 million investment in control technology over seventeen years would stop only one cancer death, the association supported the agency's approach of risk and cost assessment. Further, the group argued, there was little scientific basis for requiring the phosphorus industry to limit emissions.[57]

On February 25, 1986, the EDF, the NRDC, and the Sierra

Club filed a reply brief addressing the contention that the EPA may consider cost and feasibility in setting standards for hazardous air pollutants. The environmental groups argued that the EPA's use of a "significant risk" policy in deciding whether to set standards for various source categories was inconsistent with the CAA's mandate to protect public health with an ample margin of safety. They then renewed their request that the court remand the radionuclide regulations back to the EPA.[58]

Vinyl Chloride Decision
On July 28, 1987, before the radionuclides issue was settled by the court, Judge Robert Bork of the Court of Appeals for the District of Columbia issued a landmark decision in another case that dramatically affected the EPA's radionuclide regulations. The appeals court, in ruling on the merits of the agency's vinyl chloride regulations, held that the EPA had improperly considered factors of cost and technological feasibility in determining safety levels for the hazardous air pollutant.[59] The court wrote: "We hold . . . that the Administrator cannot consider cost and technological feasibility in determining what is 'safe.' This determination must be based solely upon the risk of health."[60] The court mandated a two-step process for regulating hazardous air pollutants in which the EPA administrator must first establish an "acceptable" level of risk based solely on health considerations before setting standards that provide an "ample margin of safety." In determining the ample margin of safety, the administrator may require further reductions in emissions to consider health risks, as well as costs and technological feasibility.

On March 17, 1988, the court of appeals granted a joint EPA, NRDC, and EDF motion to delay the issuance of final radionuclide emission standards (previously scheduled for June 6, 1988) until February 28, 1989, with a final rulemaking by August 31, 1989. Two of the rationales cited in defense of the requested extension were the vinyl chloride case[61] and the EPA's desire to study data concerning the effects of radionuclide emissions on Japanese survivors of the nuclear bomb attacks of World War II.[62]

As a result of the vinyl chloride decision, the EPA began to assess not only fatal cancers caused by radionuclides, but nonfatal cancers as well.[63] Further, because of a reexamination of the radionuclides data, on March 7, 1989, the EPA proposed four different approaches for regulating twelve source categories of the hazardous air pollutants.[64] On December 15 of that year, the eleven-year radionuclide battle seemed to have come to an end. After a series of extensive hearings and a lengthy comment period, the agency selected a final approach and issued final regulations to control emissions from the following sources: DOE facilities, licensees of the Nuclear Regulatory Commission and non-DOE federal facilities, uranium fuel cycle facilities, elemental phosphorus plants, coal-fired boilers, high-level nuclear waste disposal facilities, phosphogypsum stacks, underground and surface uranium mines, and the operation and disposal of uranium mill-tailings piles. In addition, the agency granted a reconsideration of its regulations concerning emissions from facilities licensed by the Nuclear Regulatory Commission because of possible duplication in the regulations and possible effects on medical treatments.[65]

It is interesting to note that in the agency's announcement of the final radionuclide regulations it also announced that it had reexamined the 1979 decision to list radionuclides as a hazardous air pollutant. The EPA concluded, after eleven tumultuous years of conflict, that the 1979 decision had been correct. In support of its conclusion, the agency stated that the evidence that radionuclides can cause cancer had increased since 1979 and that radiation is now considered a non-threshold pollutant—meaning that there is no truly safe level of exposure.

On November 15, 1990, President George Bush signed into law the new Clean Air Act. The new law mandates that three radionuclides sources—elemental phosphorous plants, grate calcination elemental phosphorous plants and phosphogypsum stacks—must continue to be regulated by the EPA as they were prior to the 1990 new Clean Air Act. As to non-DOE federal facilities not licensed by the NRC, coal-fired utility and industrial boilers, underground uranium mines, surface uranium mines, and disposal of uranium mill-tailings piles, the prior law will also remain in effect unless the EPA decides to apply the 1990 amendments.

The new Clean Air Act also provides that the EPA may choose not to issue radionuclide emissions standards for sources licensed by the NRC if the EPA determines that the NRC regulations provide an ample margin of safety. In April, 1991, the EPA suspended its regulations for sources licensed by the NRC but did so without the mandated determination that the NRC regulations provide an ample margin of safety.[66] The NRDC sued the EPA, maintaining that the EPA lacked authority under the new Clean Air Act for this action. The EPA defended its actions by maintaining that section 112 of the act broadly allowed the suspension and that it would be an unreasonable burden on NRC licensees to be subjected to these regulations when the results of an additional study "might lead to the finding that the existing NRC regulations provide an ample margin of safety."[67]

On September 25, 1992, the Court of Appeals for the District of Columbia found in favor of the NRDC and concluded that the EPA did not possess the authority under the new Clean Air Act to stay the radionuclide regulations. The EPA reacted by publishing, two months later, a memorandum of understanding with the NRC that outlined a plan for cooperation between the two organizations for the regulation of radionuclides.[68] Under the terms of the agreement, the EPA must examine NRC standards before it promulgates any of its own discretionary standards under the Clean Air Act. The EPA is responsible for environmental protection outside the boundaries of NRC licensees, the organizations agreed, while the NRC is responsible for environmental protection of its licensees through its licensing and regulatory authority. As of this writing, environmentalists are challenging the agreement and further litigation is possible.

Conclusion

This twelve-year saga of radionuclides battles presents a number of issues, some common to administrative agencies generally, others unique to the EPA. Confronted initially by intense political pressures, the EPA listed radionuclides as a hazardous air pollutant, not fully aware of the difficulties in developing standards for such substances. What is particularly significant in this case is the compounding effect of other economic, political, and legal influences familiar to all U.S. administrative agencies and departments. Another common theme is the inability and unwillingness of the court to factor the agency's lack of staff and budget in its decision. A final common theme is the postjudgment power play by the agency staff, which in this instance took the form of the promulgation of sham regulations that in fact increased the amount of radionuclides that could be emitted in the air.[69]

Seemingly unique to science-based organizations is the critical importance of the scientific process, which manifested itself in three ways: First, in the need for a prolonged period of time to develop the regulations; second, in the need to maintain scientific credibility, which serves as a foundation to all the agency's regulations; and third, in the importance and power of the Science Advisory Board. All of these factors came together to force the administrator to choose scientific credibility over court compliance. Also unique to the EPA are its statutes, which reward and therefore encouraged three environmental groups to join the fight against the agency. It is not surprising that the EPA, because of this tumultuous process, was very reluctant to list air pollutants as hazardous under the old Clean Air Act but instead preferred to list such substances on an "intent to designate" list that did not require immediate action and allowed time for further research.[70] Prior to the new (1990) Clean Air Act, the EPA had listed only 6 hazardous air pollutants in addition to radio-nuclides: arsenic, asbestos, benzene, beryllium, mercury, and vinyl chloride. As mentioned earlier, the 1990 Clean Air Act lists 189 hazardous air pollutants that the EPA must now regulate.

Additional examples of the use of the courts to force change in the EPA's clean air programs and policies can be found in R. Shep Melnick's work (discussed briefly in Chapter Seven). For example, Melnick examined the issue of the heights of smoke-stacks from 1973 to 1982. He analyzed the 1974 Fifth Circuit decision that held that the EPA could allow polluters to substitute the dispersion of pollutants into the air for emission reductions only when technological controls were "unavailable."[71] He then looked at the motion for contempt filed by the NRDC against the EPA when a year had passed and the EPA had not complied with the court's order.[72] The EPA scrambled to develop stack height regulations only to have Congress order changes in 1977. Final stack height rules were not promulgated until 1982—eight years after the NRDC decision.

Melnick concluded that there were three assets to the court's intervention in the dispersion issue and three liabilities.

The assets included the use of a long-range perspective, the strengthening of the bargaining power of environmental groups, and the gain of control over lower levels of the bureaucracy by political executives. The liabilities mentioned by Melnick were the entering of the judiciary in a political debate, the issuance of an extreme judicial order that showed very little understanding of the complex issues, and the slowing of the search by environmentalists for innovative ways of dealing with air pollution.

Melnick's analysis stopped in 1982. After 1982, the courts continued to refuse to defer to the expertise of the EPA staff and gave the agency little or no discretion as to how it could change stack height regulations. When the final regulations on stack heights were issued and subsequently challenged, the court, in 1988, saying that it was loath to prolong the agony of court intervention into the stack height regulatory process, upheld the majority of the provisions made in response to the previous court orders. The court did, however, remand three provisions of the regulations to the agency for further review.[73]

When portions of the regulations were remanded to the agency, the administration of the EPA was affected in several ways. The agency held public hearings, issued several interim guidance documents outlining changes in the policies and administration of the program, created an internal multidisciplinary working group, drafted new regulations, issued policy statements explaining the new regulations, implemented changes in the program, and issued status updates to the court. The EPA sought to buffer the effects of the court's order by finding innovative alternative ways of regulating industry polluters, such as "bubble plans" in which violations of specific emission levels are allowed as long as the total air quality under an EPA-designated "bubble" meets EPA standards. The agency also reconsidered options it had discarded in 1979 as being too difficult to implement and used the court decision to defend its regulations to the Office of Management and Budget. In 1992 and 1993, the issue of stack heights arose in the EPA's review of Clean Air Act state implementation plans developed by Maine, California, New Hampshire, and Montana.[74] The stack heights issue rages on today.

Diffusing Hazardous Wastes

Chapter Six

I pray for lawsuits. It's the only way I can get my regulations out of OMB [the Office of Management and Budget]. Sometimes I feel like sending environmental groups a list of our pending regulations being held by OMB with stars placed before those they should sue us on.

—EPA ENGINEER
Interview, week of May 15, 1988

Hazardous waste is an enormous challenge for the EPA. According to one study, an estimated 264 million metric tons of hazardous waste are generated annually,[1] enough to "fill the New Orleans Superdome almost 1,500 times over."[2] Most of these wastes have not been destroyed, but have been buried in landfills, lagoons, vacant lots, and other dump sites. Over time, the wastes from these sites have leaked, polluting the land, water, and air. The Office of Technology Assessment estimates that there are between 1,500 and 10,000 inactive hazardous waste sites in the United States today,[3] although many find this estimate conservative.[4]

The Office of Management and Budget Challenge

Congress mandated in the Resource Conservation and Recovery Act (RCRA)[5] that final permit standards for leaking underground storage tanks be issued by the EPA by March 1, 1985.[6] When the deadline passed and the standards had not been promulgated, a disgruntled Environmental Defense Fund (EDF) sued the EPA and the Office of Management and Budget (OMB) in the District Court for the District of Columbia.[7] The reason for the delay, the EDF asserted, was the president's Office of Management and Budget, which had been reviewing the standards for months. The EDF sought an order forcing the EPA to issue the standards and an injunction against the OMB to halt further delaying actions by the budget office in the future.

The OMB's regulatory review authority over EPA is derived from two executive orders. The first is Executive Order 12291,[8] which requires executive agencies to submit proposed rules and final rules to the OMB for review.[9] The second is Executive Order 12498,[10] which requires executive agencies to submit to the OMB for review a "draft regulatory program" describing "significant regulatory actions" the agency plans to carry out during a fiscal year.[11] It was OMB action taken pursuant to Executive Order 12291 that was the subject of the EDF lawsuit.

EPA and OMB interactions had been closely scrutinized by individuals outside the agency for years. An organization calling itself "OMB Watch" had been formed, charging that the OMB was continually abusing its power, forcing drastic policy changes under the guise of cost-benefit and risk analysis. Many environmental groups supported that concern. Moreover, the issue of underground storage tank regulations was important for environmentalists since it affected thousands of potential pollution sites, such as gas tanks buried at nearly all automobile service stations in the nation. Those environmental groups, frustrated with the Reagan administration's weakening of environmental regulations, watched the OMB-EPA underground storage tank negotiations closely, ready to pounce at any appearance of impropriety.

The EPA had been late in submitting the proposed rules to

the OMB, handing them to OMB staff members on the date of the statutory deadline, March 1, 1985,[12] anticipating that the OMB's review would be complete within ten days.[13] On March 15, 1985, EPA staff briefed OMB staff on the proposed regulations. The OMB refused to approve the regulations and on March 25, 1985, notified the EPA that it was extending its review of them. The OMB apparently wanted the EPA to gather additional information prior to promulgating the regulations even though it would delay the process. By April 10, 1985, forty days after the statutory deadline, the EPA still had not received any formal comments from OMB.[14]

At a meeting of OMB and EPA staff held on April 16, 1985, the OMB sought significant changes in the proposed regulations in four areas.[15] Generally, the OMB wanted the EPA to shift the underlying philosophy of the underground storage tank regulations away from the EPA's preferred policy of containing all leaks to the OMB's desired policy of containing only those leaks that could be demonstrated by risk analysis to threaten harm to human health. Internal disagreement and dissension within the OMB further delayed the budget office's consideration of the regulations.[16] Some OMB staff members apparently felt that the OMB should not be dictating substantive policy decisions to the EPA, while others felt the precedent being set was important to ensure that the agency followed the Reagan administration's deregulation policies then and in the future.

After two months of review, the budget office returned the regulations to the EPA, demanding revisions.[17] On May 1, 1985, the EPA issued a "Regulatory Status Report" that admitted that the storage tank rules were being delayed by OMB review.[18] The EPA begrudgingly revised the regulations and resubmitted them to the OMB two weeks later.[19] After still more acrimonious negotiation and forced rule changes, the OMB completed its review and

cleared the proposed regulations on June 12, 1985, three and
one-half months after the congressionally mandated deadline.[20]

Two days later, on June 14, 1985, EPA Administrator Lee
Thomas approved the proposed regulations, which were published in the Federal Register within the month.[21] The following
day, the agency petitioned the court for a one-year extension for
issuing the final version of the storage tank standards. The agency
said its own internal procedure, coupled with the OMB review
procedure, made it impossible to complete the regulations until
June 30, 1986. The one-year extension, the EPA said, was the
"shortest period of time" within which the EPA could reasonably
be directed to prepare final rules. The EPA described a proposed
schedule to the court that included the following target dates:

November 30, 1985: Assess public comments on the proposed
    rules (issued June 10)
February 26, 1986: Circulate draft final rule within the EPA
May 26, 1986: Review of final rule by senior EPA staff[22]

In the meantime, EDF attorneys were gearing up for their
court battle against the OMB and the EPA. They had asked the
agency's political appointee administrators to supply information
on the extent of the OMB's activity in reviewing agency rules but
were having a difficult time accumulating the information they
needed. Robert Percival, attorney for the EDF, said that the EPA
seemed "desperate to avoid inquiry" into the OMB's role in environmental policy making.[23] Percival also said that the fact that the
EPA proposed the time extension to the court showed the need
for his organization to force the issue, demanding that the EPA
make the development of final RCRA regulations a top priority.[24]

After several requests for documents from the EDF, top EPA
management officials were able to convince the court to issue a

protective order prohibiting the disclosure of portions of internal agency documents to the plaintiffs.[25] The EPA's doors were closed to the EDF. Despite this setback, the EDF was able to accumulate compelling evidence offered by disgruntled EPA career staff members, as well as by sources outside the agency. This evidence proved that the average delay in the EPA's promulgation of regulations caused by OMB review was 91 days, while the total delay for all EPA regulations reviewed by the OMB was 311 weeks, or 2,177 days. Of the 169 regulations submitted to the OMB by the EPA that were subject to statutory or judicial deadlines, 86 had been delayed by the OMB beyond the deadline.[26]

On August 12 and 23, 1985, the Justice Department filed briefs on behalf of both the EPA and the OMB. In its briefs, the Justice Department said the storage tank regulations would not be delayed further by OMB review because that review would be concurrent with the review of the regulations by senior EPA staff. Further, the Justice Department defended the review of such regulations by the OMB as a way to ensure that agencies' activities reflected the policies of the Reagan administration.[27]

Congressional Action

In October, 1985, the House Energy and Commerce Subcommittee on Oversight and Investigations, chaired by Representative John D. Dingell (D-Michigan), issued a report claiming that the OMB had unlawfully interfered with EPA regulatory activities.[28] On January 27, 1986, Senators Carl Levin (D-Michigan), David Durenberger (R-Minnesota) and Phil Gramm (R-Texas) introduced Senate Bill 2023, the Rule Making Information Act of 1986 designed to "open" the OMB's process of reviewing regulations. The bill required regulatory agencies to open a file every time a rule making was started, into which they would put all written documents they receive, such as material from the OMB, letters from outside the agency, and logs of telephone conversations concerning the regulations. In addition, the bill would limit OMB review of regulations to thirty days. Although the bill died in committee, negotiations among the OMB and the senators yielded an informal agreement to initiate procedures designed to open up the process.

On January 28, 1986, the Senate Governmental Affairs Subcommittee on Intergovernmental Relations held a hearing to examine the OMB's control over regulations. Senator Albert Gore (D-Tennessee) and Senator Levin blasted the OMB for forcing agencies to comply with its will, shaping the substance of regulations, then "ducking" any responsibility in a process that "has been hidden from the public." Levin said, "It looks like the agency is making the decision, but in fact it's OMB, on the telephone, saying these rules should be modified."[29]

In addition, Senators Gore and Levin both alleged that the Justice Department lied in documents filed with the district court in the storage tank case when its attorneys said that agencies are not bound to take OMB's advice on regulations. "To the agencies they say, 'You follow the . . . comments of OMB or your job is at risk.' To the court they say, 'Any agency head is free . . . to issue the agency rule in what ever form the agency head deems advisable,'" Levin said.[30] In response, OMB Director James C. Miller III testified that the budget office's role was "advisory" but said that regulatory agencies should take OMB comments "seriously." Miller described the process as engaging regulatory officials in "socratic dialogues."[31]

Miller then explained to the congressional committee an experimental procedure that the OMB had instigated in 1985 in which EPA officials were invited to "the majority" of meetings of OMB officials with outside parties (primarily private businesses) concerning EPA regulations. Moreover, under the new policy, letters to the OMB concerning EPA rules were forwarded to the EPA, without agency officials having to ask for them. When it was necessary to hold EPA regulations for review, Miller insisted, the average review time was twenty days.[32]

EDF attorney Robert Percival countered this testimony by maintaining that "OMB ha[d] used the regulatory review process to block and to weaken environmental regulations in defiance of statutory directives." Percival argued that the OMB should be forced to obey the law. Additionally, the EDF attorney said that the OMB should be held accountable for its policy decisions "because what OMB does behind closed doors has a direct impact on the health and safety of people throughout the nation."[33]

The Ruling on OMB Interference

On the same day as the Senate subcommittee hearing, Judge Thomas A. Flannery issued his decision in the EDF underground storage tank case. Flannery found that the court had jurisdiction over the OMB. The OMB had argued that even if it had exceeded its authority by blocking regulatory action beyond the statutory deadline, the court was powerless to remedy the situation. Judge Flannery disagreed, declaring that the OMB must "obey the law Congress sets down."[34]

Moreover, Flannery found that the delay in the issuance of the storage tank regulations had been caused by the OMB and that the OMB had no authority to cause the EPA to miss statutory deadlines. He then questioned the constitutionality of allowing the OMB to influence another agency in carrying out responsibilities delegated by Congress. "Congress enacts environmental legislation after years of study and deliberation, and then delegates to the expert judgment of the EPA Administrator the authority to issue regulations carrying out the aims of the law," Flannery wrote.[35] The OMB's activities not only encroached upon the independence and expertise of the EPA, Flannery continued, but allowed those who were unsuccessful in their lobbying of Congress to make an end-run and to influence policy after the fact. "This is incompatible with the will of Congress and cannot be sustained as a valid exercise of the President's Article II powers."[36]

The court demanded that the EPA issue the underground storage tank regulations within six months, or before June 30, 1986. The court did not issue an injunction against further OMB involvement in EPA affairs but chastised the budget office, warning that it was overstepping its boundaries.

Seven months later, the court awarded the EDF attorneys' fees of $49,700, saying that the environmental group had "acted as a catalyst forcing EPA and OMB to acknowledge that not promulgating the standards by March 1, 1985, was unlawful."[37] The attorneys' fees were paid out of the EPA "Administrator's Reserve Fund."[38] On April 17, 1987, the EPA reproposed underground storage tank regulations, fifteen months after the EDF decision and nine months after the court-ordered deadline.[39] The delay this time was not because of OMB interference but because the regulations affected an estimated 1.4 million underground storage tanks and the agency needed months to address hundreds of public comments and concerns.[40] Final underground storage tank regulations were issued in the fall of 1988, with updates and changes published in 1989, 1990, 1991, 1992, and 1993.[41]

In commenting on the court's decision, Robert Percival (the EDF attorney) emphasized to the media that the significance of the court's decision went far beyond the specific issue. "This is a fundamental shift in power between OMB and EPA," Percival said. "It makes it clear that, as a legal matter, OMB cannot do any more than just advise EPA and that EPA is free to accept or reject that advice. Nothing OMB does can slow EPA down."[42]

Senator Levin noted that "OMB has been caught with its hand in the cookie jar. The court had affirmed what OMB has steadfastly denied—that its role in reviewing rules under the executive order is more than advisory. As this court has affirmed in this case, OMB is dominating significant agency regulatory decisions."[43]

Edwin L. Dale, Jr., chief spokesperson for the OMB, commented on the case by stating simply, "[W]e don't like the language of the decision."[44] OMB staff members interviewed for this study said it was "quite a setback" for the budget office. "It makes it very difficult for us to review EPA regulations," they said, "since we often do not receive the rules until the date they were ordered by statute to be promulgated. Review now many times must be terminated ahead of time" because of the EDF decision.[45]

EPA career bureaucrats, although technically on the losing side of the decision, were delighted with the outcome of the case but were in disagreement with the OMB concerning the effect of the case. Although the judge's order forced the OMB to release the EPA's RCRA regulations within the statutorily mandated deadlines, similar action has not been seen in other statutory areas. One EPA staff member from another division said, "I pray for lawsuits. It's the only way I can get my regulations out of OMB. Sometimes I feel like sending environmental groups a list of our pending regulations being held by OMB with stars placed before those they should sue us on."[46]

While the EPA was a party in the EDF underground storage tank lawsuit, it obviously was not that agency that was the true target of the plaintiff's actions, but the OMB. (In some instances, the OMB's constant interference in the EPA's policies has been far more pervasive than court intervention.) Nevertheless, the underground storage tank court decision affected the policies and administration of the EPA and, concomitantly, affected EPA-OMB relations.

OMB interference in the promulgation of regulations by the EPA continued during the administration of President George Bush, although much of the overview of environmental regulations was carried out by a controversial cabinet-level group, headed by Vice President Dan Quayle, called the Competitiveness Council. (President Clinton abolished the Competitiveness Council within his first days as president.) In August, 1989, for example, the OMB "held hostage" an EPA rule that established new RCRA cleanup standards for solid waste management units, as well as a rule governing boilers and furnaces. One of the major controversies centered on how much contamination could remain at the site, with the OMB pushing for tolerance of greater contamination.[47] In 1990, another lawsuit was filed challenging OMB interference with Superfund regulations. That case, mentioned in the pages ahead, is still being litigated as of this writing.[48]

On February 16, 1993, EPA Administrator Carol Browner announced that under the Clinton administration, the OMB Office of Information and Regulatory Affairs will review disputes concerning environmental regulations. The review will be "a more friendly type of review" than in the past, Browner said, without giving further detail about the extent of the involvement of the OMB.[49] As of the writing of this chapter, it was rumored that Vice President Albert Gore was designing a new environmental regulation review process, but no final announcements had been made.

In other instances the EPA was not the direct target of a lawsuit, yet the agency's policies and administration were greatly affected. The Department of Energy's polluting facilities is one example.

The Department of Energy Challenge

For the last fifty years, the Department of Energy and its predecessors have been in charge of providing the nuclear materials necessary for the manufacturing of nuclear warheads for the Department of Defense. The components for such warheads have been produced by government-owned, contractor-operated facilities (GOCOs) in thirteen states. Nuclear weapons facilities of the Department of Defense take up nearly 4,000 square miles of federal lands.

In 1983, a study by the Tennessee Department of Health and Environment showed that the Department of Energy's (DOE) Oak Ridge nuclear weapons plant[50] was discharging into a tributary of the Clinch River substances full of toxic chemicals, including polychlorinated biphenyls, halogenated solvents, cyanide, mercury, acid, and radioactive materials.[51] The river, a source of drinking water for communities downstream from the DOE facility, was found by the Tennessee Valley Authority to contain 140 chemicals.[52] In addition, unlined waste pits on the DOE's Oak Ridge property were leaking toxic materials into groundwater and streams.[53]

On September 20, 1983, the Legal Environmental Assistance Foundation and the Natural Resources Defense Council sued the Department of Energy, alleging that both RCRA and the Clean Water Act had been violated by the DOE. RCRA regulations concerning the storage, treatment, and handling of hazardous wastes were not being followed by the DOE, the environmental groups alleged. Further, the discharges into streams violated the Clean Water Act, they maintained.[54]

Although the EPA was neither a plaintiff nor a defendant in the suit, the topic of DOE compliance with EPA statutes had been the subject of an ongoing disagreement between the two organizations since the late 1970s and early 1980s. For example, on November 14, 1980, Stephen H. Greenleigh, assistant general counsel for environment at the DOE, wrote to the EPA contending that the DOE need not comply with RCRA because that statute was preempted by the Atomic Energy Act.[55] In contrast, on June 22, 1983, A. James Barnes, acting general counsel for the EPA, issued an opinion concluding that RCRA, generally, does apply to DOE facilities.[56]

On July 12, 1983, Lee Thomas, then assistant administrator for solid waste and emergency response, wrote a memo to William Ruckelshaus, the EPA administrator, maintaining that the lack of interagency cooperation was causing problems in the regional offices. Thomas urged Ruckelshaus to press for an agreement with the DOE. Nothing substantive was done.[57]

Administrative Approach

On January 4, 1984, the EPA released a document entitled *The Environmental Protection Agency Federal Facilities Compliance Program: Strategy for Resolution of Compliance Problems at Federal Facilities*. In that work, the EPA stated its policy of not pursuing judicial remedies against other federal agencies for noncompliance with pollution control laws. Rather, the agency's preferred method of handling such disputes was described as "an administrative approach grounded in cooperative action." Following that philosophy, the Office of Management and Budget would be the final arbiter of such conflicts, pursuant to the Executive Order 12088.[58]

The memo also outlined a second possible administrative mechanism for resolving compliance problems between the EPA and other federal agencies pursuant to Executive Order 12146.[59] The policy outlined in the document, which named the Department of Justice as the final arbiter of disputes, was to be applied whenever a strictly legal dispute existed between agencies. Examples of possible applications included disputes concerning the interpretation of a statute and disputes concerning the applicability of statutes.

On February 22, 1984, the EPA and the DOE signed a "Memorandum of Understanding (MOU) on Responsibilities for Hazardous and Radioactive Mixed Waste Management."[60] In the memorandum of understanding, the DOE agreed to give security clearance to certain members of the EPA staff, while the EPA agreed to keep sensitive information confidential. The DOE agreed to comply with EPA regulations concerning hazardous waste generation, transportation, treatment, storage, and disposal. The memorandum of understanding also outlined procedures for implementing and modifying the agreement. Finally, the DOE agreed to develop a Hazardous Waste Compliance Plan.

Both organizations were blasted for the agreement because it showed that the DOE was willing to obey environmental laws only on a voluntary, as opposed to a mandatory, basis. "The consequences of this are extremely serious," said Representative Albert Gore, Jr. (D-Tennessee). "Citizens will be denied mandatory protection of the law [at the DOE's nuclear sites]."[61] While A. James Barnes, general counsel for the EPA, cautioned that the agreement did not prejudice the agency's view that the DOE was subject to RCRA requirements, Representative Gore called such a statement "gobbledygook."[62]

Meanwhile, the Legal Environmental Assistance Foundation (LEAF) and the Natural Resources Defense Council (NRDC) persisted in their lawsuit, and briefs were filed by all parties. The Justice Department, representing the DOE, argued that the Atomic Energy Act preempted RCRA by giving the DOE authority to manage hazardous wastes generated by federal nuclear facilities. Further, the memorandum of understanding signed by both the

EPA and the DOE allowed the federal facilities to comply voluntarily with RCRA, the Justice Department argued. "In this way," the attorneys wrote in their brief, "Congress' objectives in both RCRA and the AEA have been harmonized."[63]

The Justice Department also argued that nuclear weapons facilities should be exempt from RCRA on national security grounds. Adhering to RCRA would subject confidential data to the scrutiny of state and EPA inspectors. To do so might cause the United States government's nuclear weapons secrets to be released.[64]

The Court's Decision

On April 13, 1984, Judge Robert Taylor of the U.S. District Court for the Eastern District of Tennessee ruled that the Department of Energy must seek a RCRA permit from the EPA for the treatment, storage, and disposal of hazardous wastes.[65] The DOE also was ordered to seek permits from the EPA for pollutant discharge under the Clean Water Act. The plant managers, the court said, must bring the plant into compliance with the two laws "with all deliberate speed."[66]

The Atomic Energy Act, Judge Taylor wrote, does not exempt the DOE from complying with RCRA hazardous waste rules. The Atomic Energy Act only preempts RCRA in areas concerning nuclear and radioactive wastes. If confidential data would be endangered by putting the Oak Ridge plant in compliance with RCRA, then the DOE could request a presidential exemption from the law.[67]

On June 14, 1984, the NRDC and LEAF asked the EPA to revoke the memorandum of understanding that provided for DOE voluntary compliance with RCRA. The memorandum of understanding, the environmental groups argued, was moot given the outcome of the Oak Ridge litigation. The groups said that the EPA should instruct the DOE that wastes that are both hazardous and radioactive are subject to both RCRA and Atomic Energy Act regulations.[68] The EPA refused.

In July, 1984, the DOE and the EPA announced a new joint program "to ensure continued aggressive implementation of RCRA, to protect public health and the environment, and to define precisely those instances when application to [DOE] facilities would be inconsistent with the Atomic Energy Act."[69] To implement the court decision as well as the joint program, the EPA formed interagency working groups charged with dealing with the technical, legal, and national security issues involved in EPA regulation of DOE facilities.[70] The EPA was then to revise its RCRA policies to reflect the recommendations of the working group in two areas: first, the issue of how "mixed wastes" (wastes that are both hazardous and radioactive) should be handled and, second, the issue of how confidential information concerning national security would remain confidential in the regulatory process. Further, the DOE changed its policy on mixed wastes and acknowledged that its wastes are subject to RCRA regulations.

The EPA drafted amendments to RCRA regulations designed "to ensure that the application of state and federal hazardous waste laws to DOE facilities is not inconsistent with the Atomic Energy Act."[71] Further, the regulations discussed procedures to prevent disclosure of national security data.[72] The draft regulations also allowed the DOE to request a variance from some RCRA regulations because of the possibility of increased radiation hazards.[73] Last, the DOE drafted proposed regulations to address the issue of "mixed wastes."

In 1985, the General Accounting Office released a study that concluded that EPA-DOE coordination had improved considerably because of the Oak Ridge lawsuit. The study, which examined another DOE facility in South Carolina, found that the new procedures and agreements forged in the meetings of the two agencies in response to the Oak Ridge suit helped spur other DOE nuclear plants to comply with RCRA regulations. The DOE became more cooperative with the EPA, the General Accounting Office concluded, because of the lawsuit and the revision of the memorandum of understanding in response to the suit.[74] One year later, however, the General Accounting Office revised its position and found that when viewed as a whole, "federal agency performance in implementing RCRA has not been exemplary."[75] In 1991, an official with the Office of Technology Assessment blasted the DOE's handling of its waste problems and highlighted before Congress the agency's lack of information, trained personnel, and technology to deal with environmental problems.[76]

In the last few years the EPA has attempted to improve the regulation of DOE sites. First, the agency extended the policy that mixed wastes are to be treated as hazardous wastes by requiring states with responsibility for hazardous waste programs to demonstrate authority to regulate the hazardous components of mixed wastes.[77] Next, the agency issued policies concerning the enforcement of the EPA's RCRA regulations at federal facilities.[78] Last, the EPA issued policies outlining procedures for settling RCRA disputes between the EPA and other federal agencies.[79]

On October 6, 1992, President George Bush significantly increased the EPA's and the states' power in dealing with the DOE and other federal organizations by signing into law the Federal Facilities Compliance Act.[80] The new law was enacted partly in response to a Supreme Court decision issued five months earlier that concluded that RCRA did not allow fines or penalties to be assessed against federal facilities.[81] The law expressly waives the sovereign immunity of federal facilities under RCRA, thus making it clear that the EPA and the states may assess fines and penalties against government entities such as the DOE for violations of that law. (An exception was made for mixed hazardous and radioactive wastes generated and stored at DOE nuclear facilities: the DOE has three years to comply with RCRA regulations pertaining to these wastes before enforcement actions can be taken against it.) The state of Washington lost little time in implementing the law: On March 11, 1993, the Washington Department of Ecology assessed fines totaling $100,000 against the DOE for RCRA violations at its Hanford nuclear site.[82]

The situation at the DOE Oak Ridge plant will remain an ongoing dispute into the next decade. In 1990, for example, engineers had begun to complete a $66 million project to cover ninety-two acres of chemical burial grounds with caps made from plastic liners and clay.[83] But just as these wastes were being cleaned up, PCBs were found in monitoring wells on the Oak Ridge reservation.[84] In response to this and other DOE environmental problems, the EPA moved its Office of Federal Activities, which serves as a liaison to the DOE and other federal agencies, to the Office of Enforcement and Compliance Monitoring. The move was meant to gain greater visibility for the Office of Federal Activities and to emphasize the EPA's commitment to environmental law compliance by other federal organizations.[85]

Today, an estimated 3,000 inactive DOE waste sites must be cleaned up. The DOE maintains that it has entered into nearly sixty agreements with the EPA and individual states that establish schedules for such cleanups. While the DOE projects that the cleanup costs will be $81 billion, the General Accounting Office estimates total costs at $155 billion. Still others project cleanup costs at more than $200 billion.

The issue of federal facilities and the EPA was addressed in court in 1990. In September, 1989, the Conservation Law Foundation of New England notified the EPA of its intent to file suit over the EPA's management of its federal facilities docket and the agency's lack of action in response to a congressional mandate to assess hundreds of federally owned hazardous waste sites. The case went to court, and on July 30, 1990, the U.S. District Court for the District of Massachusetts found that the EPA had missed a statutory deadline for listing all federal facilities with potential hazardous waste problems by over a year. Although the court initially refused to order the agency to abide by a new schedule urged by the plaintiffs because "there remain[ed] issues of fact concerning the feasibility of the potential [congressionally mandated] deadlines," a deadline of July, 1992, was later established to complete assessments of the sites, and a deadline of July, 1993, was established to decide whether any of the federal facilities should be placed on the national priority list of hazardous waste sites.[86]

The EPA proceeded with actions aimed to comply with the court's deadlines. In November, 1991, however, the U.S. Court of Appeals for the First Circuit reversed the lower court's decision and held that the environmental groups lacked standing to sue, since they had requested a ruling that would affect federal facilities nationwide.[87] Despite the reversal, EPA officials announced that they would still try to meet the deadlines imposed by the court.[88] At the same time, environmentalists vowed to appeal the decision and to file individual lawsuits in those areas of the country where their members have standing to sue.[89]

As the issue of compliance by federal facilities was rearing its ugly head, so too were other challenges to hazardous waste policy. One of those challenges concerned the development and continual updating by the EPA of a National Contingency Plan for hazardous waste spills.

The National Contingency Plan Challenge

Section 9605 of the Comprehensive Environmental Response, Compensation and Liability Act (CERCLA or Superfund)[90] mandated the development by the EPA of a National Contingency Plan

(NCP) by June 9, 1981.[91] The NCP was to outline the federal government's response to oil spills, hazardous substance spills, and waste dump sites. Although the EPA had completed several drafts of the NCP by the June 9 statutory deadline, it failed to meet the final deadline because the Reagan administration ordered major revisions.[92] Not surprisingly, the plan had been held for review by the Office of Management and Budget and President Reagan's National Response Team for six months.[93]

When the EPA failed to meet the statutory deadline, the Environmental Defense Fund (EDF) and the state of New Jersey filed suit to force the agency to issue a plan.[94] The District Court for the District of Columbia granted the EDF's motion for summary judgment, calling the fact that the EPA had ignored congressional intent "straight forward and uncontroverted." The judge ordered the EPA to produce the NCP in draft form within thirty days and a final NCP within ninety days.

On March 12, 1982, exactly thirty days after the court's decision, the EPA published a proposed NCP. EPA Administrator Anne Gorsuch announced in a press conference that although "there was a temptation to write an encyclopedic manual," the NCP's provisions were "concise, its language non-technical, and its requirements flexible. Simply put, the NCP exemplifies regulatory reform in the Reagan Administration."[95] Christopher De-Muth, executive director of the Presidential Task Force on Regulatory Relief, said the NCP proves that federal regulations "need not be cumbersome or costly."[96]

The plan was immediately praised by the chemical industry and harshly criticized by environmental groups and some members of Congress. The Chemical Manufacturers' Association said the EPA had "done a very good job in stating the general factors that must be considered in developing site-by-site remedies in a very clear and concise fashion."[97] By contrast, the EDF, noting that the specific cleanup standards of the Carter administration had been dropped from the plan, said that the EPA appeared to have put into effect "the least cost solution instead of the most cost-effective means of protecting public health and the environment."[98] Khristine Hall, the EDF attorney, blasted the plan: "Instead of providing goals, it provides methods. The criteria are so loose we are afraid they will not be enough to protect public health and the environment."[99]

Representative James Florio (D-New Jersey) called the NCP a "blueprint for further inaction and delay" because it allowed the "EPA to take minimal action or no action at all at some of the sites. This is absolutely contrary to the intent of the law," he said.[100] Representative John Lafalce (D-New York), who represents the district in which the toxic Love Canal site is located, labeled the NCP as a "step backward, months after a decision was due."[101]

The EPA's Return to Court

In response to such public criticism, the EPA petitioned the District Court for the District of Columbia to reconsider its order mandating a final NCP sixty days after the issuance of the draft NCP. The EPA asked for at least a sixty-day extension of the court's previous deadline to garner public comments, and an additional undetermined amount of time to revise the final plan in response to such comments. The EPA said it "will likely be impossible to complete . . . [the NCP] within [the remaining] thirty days."[102] The court granted the EPA only a fifteen-day extension, chastising the agency for waiting until the last minute to file its motion, "significantly muting . . . [its] claims of hardship."[103]

The EPA responded to the court's new decision in three ways. First, the EPA extended the public comment period by fifteen days to April 28, 1982.[104] During that extended period, the agency received over a hundred comments, totaling 1,000 pages.[105] Second, the EPA appealed the court's decision to the U.S. Court of Appeals for the District of Columbia Circuit, saying that it did not believe it could review and analyze all the comments, determine necessary changes, prepare a response to all the significant comments, and publish the final plan with responses in the Federal Register by the newly ordered date of May 28, 1982.[106] Third, the EPA filed an affidavit with the original court, the U.S. District Court for the District of Columbia, stating again that it would be impossible for the agency to comply with the court order because it would take 90 to 120 days for EPA to issue the final plan. The agency asked for a modification of the court's order or, in the alternative, a stay of the decision pending appeal.[107]

During this time, the EPA and the EDF were engaged in negotiations. The two groups finally agreed that the EDF would ask the district court for an extension to July 16, 1982, if the EPA would file a motion to remand the case to that court.[108] The EPA filed the motion. On May 28, 1982, the district court gave the EPA a forty-five-day extension, until July 16, to issue the NCP. Judge John Pratt also ordered the EPA to submit progress reports to the court on June 7 and June 25. The June 7 progress report, Judge Pratt ordered, was to include a description of "the extraordinary steps being taken [to ensure] . . . expeditious implementation of the July 16 deadline."[109]

On July 16, 1982, the EPA issued the NCP in final form; three days later, the EPA informed the court of its action. The agency came very close to missing the July deadline, however, because of a "high-level turf fight" among the EPA, the Department of the Interior, and the Commerce Department concerning which federal agencies should serve as trustees of natural resources eligible for damage compensation under Superfund.[110] The arbiter of the dispute was the Office of Management and Budget. The final NCP listed both the Interior and Commerce departments as "co-trustees" of natural resources.

Changes incorporated in the final NCP included expanded roles for states in hazardous waste cleanup; a provision that selection of a site remedy must be governed not only by cost, but also by technical and environmental "soundness"; and a division of responsibilities for responses among the EPA, the Coast Guard, the Federal Emergency Management Agency, the Defense Department, and the Department of Health and Human Services, in response to an executive order from President Reagan concerning the Superfund program. The final plan did not prescribe a universal cleanup standard as was urged by environmental groups.

By statute, the NCP was to take effect sixty days after its publication in the Federal Register, unless Congress took action to stop it. When the sixtieth day, October 1, 1982, passed and Congress had not acted, the plan became effective. One environmental newspaper, however, reported that the EPA was unaware that the plan had become operational.[111] Khristine Hall, attorney for the EDF, commented that the agency's action "indicate[d] that the National Contingency Plan is too vague to be useful because they [the EPA] haven't even bothered to keep track of whether it's in effect."[112]

On October 14, 1982, the Environmental Defense Fund and the state of New Jersey filed yet another lawsuit against the EPA, seeking review of the new NCP by the U.S. Court of Appeals for the District of Columbia. In filing the suit, the EDF said the plan was "too vague and leaves too much discretion to the EPA on how to proceed with hazardous waste sites and on the degree of cleanup."[113]

A month later, a subcommittee of the House Energy and

Commerce Committee held hearings to examine the EPA's administration of Superfund sites in Missouri and Arkansas. In the course of the proceedings, the NCP was blasted by environmentalists and congresspersons. Ellen Silbergeld, chief toxics scientist at EDF, testified that the NCP was "very defective." The lack of explicit cleanup standards in the NCP had already resulted in hazardous waste site cleanups that failed to protect human health and wasted public funds, she said. The EDF publicly urged the EPA to rewrite the plan to include specific guidelines for cleanup.[114]

On December 7, 1982, the court awarded the EDF $14,285.04 for attorneys fees and expenses incurred in its successful NCP lawsuit against the EPA. The environmental group filed for this award under the Equal Access to Justice Act, which requires a party seeking such an award to submit a request to the court within thirty days of final judgment. The EPA argued that since summary judgment against them had been entered on February 12, 1982, and the EDF had not filed with the court until July 30, 1982, the application was untimely. Using the date on which the EPA had actually complied with its order (July 16, 1982) as the date of final disposition of the case, however, the court held that the application was reasonable.

EDF, New Jersey, and EPA Settlement

On February 1, 1984, the EPA, the state of New Jersey, and the EDF signed a settlement agreement concerning the NCP. The EPA agreed to the following:

1. Amendments to the NCP to require that, first, relevant quantitative health and environmental standards and criteria developed by the EPA under other programs would be used in determining the extent of remedy needed and,

second, if such standards or criteria were substantially ad-
justed (e.g., for risk level or exposure factors), then the lead
agency would explain the basis for the adjustment

2. Amendments to the NCP to allow facilities presently owned
    by the United States or its agencies to be included in the
    NCP

3. Amendments to the NCP to require the development of
    community relations plans for all Superfund-financed re-
    sponse actions, to require public review of feasibility stud-
    ies for all Superfund-financed response measures, and to
    provide comparable public participation for private-party
    response measures taken pursuant to enforcement actions

4. A rule addressing the issue of whether response activities
    must comply with other federal, state, or local environmen-
    tal laws[115]

On November 20, 1985, the EPA issued a revised final
NCP.[116] Although the NCP contained the provisions agreed to in
its settlement agreement with the EDF and the state of New Jersey,
the EDF complained that the agency had complied only with the
strict letter of the agreement and had left several major loopholes
in the plan.[117] For example, the plan contained a negotiated "how
clean is clean" policy that outlined the extent to which Superfund
cleanup actions had to comply with environmental laws and
regulations. Nevertheless, the plan allowed the EPA to waive
applicable requirements under several circumstances. EDF attorney Jane Bloom said that this and other loopholes "would
allow sites not to meet existing environmental standards" and
would not ensure that permanent cleanups would be implemented.[118] The EPA did, however, remove the original plan's
prohibition against listing federal facilities on the National Priorities List, a change that environmental groups favored.

The issue of the National Contingency Plan did not die in 1985. The following year, Congress passed amendments to CERCLA that forced the EPA to develop new requirements for remedy selection in Superfund cleanups.[119] Under the Superfund Amendments and Reauthorization Act of 1986, the EPA was to revise the NCP by early 1988. That plan was "held hostage" by the Office of Management and Budget, however, because of the EPA's unwillingness to make major changes as requested by the office.[120] In response to yet another court-ordered deadline, the EPA issued a 574-page plan on February 6, 1990—the first major overhaul of the Superfund plan since 1985.[121] The plan went into effect on April 9, 1990.[122] Not surprisingly, two months later lawsuits were filed by several states and private businesses challenging specific provisions of the NCP and alleging further interference by the Office of Management and Budget with the NCP. Oral arguments were heard in February, 1993. As of this writing, the case is still in court.[123]

From many perspectives, the NCP lawsuits were positive forces prompting more thorough national hazardous waste planning. Indeed, one consistent thread in this study is that court intervention into the policies and administration of a bureaucracy can indeed be beneficial. The following brief case study, prompted by a reporter's Freedom of Information Act request, further illustrates this point.

The Freedom of Information Act Challenge

In the early 1980s, the EPA changed its policy concerning the disclosure of the names of recipients of notices sent under CERCLA, in response to a lawsuit by a journalist.[124] Under Administrator Anne Gorsuch, the EPA had taken the position that hazardous waste was essentially under control and that excessive regulation of industry, not pollution, was the largest problem the EPA needed to address. Therefore, when Neil J. Cohen, a journalist, filed requests with the EPA under the Freedom of Information Act to acquire copies of Superfund letters sent to individuals, corporations, and government agencies, the agency essentially refused to cooperate.

The EPA released the body of the letters to Cohen but maintained that the identities of the addresses were exempt from disclosure under the Freedom of Information Act. The EPA said that release of such information would be an "unwarranted invasion of privacy" and would reduce the cooperation of those parties in voluntary cleanup of hazardous wastes.[125] Cohen sued, arguing that disclosure would have the opposite effect since public opinion would force the responsible parties into action.

Judge William B. Bryant of the U.S. District Court for the District of Columbia disagreed with the EPA and found in favor of Cohen. Bryant said that the EPA had failed to prove that the release of the information in question would interfere with the EPA's enforcement function by "resulting in concrete adverse consequences."[126] The court also disagreed that releasing the names would be an invasion of privacy.

Prior to a resolution of the *Cohen* dispute, Anne Gorsuch was removed as administrator of the EPA (as previously mentioned) partly because of allegations of mismanagement and "sweetheart deals" with polluting industries. When William D. Ruckelshaus was reinstated as EPA administrator, he immediately sought to open the lines of communication between the agency and the public. It was this fact, coupled with the *Cohen* decision, that prompted the EPA to issue a memorandum on January 16, 1984, to regional offices. This memorandum said that the agency was establishing a new policy as a result of the *Cohen* decision and the administrator's new approach of conducting business in a more open atmosphere, and that this new policy would be "an effort to increase public pressure on parties . . . [to promote] voluntary cleanup of hazardous waste sites." The memorandum then directed the regional offices to release the names of such parties unless the "disclosure of a particular name . . . [would] cause such interference with an ongoing enforcement proceeding that discretionary disclosure . . . [was] clearly unwarranted" and such interference could be documented in detail.[127]

Contrary to previous EPA policy, the memorandum maintained that there was "a strong current of opinion" in private industry that releasing the names would promote voluntary cleanup among parties who might not otherwise come forward. Moreover, the new policy change was "more consistent with the general efforts of the agency to open up more of the enforcement process to the interested public and would save agency personnel the administrative burden of preparing and defending denials to the increasing number of requests."

The memorandum outlined new agency procedures to implement the policy, including the following:

"Quality assuring" the list of potentially responsible parties every six months

Notifying EPA headquarters whenever a decision was made not to disclose a name

Consulting with the regional counsel when additional information was requested for a decision on whether disclosure would interfere with site enforcement

Submitting the names to the applicant with an explanation of how the EPA defined potentially responsible parties and the purposes of sending notice letters

Including with the list a disclaimer concerning the liability of the parties on the list

Using the term *potentially responsible parties* when referring to names on the list if none have been found liable

Thus, in response to the *Cohen* decision and other factors, the EPA reversed not only its actions concerning the release of names of individuals, corporations, and government entities involved in Superfund actions, but also its underlying policy and procedures.

Conclusion

This study indicates that, contrary to the general picture painted by many of today's judicial scholars, the partnership of courts and public agencies has many positive attributes. In particular, the courts have been strong instruments of counterforce used by environmental groups (and other entities) when political and economic conditions made it difficult to gain access to decision makers in the executive branch. The bureaucratic politics of the Reagan administration were major factors in these difficulties of access.

Similarly, although it is true that the organizations involved (the Office of Management and Budget, the Department of Energy, and the EPA) all engaged in postjudgment power plays, read court orders narrowly, and were able to curb litigants' access to vital information, the court decisions served as catalysts for positive changes in national environmental policy. The EPA became more accessible to the public because of the Freedom of Information Act case, became less susceptible to interference by the Office of Management and Budget (in one narrow area) because of the underground storage tank case, published a tighter, more environmentally sound document because of the National Contingency Plan case, and gained greater authority over federal government polluters in the Legal Environmental Assistance Foundation case. This is true even in cases in which the EPA was not the prime target of the lawsuit.

None of these examples involved the EPA as a plaintiff, yet the agency has compiled a remarkable record of successes by using the courts to establish precedents in its Superfund program. Indeed, one environmental journal concluded that the shape of CERCLA has been determined not in EPA internal rule makings but in the courts, with "each week bring[ing] another significant decision."[128] Some have gone so far as to maintain that the courts, generally, have been too extreme in their deference to the EPA in the agency's interpretation and implementation of CERCLA.[129] The litigation outcomes have been termed "one-sided, with government interpretation of the statute carrying practically every decision."[130] Ironically, however, despite the EPA's great successes in court, the Superfund program continues to be an administrative nightmare for the agency.[131] On February 11, 1993, for example, President Clinton, in a speech to a group of businesspersons, called the Superfund program "a disaster." He noted, "All the money goes to the lawyers and none of the money goes to clean up the problems that it was designed to clean up."[132] Five days later, EPA Administrator Carol Browner announced that the Superfund program would be reevaluated since it had "not functioned as was once hoped."[133]

Out of the Sample and Into the Universe

Chapter Seven

*Does anyone know . . . where we can go to find
light on what the practical consequences of these
decisions have been?*
—JUSTICE FELIX FRANKFURTER

The literature is replete with works by scholars arguing about
the appropriateness of judges intervening in policy and administrative disputes. While a few researchers have examined what
happens when judges do intervene in a specific instance or
two, they have been less attentive to the cumulative changes
in policies and administration in individual regulatory agencies
that may result from such judicial activity (see Table 6).[1] This
book has demonstrated that federal courts and the people who
brought them into the policy process have significantly affected
the policies and administration of the EPA in several statutory
areas. The case studies presented in the previous chapters to
demonstrate the complexity and diversity of the topic are just
a few of the hundreds of EPA cases examined in this study. Let
us now move out of the sample and into the universe to examine, first, how federal courts as a whole have affected the EPA
and, second, the policy and administrative consequences of such
judiciary-agency interaction.

Table 6
The Possible Impacts of the Judiciary

Author/Year	Findings and Conclusions
Bazelon, 1977	There is a new collaborative "partnership" between reviewing courts and administrative agencies
Stewart, 1975	A procedural remand can be used by a judge to curb the uncontrolled discretion of administrative agencies
Horowitz, 1977, 1983; Wood, 1982; Rosenbloom, 1983; Johnson and Canon, 1984; Yarbrough, 1985; O'Leary and Wise, 1991	There are often unintended consequences, unanticipated questions, and unforeseen problems of court decisions involving public agencies
Hale, 1979; O'Leary and Wise, 1991	There are anticipated and unanticipated budgetary costs of implementing a court decision
Allerton, 1976; Diver, 1979; Frug, 1979; Hale, 1979; Yarbrough, 1982; Horowitz, 1983; Melnick, 1983; Moss, 1983; Rothman and Rothman, 1984; Straussman, 1986; Wildavsky, 1988; O'Leary and Wise, 1991	Special legislative appropriations are needed at times to provide the funds necessary to implement a court decision
Allerton, 1976; Hale, 1979; Horowitz, 1983; Straussman, 1986	Often funds must be taken from other programs and channeled into the program that is the subject of a court decision

Fisher, 1975; Hale, 1979; Harriman and Straussman, 1983; Taggert, 1989; Chilton and Talarico, 1990; O'Leary and Wise, 1991	Court decisions may yield a transfer of budgetary power from an administrator to a judge. When this occurs the budgetary discretion of administrators is decreased
Hale, 1979	Court decisions can frustrate budgetary retrenchment and can encourage budgetary games
Hale, 1979; Straussman, 1986	Court decisions may yield opportunities for budgetary enhancement
Cramton, 1976; Horowitz, 1983; Rosenbloom, 1983	Judges may become invested in the outcome of litigation and may lose their cloak of neutrality
Cramton, 1976; Wood, 1982; Horowitz, 1983; Melnick, 1983; Rosenbloom, 1983	Judges often deal with subject matter outside their areas of expertise
Chayes, 1976; Frug, 1978; Fiss, 1979; Wood, 1982; Horowitz, 1983; Cooper, 1988; O'Leary and Wise, 1991	Judicial decisions concerning public agencies often include detailed judicial supervision of those organizations (including ongoing, affirmative decrees) with frequent judicial interaction with agency staff

(continued)

Table 6. The Possible Impacts of the Judiciary *(continued)*

Author/Year	Findings and Conclusions
Frug, 1978; Melnick, 1983; Rosenbloom, 1983	Judges have been aggressive and active in their oversight of administrative agencies
Melnick, 1983, 1985	Judges often refuse to defer to administrators' expertise
Glazer, 1978; Pfeffer and Salancik, 1978; O'Leary and Wise, 1991	Judicial activity can lead to a reduction in the power of administrators, a reduction in the authority of administrators, and theoretical knowledge being given greater weight by a court than administrative knowledge
Glazer, 1978; Wood, 1982; Melnick, 1983	Judicial activity can lead to a court making "wrong" or "bad" policy
Glazer, 1978; Pfeffer and Salancik, 1978	Judicial activity can lead to increased power of the legal profession

Rosenbloom, 1983; O'Leary and Wise, 1991	Judicial interaction with administrative agencies can jeopardize representative democracy
Allerton, 1976; Diver, 1979; Frug, 1979; Hale, 1979; Horowitz, 1982; Yarbrough, 1982; Melnick, 1983; Moss, 1983; Rothman and Rothman, 1984; Straussman, 1986; Wildavsky, 1988; O'Leary and Wise, 1991	A negative judicial decision can be used by a public organization to strengthen its position
Glick, 1970; Johnson and Canon, 1979; Yarbrough, 1985	Judges must often rely on other courts and other organizations to supervise the implementation of a court decision
Johnson, 1979	A court order can dictate issues that must be considered by public organizations
Bullock and Lamb, 1984	The filing of a lawsuit can confirm and strengthen government policy

Note: For full documentation of authors' works cited, refer to the Bibliography.

Judicial Involvement

Other authors have examined the use of the courts to promote changes in environmental policies. The important role that
courts have played in helping to formulate, modify, and clarify
environmental policy, generally, in the decade of the 1970s was
documented by Lettie M. Wenner.[2] The use of courts to modify
DDT policy was the focus of Christopher J. Bosso, Frank Graham,
and Thomas R. Dunlap in their individual studies.[3] The impact of
the courts on federal regulation of vinyl chloride was described
by David Doniger.[4] Law review articles on specific court cases are
numerous.[5] R. Shep Melnick, in his analysis of six case studies
concerning one statute, the Clean Air Act, paints a portrait of
judges becoming increasingly aggressive in shaping pollution
control policy, abandoning their traditional deference to bureaucratic expertise.[6]

An examination of the spectrum of cases involving the EPA
yields a different conclusion than is presented in much of the
literature. Judges have been neither totally aggressive and active
in their oversight of the EPA, nor totally passive. Rather, judicial
interaction with the agency falls along a continuum, ranging from
cases with little or no judicial involvement that triggered changes
in the EPA, to cases involving active and aggressive judges that
also triggered changes in the EPA. The five major groups of cases
along the continuum are presented in Table 7 with individual
case examples. They consist of the following:

1.   Cases in which the mere filing of a lawsuit, without judicial
     action, has evoked a change in the EPA
2.   Cases in which courts have upheld the agency's position
     completely without yielding changes in the agency's pol-
     icies and administration

3. Cases in which judges who have been passive and unwilling to intervene in the affairs of the EPA have issued decisions that nonetheless have affected the agency's policies and administration
4. Cases in which judges have legitimately used their discretionary powers deliberately to affect agency actions
5. Cases in which judges have exceeded acceptable judicial boundaries to evoke changes in the agency[7]

This conclusion demonstrates the problems inherent in attempting to generalize from an examination of only one statutory area as Melnick did in his study of the courts and the EPA under the Clean Air Act. While the findings of this study do not necessarily negate a conclusion that *some* judges have become increasingly deliberate and aggressive in shaping regulatory policy, it is clear that a sweeping conclusion that judges generally have become increasingly deliberate and aggressive is not supported by the totality of the evidence. By adding the other pieces of the puzzle, a different picture, as well as the logical conclusions, emerge. Thus, the courts have been neither entirely passive nor totally aggressive. Instead, the actions of judges may be placed along a continuum.

The Filing of Lawsuits

At one end of the judicial impact spectrum are cases in which the mere filing of a lawsuit, without judicial action, has evoked a change in the EPA's policies and administration. In this context, the federal courts have been used as tools by plaintiffs to catch the agency's attention and to impress upon the EPA the seriousness of the plaintiff's grievances. In the formaldehyde case mentioned in Chapter Four, for example, the EPA reversed what career staff members referred to as a "purely political decision"[8] not to

Table 7

Patterns of Judicial Involvement in EPA Policies and Administration

Category	Examples

1. Filing of lawsuit, without judicial action, evoked change in EPA policy and/or administration.	*NRDC and APHA v. EPA*
	  EPA accelerated its studies of formaldehyde; judge refused to issue order and dismissed suit. EPA regulated formaldehyde.
	Shell Oil v. EPA
	  Filing of lawsuit prompted EPA policy reversal concerning liquids in landfills. Subsequent lawsuits and political pressures yielded a second policy reversal.

2. Courts have upheld EPA position without yielding change in EPA policy or administration.	*U.S. v. Chem-Dyne; U.S. v. NEPACCO; U.S. v. Ward; U.S. v. SCRDI; U.S. v. Conservation Chemical; U.S. v. Argent Corp.; U.S. v. Cauffman; U.S. v. Maryland Bank and Trust; U.S. v. Mirable; U.S. v. Carolawn; In Re: T.P. Long Chemical Co.; U.S. v. A&F Materials, Inc.; U.S. v. Ottati & Goss; U.S. v. Reilly Tar; U.S. v. Waste Ind.; U.S. v. Seymour Recycling Corp.; U.S. v. Vertac Chemical Corp.; U.S. v. Hardage; U.S. v. M/V Big Sam; U.S. v. Lebeouf Bros. Towing; U.S. v. Tex-Tow; U.S. v. Price; U.S. v. Bear Marine Services; U.S. v. Dickerson; U.S. v. Miami Drum; U.S. v. Tyson; U.S. v. Northernaire Plating; Long Pine Steering Committee v. EPA; U.S. v. Western Processing; Wheaton Industries v. EPA; J.V. Peters v. Administrator; Artesian Water v. Govt. of New Castle County; U.S. v. Standard Equipment; Eagle-Pitcher Industry v. EPA; Cadillac Fairview/California v. Dow Chemical*
	  CERCLA (Superfund) cases determined standards of causation and liability for hazardous waste cleanup.
	State Water Control Board v. Train; U.S. v. City of Detroit; Township of Franklin Sewerage Authority v. Middlesex County Utilities Authority
	  In these CWA NMP cases, judges and EPA together implemented the policy, forcing municipal compliance with the act, establishing pro-EPA precedents, assessing penalties, and scheduling corrective actions.

3. Passive judges, reluctant to intervene in EPA affairs, issued decisions that nonetheless affected EPA policy and/or administration.

NRDC & AFL-CIO v. EPA
  Judge invalidated EPA's voluntary testing agreement process under TSCA; terminated 21 industry-EPA agreements.

LEAF v. Hodel
  Judge interpreted provisions of RCRA and AEA as mandating DOE compliance with EPA regulations; increased EPA's power and authority.

Illinois v. Costle
  Judge ordered EPA to promulgate regulations mandated by RCRA and issued an ongoing, affirmative decree, thereby accelerating the pace of EPA actions.

EDF v. Costle
  Judge remanded SDWA organics regulations back to agency because of uncertainty in a highly technical area.

National Wildlife Federation and Colorado Wildlife Federation v. EPA
  Judicially approved consent decree concerning SDWA underground injection control program spurred nationwide regulation by EPA of injection wells.

4. Judges legitimately used discretionary powers deliberately to affect EPA policy and/or administration.

NRDC v. Costle
  Court refused to defer to expertise of EPA staff, read into TSCA an implied time frame of "reasonableness," ordered EPA to meet with environmental groups to develop compliance schedule, and denied request for 30-day extension. Decision involved an ongoing, affirmative decree and detailed judicial supervision of EPA. Agency was placed on compliance schedule and ordered to provide semiannual status updates to court.

continued

Table 7. Patterns of Judicial Involvement in EPA Policies and Administration *(continued)*

Category	Examples
	EDF v. EPA
	Judge ordered EPA to meet with all parties to plan regulation of PCBs under TSCA. Lawsuit yielded a jointly developed plan that was jointly implemented. Plaintiffs and judge supervised implementation of decree.
	NRDC v. EPA (The "Flannery Decision")
	Judge structured the CWA suit by modifying settlement prior to approval to include supervision of EPA by plaintiffs.
	Sierra Club v. Ruckelshaus
	Judge ordered EPA to meet with plaintiff to develop a mutually agreeable compliance schedule for regulation of radionuclides under CAA.
	EDF v. Gorsuch
	Judge agreed to ¼ of EPA-requested time extension for production of National Contingency Plan as mandated by CERCLA Superfund); judge later ordered agency to explain the "extraordinary steps" it was taking to comply with his order.
	Mumford Cove Assn., Inc., v. Town of Groton; U.S. v. City of Moore; U.S. v. Metropolitan District Commission
	Judges asserted themselves to help further or settle cases under CWA NMP.
	Coben v. EPA
	Judge refused to defer to judgment of EPA staff and held that agency failed to prove that a release of Superfund information to a journalist would result in concrete harm. Ordered release of information.

5. Judges either have gone beyond normal patterns of judicial behavior or have violated accepted judicial boundaries to evoke change in the agency.

NRDC v. Costle

Judge refused to defer to expertise of EPA on testing of chemicals under TSCA; ordered plaintiff environmental group to enforce order by commencing new action should EPA not comply with court mandate; and waived congressionally mandated 60-day notice provision in direct violation of statute. Judge coupled detailed judicial supervision (through an ongoing affirmative decree) with supervision by plaintiffs.

Illinois v. Gorsuch

Court declared EPA had violated APA by effectively suspending a regulation, even though the agency had already reversed its action. Court curbed EPA's uncontrolled discretion.

EDF v. Thomas

Court used its jurisdiction over EPA to send message to OMB that its holding of EPA regulations past a statutory deadline was unconstitutional and to let OMB know what was expected of it.

Monsanto v. Gorsuch

Judge doubled statutorily established notice requirement for EPA, refused to defer to expertise of EPA staff, enjoined agency from implementing parts of FIFRA, and denied stay pending appeal.

Union Carbide v. Ruckelshaus

Judge aggressively and uncompromisingly refused to yield not only to the EPA but to the Supreme Court in interpretation of FIFRA.

regulate the chemical in response to the filing of a lawsuit.[9] In another instance, the mere filing of a lawsuit prompted an EPA policy reversal concerning the placement of liquids in landfills. Subsequent lawsuits coupled with political pressures yielded a second reversal of policy on liquids in landfills.[10]

The Courts' Approval of the EPA

Second, in hundreds of cases, federal courts have given legal approval to EPA decisions without yielding changes in the agency's policies and administration. Examples can be found in judicial interpretations of the Superfund statute during its early years, when courts agreed with virtually every interpretation of the act by the EPA.[11] Other examples can be found in the EPA's implementation of its Clean Water Act National Municipal Policy in which judges and the EPA have banded together to force municipal compliance with the Clean Water Act, to establish pro-EPA precedents, to assess penalties, and to schedule corrective actions. In both sets of cases, judicial support of the EPA's statutory interpretations served to confirm and strengthen government policy.[12] (See Table 7 for specific cases.)

Passive Judicial Review

Third, federal courts have had an impact on the policies and administration of the EPA simply because of the nature of judicial review. In these instances, even the most passive judges, at times, have affected the discretion and autonomy of the agency. A typical example is a case in which the EPA was sued for not meeting a statutory deadline for promulgating regulations under the Resource Conservation and Recovery Act. By straightforwardly interpreting the statute, finding that the EPA had missed the deadline, and issuing an ongoing, affirmative decree, the judge prompted an acceleration of the pace of EPA actions.[13] (Additional examples can be found in Table 7.)

Discretionary Judicial Powers

In a fourth set of circumstances, judges have used their discretion and authority to push the agency in a specific direction. Included in this group are judicial efforts to manage the agency's response to a court order, judicial denial of agency requests during and after litigation, and judicial attempts to force the EPA to take a second look at its actions. In one case, for example, the court read into a statute an implied time frame of "reasonableness" within which the agency was to develop final regulations, even though no such time limit was imposed by the statute. The court then ordered the EPA to meet with the plaintiff environmental group to develop a compliance schedule. The case involved an ongoing, affirmative decree[14] and detailed judicial supervision.[15] The agency was placed on a compliance schedule and ordered to provide the court with semiannual status updates.[16] (Table 7 contains additional examples.)

Active, Aggressive Judicial Actions

Finally, in the smallest minority of cases, judges have actively and aggressively intervened in the administration and policies of the EPA.[17] This group includes cases in which judges have overstepped their statutory bounds, have questioned the scientific and policy expertise of EPA staff, and have aggressively pushed the EPA into action. In the toxics case mentioned in Chapter Four, for example, after refusing to defer to the scientific expertise of EPA administrators,[18] the judge ordered the plaintiff environmental group to enforce the court order by commencing a new action should the EPA not comply with the court mandate.[19] To facilitate the filing of a new lawsuit against the EPA, the judge waived a congressionally mandated provision for sixty days' notice, in direct violation of the statute. In this instance, the judge coupled detailed judicial supervision of the agency (through an ongoing affirmative decree) with supervision by the plaintiffs.[20] (See Table 7 for additional examples.)

The Impact of Federal Court Decisions on the Administration of the EPA

Federal court decisions have affected the administration of the EPA in several ways: Prompting a redistribution of budgetary and staff resources within the EPA, reducing the discretion and autonomy of EPA administrators, increasing the power of the EPA legal staff, decreasing the power and authority of EPA scientists, and selectively empowering certain organizational units within the EPA. In addition, court decisions have yielded an increase in external power and authority for the EPA as a whole.[21]

Court Orders and the Redistribution of Resources
Federal court decisions have served to redistribute resources within the EPA. The redistributive consequences of court decisions were predicted by Donald Horowitz, George Hale, and Jeffrey Straussman and have been observed in other agencies by W. S. Allerton and Louis Fisher.[22] The conclusions of this section are based on an examination of the implementation of EPA cases, as well as interviews with members of the EPA staff, Office of Management and Budget staff, and Congressional Budget Office staff.

With one exception, the EPA has not received additional staff or funds from Congress to enable it to comply with specific court decisions.[23] There are several reasons for this fact. First, the EPA's budget and planning cycles are two to three years ahead of the current fiscal year. The implementation of most EPA court orders does not exceed that length of time. Therefore, when a court decision mandating EPA action is issued, there usually is no opportunity to include in the budget requests for additional agency resources for complying with the court orders.

Second, in this time of fiscal austerity, there is very little "extra" money in the federal budget. This has caused the process for review of requests for additional funds to become very strict and cumbersome. For EPA requests there are six layers of hurdles that must be jumped before supplemental funds will be approved: the division level, the office director level, the assistant administrator level, the administrator level, the Office of Management and Budget, and Congress. Very few requests make it through the process. One former budget director at the EPA put it this way: "The supplemental process is too slow. OMB is too stingy. And, with a $6.94 billion budget, most court cases aren't *that* expensive to comply with. It is just too hard to get additional funds and people . . . and politically unpopular. Supplementals are never requested."[24]

Third, for court orders of longer duration that are issued in time to be incorporated into a budget cycle, the case is discussed in agency hearings with the Office of Management and Budget as well as in congressional appropriation committee hearings. The EPA is often asked how much it needs to comply with a court order, but there is never a line item dedicated to the court decision. Rather, the court order bumps, or delays, other items from getting funded. As mentioned previously, when the former EPA administrator, Anne Gorsuch, attempted to cut the EPA budget by 30 to 40 percent, she began by listing agency priorities: Court orders were at the top of the list of "untouchables," followed by statutory mandates. All other programs and priorities dropped to the bottom and were subject to budgetary cuts.[25] This fact confirms Hale's proposition that court orders can frustrate budgetary retrenchment.[26]

Reprogramming

The typical EPA budgetary response to a court order is called "reprogramming," in which funds, and sometimes personnel, are moved from program to program within an office, or even from office to office. Here, too, as funds are earmarked for court orders, other less pressing priorities are halted because of the lack of funding. "Sometimes it is painful to cut one part of a program for another," the former EPA budget director said, "but it has to be done to comply with the court decision. The administrator must make tough choices as to where the money will come from. Something in the current year just doesn't get done."[27]

The EPA also has two funds it has drawn from to meet the expenses associated with court orders: the administrator's discretionary fund and the "other contractual services" fund. When an award of attorneys fees is made by a court to an environmental group, it is usually paid out of the EPA administrator's discretionary fund.[28] When consulting firms need to be hired to do work to comply with a court order, they are usually paid out of the "other contractual services" fund.[29]

EPA staff members reported relying more often on consulting firms to perform work necessary to comply with court orders because of the lack of specialized internal resources readily available on short notice for such a task. There are several consequences, both positive and negative, of this increased use of consultants. On one hand, it is an expeditious way to meet rapid change in the agency without greatly disturbing the status quo. Experts can be brought in on a short-term basis without hiring permanent employees. On the other hand, as this use of consultants has grown, there has been a gradual erosion of the EPA's in-house expertise. In hiring new staff members, EPA managers now look "less for technical geniuses" and more for generalists who can oversee and communicate with technical consultants. This has affected morale, as members of the EPA technical staff at times resent not being able to use their expertise.[30]

The Negative Reaction of the Office of Management
and Budget and the Congressional Budget Office
Members of the Office of Management and Budget staff who overview the EPA budget do not like court decisions for three primary reasons. First, they are sometimes impossible to implement. Second, a court decision limits the flexibility of the Office of Management and Budget as far as what it can and cannot cut from the EPA's budget. Third, court decisions "reflect badly on the administration," although one member of the Office of Management and Budget admitted that "you may see a smile on my face when certain EPA regulations are overturned."[31]

Members of the Congressional Budget Office staff expressed a dislike of court decisions for two different reasons. First, one of the responsibilities of the Congressional Budget Office is to review the EPA's performance and success in reaching predetermined goals from year to year. When an unexpected court order is issued, it may displace a priority program objective. At the end of the fiscal year, work that was supposed to have been completed may have been halted, wreaking havoc on the performance auditing process. Second, Congressional Budget Office staff members reported that congresspersons sometimes become angry with the EPA when their pet pork barrel projects are dropped because the EPA has reprogrammed funds to comply with court decisions.[32]

Reduction in Discretion and Autonomy

From an administrative perspective, courts have reduced the discretion, autonomy, power, and authority of EPA administrators.[33] In the words of a former deputy administrator of the EPA, the courts "torque the agency around."[34] Oftentimes new programs are never implemented because resources are devoted to meeting court demands. In addition, court decisions affect EPA planning activities. As one EPA staff member said, "you can't plan for a court remand."

Moreover, court decisions can be broad and vague, affecting more than they need to. An example is the case concerning trade secrets and the Federal Insecticide, Fungicide and Rodenticide Act presented in Chapter Three.[35] In that instance, a judge held that the statute was unconstitutional because Congress had exceeded its regulatory authority and violated the Fifth Amendment's prohibition against the taking of property without just compensation. The court issued a permanent injunction barring the EPA from carrying out four provisions of the statute. EPA attorneys agreed that the court could have reached the same conclusion without nullifying all four statutory sections.[36]

Increase in Power of Legal Staff

The proliferation of court decisions concerning the EPA has forced what one staff member called "non-user-friendly" regulations.[37] The Office of General Counsel often rewrites regulations, notices, and proposals in anticipation that a lawsuit is imminent. Lawyers have the last word in most EPA actions, supporting the commonsensical theories of Nathan Glazer and Jeffrey Pfeffer and Gerald R. Salancik that an organization that faces or initiates a number of lawsuits will experience a gain in the power and influence of attorneys.[38]

Decrease in Power and Authority of Scientists

From a scientific perspective, the effect of court decisions on the EPA has important implications. The major issue here is not so much that judges are making scientific decisions but that judicial decisions are interrupting scientific processes. The EPA's process of developing regulations is what James Thompson calls "long-linked," involving serial interdependence.[39] Certain actions must build on other actions before final products can be issued. For example, scientific studies must be completed, data must be collected, and then the data must be analyzed prior to technical regulations being developed. There is a need for peer scientific review. Often the EPA either cannot comply with the court decision because these foundation steps have not been completed, or it skips needed steps and issues poorly conceived standards. Time constraints are exacerbated.

An example can be found in *Sierra Club v. Ruckelshaus,* examined in Chapter Five, in which the EPA was ordered by a court to issue regulations under the Clean Air Act to regulate radionuclides. The EPA requested nine years to develop a scientific basis for the regulations; instead a judge gave them 180 days. The agency issued the regulations, bypassing the typical review by its Science Advisory Board. When the advisory board finally reviewed the regulations, it found them scientifically flawed. The EPA administrator responded by withdrawing the regulations and was held in contempt of court. To purge itself of the contempt of court citation, the agency issued "sham" regulations that conformed with the letter of the court's order but, in fact, increased the amount of radionuclides that could be emitted into the atmosphere.

Positive Affect on EPA Administration
Despite these negative effects of federal court decisions, most members of the EPA staff within program offices involved in court cases reported several positive consequences of court decisions from their "micro" or individual organizational unit perspective. These positive attributes included the following:

1. *An increase in power for program offices within the EPA.* A court mandate always gets the attention of upper-echelon managers at the EPA. Offices that usually find their ideas concerning programmatic changes lost in the EPA bureaucratic maze find that their ideas are listened to if tied to the implementation of a court decision.
2. *An increase in resources for certain program offices, almost always derived from reprogramming.* As funds are needed to implement a court order, they usually are taken from other programs and offices within the EPA. The EPA program charged with implementing a court order is the beneficiary in this budgetary redistribution process.
3. *An increase in staff motivation and morale.* As workers band together to accomplish the goal of complying with court orders, they become more focused and directed. Staff members expressed great pride in implementing a court order in a timely fashion. Staff persons in an EPA regional office, for example, expressed joy when their actions prevented the regional administrator from being thrown in jail for contempt of court.
4. *A lifting of administrative burdens and prolonged review*

by the Office of Management and Budget. Internal agency approval procedures are streamlined in an effort to expeditiously comply with court mandates. The same phenomena has been seen with OMB approval of regulation changes. In the case discussed in Chapter Six, *Environmental Defense Fund v. Thomas,* the Office of Management and Budget was chastised by a judge for holding EPA underground storage tank regulations "hostage." EPA staff members found that after that decision the Office of Management and Budget no longer delayed the promulgation of such regulations, although spillover effects were not seen in other EPA programmatic areas.

5. *An increase in external power, authority, and discretion for the EPA as a whole.* As pro-EPA precedents are decided, the EPA gains legitimacy. The agency's power over the entities it regulates, as well as other federal agencies, has increased.

Three examples of these five positive effects merit attention. First, in the Clean Water Act case concerning the regulation of toxic chemicals discussed in Chapter Two, EPA staff members reported that the court-approved program was administratively more efficient and environmentally more sound than the agency's previous program. Moreover, the court order sparked positive interest in Congress, yielding both an increase in agency resources and a codification of the judiciary mandated changes. (It should be noted, however, that this 1977 example is the only instance in which Congress provided additional funds for implementation of a specific court order involving the EPA.) The case was heralded by EPA staff as a way to "focus on getting something done." With the pressures and the resources the court order brought, "people were motivated better; consequently the final product was better."[40]

Second, in the Superfund Freedom of Information Act case in which a judge ordered the EPA to release the names of alleged polluters to a reporter (discussed in Chapter Six), the agency complied by changing both its policy and its procedure on the subject. The result was a streamlined agency operation that members of the EPA staff viewed as being more responsive to the public.[41]

Third, in the Resource Conservation and Recovery Act and Clean Water Act case presented in Chapter Six concerning the EPA's regulation of Department of Energy facilities, a judge ordered the Department of Energy to apply for EPA permits. Although the EPA was neither a plaintiff nor a defendant in the suit, the decision had a positive effect on the EPA's policies and administration, increasing the EPA's power and authority over the Department of Energy. Moreover, according to a study by the General Accounting Office, the decision had unanticipated positive effects as the EPA acquired further leverage over other Department of Energy facilities, yielding greater compliance by the Energy Department with EPA statutes and regulations.[42] (The discovery of hundreds of Department of Energy waste sites in the late 1980s and the early 1990s, however, indicates that the department's compliance was extremely limited. See Chapter Six.)

The Impact of Federal Court Decisions on the EPA's Policies

Perhaps the most significant impact of federal court decisions on the EPA has been on policy. From a "macro" or agencywide perspective, compliance with court orders has become one of the agency's top priorities, at times overtaking congressional mandates. The courts have dictated which issues get attention at the EPA. In an atmosphere of limited resources, coupled with unrealistic and numerous statutory mandates,[43] the EPA has been forced to make decisions among competing priorities. With few exceptions, court orders have been the "winners" in this competition.

From a "micro" or individual organizational unit perspective, compliance with court orders also has become the top priority of many EPA divisions. For example, in nearly every case examined, EPA staff members reported concentrating the majority of their efforts on implementing court decrees. Other programs and priorities became secondary or were dropped. Moreover, members of the EPA staff developed specific programmatic policies and changed regulations in response to court decisions.

Such judicial dominance over the formulation of EPA policy has grave ramifications in two respects. First, as Donald Horowitz observed, courts by their very nature are narrowly focused on the issues presented in a case.[44] Yet those narrow court-generated issues have become the EPA's highest priorities. As a consequence, the most pressing environmental problems are not necessarily those addressed by our nation's environmental agency. Matters suitable for litigation are the "squeaky wheels that get the grease," while other important environmental problems fall by the wayside. Huge amounts of resources have been dedicated to meeting court decisions, when the environmental and health benefits, at times, have been marginal. An example is the Clean Air Act radionuclides case, examined in Chapter Five, in which $7.6 million and 150 staff work years were spent over a six-year period to develop regulations that would prevent one cancer death every thirteen years.[45]

Second, from the perspective of representative democracy, judicial dominance over EPA policies is problematic.[46] Court orders can differ from the mandates of our elected congressional representatives. Moreover, judicial dominance of agency policy makes it difficult for those not a party to a lawsuit to participate in the EPA regulatory process.[47] In the Clean Water Act's Flannery Decision, for example, the EPA carried out programs and processes ordered by a court-modified consent decree that were beyond those mandated by Congress. Congress reacted by amending the Clean Water Act to adopt the provisions of the consent decree.[48] A second example is found in Melnick's work, in which a judge, basing his decision on a vague preamble to the Clean Air Act, ordered the EPA to implement a program to prevent the significant deterioration of air. The agency complied, and Congress then amended the act to mandate the program.

Conclusion: A View to the Future

This work has demonstrated that the impact of federal court decisions on the policies and administration of the United States Environmental Protection Agency has been multifaceted and complex. The decisions of courts have been neither entirely positive nor totally negative. Rather, the decrees of judges fall along a continuum, ranging from confirming and legitimizing the actions of the EPA to bringing about change in the agency's policies and administration.

From an agencywide policy perspective, however, the impact of court decisions on the EPA is problematic. Compliance with court orders has become one of the agency's top priorities, at times overtaking congressional mandates and threatening representative democracy. Clearly litigation is not the best way to formulate environmental policy or to determine our nation's environmental priorities. The problems lie primarily with Congress, with interest groups, with the judicial system, and with the EPA. These problems pose a number of challenges for the future—challenges that could either overwhelm and cripple an already ailing EPA or, conversely, if properly addressed, serve as catalysts to launch the agency toward a dynamic and effective third decade.

First, much of the responsibility for the negative effect of court decisions on the development of environmental policy and the administration of environmental laws within the EPA must lie with Congress. Congress created the EPA's statutes, which allow the agency to be second-guessed by outside groups. Congress set the numerous and unrealistic statutory deadlines, making the EPA an "easy mark" for litigation. And Congress created incentives for abundant incremental litigation against the EPA by liberally allowing and rewarding narrowly focused citizen suits.

Our environmental laws must be reexamined and refined. Our environmental problems must be prioritized using political, economic, legal, and health inputs, thus utilizing a holistic or integrated approach, not a piecemeal, incremental approach. In addition, a greater emphasis on pollution prevention in our laws is essential. These will not be easy tasks, for the problems are growing more challenging and the decisions more difficult every day.

Second, while it is important to preserve the rights of interest groups to file lawsuits against the EPA in instances, for example, where the agency's actions have been arbitrary, capricious, or in flagrant violation of law, the challenge for those filing under citizen suit provisions[49] will be to rethink whether they are truly acting in the public interest. Of course defining "the public interest" is a quest that has defied students of public policy since the beginning of time. But on a very simple level, it is clear that anti-EPA plaintiffs must look beyond the "quick fix" and the instant gratification that winning a suit against the agency may bring. Such suits can be mere "Band-Aid solutions" that exacerbate existing problems within the agency and in the long run slow entire regulatory processes. Planning becomes impossible.

And without planning the EPA is reduced to a dedicated yet ineffective group of "keystone cops" rushing from one crisis to another.

Third, obvious institutional influences come into play when court decisions affect public agencies, including the fact that judges of EPA court cases are typically "chained" to the issues developed by attorneys representing their clients' narrow interests. The judicial system generally is not designed to allow a full analysis of the public policy implications of specific court decisions. Moreover, individual judges at times contribute to the negative effects of federal court decisions on the EPA. In some instances judges have overstepped their statutory bounds to force change in the agency. In other instances, judges have aggressively pushed the EPA in a specific direction seemingly based on their own personal biases. A 1991 study, for example, suggests that judges appointed by President Ronald Reagan have a greater inclination than those appointed by President Jimmy Carter to adopt positions that would reduce the burden of compliance with the Clean Air Act and the Clean Water Act on industries.[50] Federal Judge Patricia Wald has written:

> Despite much protestation to the contrary, a judge's origins and politics will surely influence his or her judicial opinions. Judges' minds are not compart- mentalized: their law-declaring functions cannot be performed by some insulated, apolitical internal mechanism. However subtly or unconsciously, the judge's political orientation *will* affect decision- making.[51]

Accordingly, one challenge for judges will be to keep personal biases in check. When appropriate, judges should urge the use of the political and administrative processes for resolving EPA disputes.

Finally, turning to the EPA, several of the agency's enforcement programs already rely heavily on nonjudicial (administrative) enforcement tools to compel violating facilities to comply with environmental regulations. Given the fact that such tools give the agency more flexibility while simultaneously allowing input from a broad spectrum of society, the use of administrative orders should, and will, grow. The proliferation of such internal orders will also allow the agency to take into consideration a wider variety of factors not accessible in narrowly drafted lawsuits.

The most difficult challenge for the EPA, however, will be to develop further nonjudicial methods for resolving environmental disputes. Negotiated rule making, where diverse interested parties discuss their goals and expectations before and during rule making (as opposed to a court challenge after rule promulgation), has already been used sparingly at the EPA. Although refinements in the process are needed, it should be used more often where appropriate. Other promising alternatives include advisory committees, roundtables, policy dialogues, informal meetings, mediation, and arbitration.[52]

Of course, there will always be instances when the only way to force compliance with our pollution laws is to seek a court order. But given the slow, incremental nature of the judicial process, the unanticipated consequences of judicial decisions, and the increasing complexity of our environmental problems, we must be more demanding in designing our solutions, moving beyond our dependence on litigation as a means of resolving environmental disputes. Only then will the EPA have a fighting chance for success in its third decade as our nation's most important public environmental organization.

Abbreviations for Notes and Bibliography

Bankr.	Bankruptcy Court
BNA	Bureau of National Affairs
C.A.	Court of Appeals
C.A. DC.	Court of Appeals for the District of Columbia
CC.A. DC.	Circuit Court of Appeals for the District of Columbia
C.D. CA.	Central District of California
C.F.R.	Code of Federal Regulations
Cir.	Circuit
Cong. Rec.	Congressional Record
Ct.	Court
DC.	District of Columbia
DC. Cir.	District of Columbia Circuit
D.C. DC.	District Court of the District of Columbia
D.C. DE.	District Court of Delaware
D.C. MA.	District Court of Massachusetts
D.C. MD.	District Court of Maryland
D.C. NM.	District Court of New Mexico
D. CO.	District of Colorado
D.C. W. TX.	District Court of West Texas
D. MA.	District of Massachusetts
D. MN.	District of Minnesota
D. NH.	District of New Hampshire
D. NJ.	District of New Jersey

D. SC.	District of South Carolina
E.D. AR.	Eastern District of Arkansas
E.D. MI.	Eastern District of Michigan
E.D. MO.	Eastern District of Missouri
E.D. NC.	Eastern District of North Carolina
E.D. PA	Eastern District of Pennsylvania
E.D. TN.	Eastern District of Tennessee
E.D. VA.	Eastern District of Virginia
ELI	Environmental Law Institute
ELR	Environmental Law Reporter
EO	Executive Order
ERC	Environmental Reporter Cases
Fed. Reg.	Federal Register
F.2d	Federal Reporter, Second Series
F.Supp	Federal Supplement Reporter
H.R.	House of Representatives
L.Ed.2d	Lawyers Edition, U.S. Supreme Court Reports, Second Series
N.D. CA.	Northern District of California
N.D. IL.	Northern District of Illinois
N.D. OH.	Northern District of Ohio
N.Y.S.2d	New York Supplement Reporter, Second Series
PL	Public Law
S.	Senate
S.Ct.	Supreme Court Reporter (U.S.)
S.D. FL.	Southern District of Florida
S.D. IL.	Southern District of Illinois
S.D. IN.	Southern District of Indiana
S.D. NY.	Southern District of New York
S.D. OH.	Southern District of Ohio
S. Rept.	Senate Report
Stat.	Statute

U.S.	United States; United States Supreme Court Reports
U.S.C.	United States Code
U.S.L.W.	United States Law Week
W.D. MI.	Western District of Michigan
W.D. MO.	Western District of Missouri
W.D. OK.	Western District of Oklahoma
W.D. PA.	Western District of Pennsylvania
W.D. WA.	Western District of Washington

Citation Format

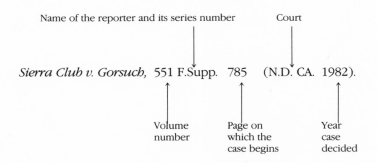

Name of the reporter and its series number   Court

Sierra Club v. Gorsuch, 551 F.Supp. 785 (N.D. CA. 1982).

Volume number   Page on which the case begins   Year case decided

Notes

Preface

1. It should be noted that I did not include in this study less-litigated EPA statutory areas, cases that have affected the EPA but were not fully litigated, additional decisions that have affected the agency even though the EPA was neither a plaintiff nor a defendant, and most unpublished court decisions (for example, numerous Superfund cases litigated between private parties in which EPA statutes were interpreted, suits filed by states against polluters, and citizens' suits filed directly against polluters).

2. I accessed the *Bureau of National Affairs Environment Reporter* via the Lexis legal data base. In addition, I examined issues of *Inside EPA*. Whenever possible, I verified the information contained in these documents through interviews with members of the EPA staff.

3. Donald T. Campbell, "Degrees of Freedom and the Case Study," *Comparative Political Studies* 8 (1975): 178–93; Robert K. Yin, "The Case Study Crisis: Some Answers," *Administrative Science Quarterly* 26 (March 1981): 58–65; Robert K. Yin, "The Case Study as Serious Research Strategy," *Knowledge* 3 (1981): 97–114; Robert K. Yin, "Studying Phenomenon and Context across Sites," *American Behavioral Scientist* 26 (1982): 84–100.

4. Ibid.; Barry Bozeman, "Retrospective Technology Assessment" (unpublished paper, 1985).

5. Robert K. Yin, *Case Study Research: Design and Methods* (Newbury Park, Calif.: Sage Publications, 1989); Robert K. Yin and Karen A. Heald, "Using the Case Survey Method to Analyze Policy Studies," *Administrative Science Quarterly* 20 (1975): 371–81.

Chapter One

1. For an interesting insight into Yannacone's philosophy of the use of courts to force social change, see Victor J. Yannacone, "Sue the Bastards," in *Earth Day: The Beginning*, ed. Staff of Environmental Action (New York: Bantam, 1970).
2. *Environmental Defense Fund v. Ruckelshaus*, 439 F.2d 584 (1971).
3. William K. Stevens, "2% of G.N.P. Spent by U.S. on Cleanup," *New York Times*, December 23, 1990, A:13.
4. Graham Hueber, "Americans Report High Levels of Environmental Concern, Activity," *Gallup Poll Monthly* 307 (April, 1991): 6–12.
5. See, for example, R. Shep Melnick, *Regulation and the Courts: The Case of the Clean Air Act* (Washington, D.C.: Brookings Institution, 1983); Gerald E. Frug, "The Judicial Power of the Purse," *University of Pennsylvania Law Review* 126 (1978): 715; David Rosenbloom, *Public Administration and Law* (New York: Marcel Dekker, 1983); R. Shep Melnick, "The Politics of Partnership," *Public Administration Review* 45 (1985): 653–60.
6. Abram Chayes, "The Role of the Judge in Public Law Litigation," *Harvard Law Review* 89 (1976): 1281.
7. David L. Bazelon, "The Impact of Courts on Public Administration," *Indiana Law Journal* 52 (1977): 101; R. Shep Melnick, "The Politics of Partnership"; Martin M. Shapiro, *Who Guards the Guardians? Judicial Control of Administration* (Athens: University of Georgia Press, 1988).
8. See Harry Eckstein, "Case Study and Theory in Political Science," in *Political Science: Scope and Theory, Volume 7*, ed. Fred I. Greenstein and Nelson W. Polsby (Reading, Mass.: Addison-Wesley, 1975); see also Arend Lijphart, "Comparative Politics and the Comparative Method," *American Political Science Review* 65 (1971): 682–93.
9. No claim is made that the results of the study at hand can be generalized to other agencies or to courts as a whole. Multiple replications of this study, with cross-agency comparisons, are needed before such assessments can be made. This study is nonetheless useful because it presents court-EPA interactions in high relief during periods when the EPA and individuals involved in its policy making pressed the agency's legal behavior to its limits.
10. J. Clarence Davies and Barbara Davies, *The Politics of Pollution* (Indianapolis: Bobbs-Merrill, 1975).
11. Edwin Diamond, "What Business Thinks," *Fortune* 81, 2 (1970): 118–72.

12. "Plan for the Environment," *New York Times,* July 12, 1970, 4:12.
13. Robert Smith, "Nixon Picks Chief of Pollution Unit," *New York Times,* November 7, 1970, 1:1.
14. "Utah Senator Reproves Environmental Agency," *New York Times,* April 23, 1981, B:8.
15. See, for example, Ronald L. Claveloux, "The Conflict between Executive Privilege and Congressional Oversight: The Gorsuch Controversy," *Duke Law Journal* 1983 (1983): 1333–58. For a discussion of how President Reagan's deregulation efforts affected the EPA, see Richard A. Harris and Sidney M. Milkis, *The Politics of Regulatory Change: A Tale of Two Agencies* (New York: Oxford University Press, 1989).

    For an interesting contrast, see Marc K. Landy, Marc J. Roberts, and Stephen R. Thomas, *The EPA: Asking the Wrong Questions* (New York: Oxford University Press, 1990), where it is argued that the EPA has been allowed to ask questions that are too narrow and to give answers that are incorrectly simplistic concerning our nation's environmental problems.
16. Bruce A. Ackerman and William T. Hassler, *Clean Coal/Dirty Air* (New Haven, Conn.: Yale University Press, 1981).
17. The bills were H.R. 3847, S. 533, S. 2006, and S. 171.
18. *BNA Environment Reporter,* March 5, 1993, 2862.
19. *Air and Water News,* July 26, 1971.
20. "Environmental Protection Head Picks New York Regional Chief," *New York Times,* September 2, 1971; "Setback for the EPA," *New York Times,* September 13, 1971.
21. Ibid. It should be noted that many herald the political appointee system as a positive way of making the agency more responsive to the electorate.
22. Office of Federal Register, *The United States Government Manual* (Washington, D.C.: Government Printing Office, 1991–1992), 549.
23. Not all programs or parts of programs are mentioned.
24. Interview of William K. Reilly as quoted in Brian Polkinghorn, "The Influence of Regulatory Negotiation on EPA as an Institution." (Draft Ph.D. dissertation, Department of Social Science, Maxwell School of Citizenship and Public Affairs, Syracuse University, April, 1993).
25. See Phillip J. Cooper, *Public Law and Public Administration* (Englewood Cliffs, N.J.: Prentice-Hall, 1988); Marc Galanter, "Why the Haves Come Out Ahead: Speculations on the Limits of Legal Change," *Law and Society Review* 9 (1974): 95.
26. For an analysis of the successes and failures of interest groups in

court, see Lee Epstein and C. K. Rowland, "Debunking the Myth of Interest Group Invincibility in the Courts," *American Political Science Review* 85 (March, 1991): 205–17.

27. See Judge Gerald Harwood, "Hearings before an EPA Administrative Law Judge," *Environmental Law Reporter,* November, 1987, 10441.

28. 40 C.F.R. section 22.

29. Administrative law judges preside over hearings that are by statute "required on the record after opportunity for an agency hearing." Administrative Procedure Act, 5 U.S.C. section 554(a). Administrative law judges may also preside over other hearings.

30. The administrator usually delegates this duty to the judicial officer. See Harwood, "Hearings."

Chapter Two

1. Federal Water Pollution Control Act (Clean Water Act), PL 92-500, October 18, 1972; amended by PL 93-207, December 28, 1973; PL 93-243, January 2, 1974; PL 93-592, January 2, 1975; PL 93-238, March 23, 1976; PL 94-273, April 21, 1976; PL 94-558, October 19, 1976; PL 95-217, December 28, 1977; PL 95-576, November 2, 1978; PL 96-148, December 16, 1979; PL 96-478 and PL 96-483, October 21, 1980; PL 96-561, December 22, 1980; PL 97-35, April 2, 1982; PL 97-216, July 18, 1982; PL 97-272, September 30, 1982; PL 97-440, January 8, 1983; PL 98-45, July 12, 1983; PL 98-623, November 8, 1984; PL 99-396, August 27, 1986; PL 100-4, February 4, 1987; PL 101-340, July 31, 1990.

2. FWPCA section 307(a), 33 U.S.C. section 1317(a)(Supp. V 1975).

3. FWPCA section 307(a)(1), 33 U.S.C. section 1317(a)(1)(Supp. V 1975).

4. FWPCA section 307(a)(2), 33 U.S.C. section 1317(a)(2)(Supp. V 1975).

5. Ibid.

6. FWPCA section 307(a)(6), 33 U.S.C. section 1317(a)(6)(Supp. V 1975).

7. Khristine L. Hall, "The Control of Toxic Pollutants under the Federal Water Pollution Control Act Amendments of 1972," *Iowa Law Review* 63 (1978): 616.

8. 38 Fed. Reg. 24344 (September 7, 1983). *Black's Law Dictionary* provides this definition of a consent decree: "A decree entered . . . on consent of both parties; it is not properly a judicial sentence, but is in the nature of a solemn contract or agreement of the parties, made under the sanction of the court, and in effect an admission by them that the decree is a just determination of their rights upon the real facts of the case, if such facts had been proved. It binds only the consenting parties and is not binding on the court."

9. 38 Fed. Reg. 24344 (1983).

10. *NRDC v. Train,* 6 ERC 1702 (1974); rev'd 519 F.2d 287 (1975).

11. Ibid. at 1704.

12. *NRDC v. Train,* 8 ERC 1233, 519 F.2d 287 (1975).

13. Briefs of environmental and industry objectors, EPA Docket No. 1, as cited in Hall, "Control of Toxic Pollutants," 609.

14. 41 Fed. Reg. 23577 (1976).

15. *NRDC v. Train,* 8 ERC 2120 (1976).

16. Ibid.

17. See Hall, "Control of Toxic Pollutants."

18. Water pollution has two major origins: point sources and nonpoint sources. The EPA defines point sources as specific points of discharge, such as outfall pipes from industrial facilities or sewage treatment plants. Examples of nonpoint sources are runoff from city streets, from construction sites, from farms, and from mines.

19. *BNA Environment Reporter,* May 7, 1976, 14.

20. See note 8, supra.

21. *BNA Environment Reporter,* June 4, 1976, 193.

22. *BNA Environment Reporter,* June 11, 1976, 217.

23. *NRDC v. Train,* 8 ERC at 2121 (1976).

24. *NRDC v. Costle,* 561 F.2d 904 (1977).

25. PL 95-217, 91 Stat. 1566.

26. 123 Cong. Rec. S. 19647–48 (daily ed. December 15, 1977). See also S. Rept. 95-370 at 56 (noting committee approval and endorsement of strategy contained in decree), reprinted in *U.S. Code Cong. & Ad. News* (1977): 4380.

27. Section 307(a)(1); added by section 53(a) of the Clean Water Act of 1977, 91 Stat. 1589.

28. Section 301(b)(2)(C); added by section 42(a) of the Clean Water Act of 1977, 91 Stat. 1582.

29. Section 307(a)(2); added by section 53(a) of the Clean Water Act of 1977, 91 Stat. 1590.

30. Section 301(b)(2)(C); added by section 42(a) of the Clean Water Act of 1977, 91 Stat. 1582.

31. *NRDC v. Costle,* 12 ERC 1181 (1978).

32. *NRDC v. Costle,* 12 ERC 1833 (1979); *Environmental Defense Fund v. Costle,* 636 F.2d 1229, 14 ERC 2161 (1980).

33. Ibid.

34. *NRDC v. Costle,* 12 ERC 1833 (1979).

35. *NRDC v. Costle,* 12 ERC at 1841 (paragraph 7(b) of consent decree).

36. *EDF v. Costle,* 636 F.2d 1229, 14 ERC 2161 (1980).

37. *NRDC v. Gorsuch,* 12 ELR 20371 (1982). It is interesting to note that the EPA argued in the instant case that "there is no basis in fact, law or policy for holding that the decree constitutes an impermissible exercise of judicial power." The EPA pointed to the fact that "the then-Administrator not only consented to its terms in order to avoid risks of continued litigation, but exercised his independent judgment that the decree provided an appropriate means of implementing the Act."

38. *Citizens for a Better Environment v. Gorsuch,* 718 F.2d 1117 (1983), 19 ERC 2057, 2068–74 (1983).

39. 19 ERC at 2068–69.

40. Ibid. at 2069.

41. Ibid. at 2071.

42. Ibid.

43. Ibid. at 2072.

44. Ibid. at 2073.

45. Ibid. at 2073–74.

46. *Union Carbide v. NRDC,* 467 U.S. 1219, 81 L.Ed.2d 373, 104 S.Ct. 2668 (1984).

47. *BNA Environment Reporter,* November 2, 1984, 909.

48. *Implementation of the Clean Water Act (A Case Study of Lawmaking by Rulemakers),* House Public Works and Transportation Subcommittee on Investigation and Oversight, 97th Cong., 2d sess., December 5, 1982, 30.

49. Douglas Costle, "Statement of Douglas Costle," *Implementation of the Federal Water Pollution Control Act: Hearings before the Subcommittee on Oversight and Review of the House Committee on Public Works and Transportation,* 96th Cong., 2d sess., 1980, 906–7.

50. EPA's Memorandum in Opposition to Intervenor's Joint Motion to Vacate, or Alternatively, to Revise the Decree and in Support of Defendant's Cross-Motion to Modify the Decree, August 3, 1981, p. 26, archived at the District Court for the District of Columbia.

51. Ibid.

52. Affidavit of Lewis S. W. Crampton, filed in support of EPA's Cross-Motion to Modify the Decree, March 5, 1982, archived at the District Court for the District of Columbia.

53. NRDC's Memorandum in Opposition to Defendant's Cross-Motion to Modify Consent Decree, March 29, 1982, p. 2, archived at the District Court for the District of Columbia.

54. *NRDC v. Gorsuch,* 17 ERC 2013 (1982).

55. Ibid. at 2015.

56. Ibid.

57. Ibid. at 2015–16.
58. Ibid.
59. Ibid. at 2016.
60. Ibid.
61. Ibid.
62. *Citizens for a Better Environment v. Gorsuch,* 718 F.2d 1117; 19 ERC 2057 (1983).
63. *BNA Environment Reporter,* May 14, 1982, 23.
64. EPA's Motion for Partial Relief from Court's Order on May 7, 1982, filed June 21, 1982, archived at the District Court for the District of Columbia.
65. Ibid.
66. See Bradford W. Wyche, "The Regulation of Toxic Pollutants under the Clean Water Act: EPA's Ten Year Rulemaking Nears Completion," *Natural Resources Lawyer* 15 (1983): 511.
67. Ibid. Wyche discusses the fact that Flannery technically lacked the jurisdiction to rule on the EPA's motion for partial relief, since the decision had already been appealed by the intervenors. Accordingly, the EPA asked the court of appeals to remand the case to enable Flannery to modify the decree. The appeals court acquiesced. After Flannery's modification, however, industry groups renewed their appeal.
68. *BNA Environment Reporter,* November 12, 1982, 1027. A similar case with a different twist is the 1983 case, *NRDC v. EPA,* in which the court ordered a ninety-day extension of deadlines for compliance in establishing limits for effluent from electroplating operations and general pretreatment standards under the CWA "to accommodate the unique management problems imposed upon the *court* by the complex issues involved by various suits challenging the rules and standards" (emphasis added); 48 Fed. Reg. 2775 (1983).
69. *NRDC v. Administrator,* 595 F. Supp. 65 (1984).
70. *NRDC v. Thomas,* 801 F.2d 457 (1986).
71. The decree was modified on August 2, 1983; January 6, 1984; July 5, 1984; January 1, 1985; April 24, 1986; and January 8, 1987. See 52 Fed. Reg. 42522 (1987).
72. 52 Fed. Reg. 42522 (1987).
73. The advantages to environmentalists under the settlement agreement were twofold. First, sixty-five pollutants were regulated, as opposed to the nine originally proposed by the EPA. Moreover, the agreement required the EPA to regulate pollutants not susceptible to treatment by publicly owned treatment works (POTWs) or that inter-

fered with, passed through, or were otherwise incompatible with
POTW systems. Second, the decree put the EPA on a "tight court-
enforceable schedule" for promulgating the new regulations. Hall
wrote: "Past experience with EPA's implementation of the FWPCA . . .
taught environmental groups that EPA often misses statutory deadlines or delays action unless under the gun of a court-ordered schedule that is then enforceable through a contempt of court action.
Drawing on this experience with EPA, the plaintiffs in the settlement
insisted on the inclusion of a tight schedule for the promulgation of
the limitations." Hall, "Control of Toxic Pollutants," 616.

74. Interviews with EPA staff members, EPA headquarters, week of
May 15, 1988. Also mentioned in Hall, "Control of Toxic Pollutants."
75. Interviews with EPA staff members, EPA headquarters, week of
May 15, 1988. Also mentioned in *EDF v. Costle,* 636 F.2d 1229, 1235–
36 (1980).
76. Interviews with EPA staff members, EPA headquarters, week of
May 15, 1988. Also mentioned in Hall, "Control of Toxic Pollutants."
77. Interviews with EPA staff members, EPA headquarters, week of
May 15, 1988. Also mentioned in Hall, "Control of Toxic Pollutants,"
and *EDF v. Costle,* 636 F.2d 1229, 1235–36 (1980).
78. See note 75, supra.
79. Interviews with EPA staff members, EPA headquarters, week of
May 15, 1988. Also mentioned in Hall, "Control of Toxic Pollutants."
80. Interview with EPA staff members, EPA headquarters, week of May 15,
1988.
81. Ibid.
82. On July 27, 1988, a federal district court issued an order that set
deadlines by which the EPA was mandated to decide whether it
would regulate dioxins in discharges from pulp and paper mills.
Under the order, the agency was ordered to conduct a risk assessment by April 30, 1989. The agency was then ordered to take action
on the pollutant within a year of undertaking the risk assessment. The
agency also was ordered to prepare guidance on issuing pollutant
discharge permits for paper and pulp mills by April 30, 1990. *EDF v.
Lee Thomas,* 657 F.Supp. 302 (D.C. D.C. 1987). Tighter dioxin discharge limits are scheduled to be imposed for sixty-six paper mills,
although they are strongly resisted by the paper and pulp industry.
States are developing their own water quality criteria for dioxin,
subject to EPA approval. In 1991–92, Congress was studying a bill
proposed by Representative Robin Tallon (D-South Carolina) that
would establish a minimum federal dioxin standard based on a

lifetime cancer risk of one in one million; H.R. 2084, 102d Cong., 1st sess., 1991. On December 3, 1992, EPA Administrator William Reilly announced a final rule setting federal standards for toxic pollutants, including dioxin, for states that have not established their own standards (57 Fed. Reg. 60848). The dioxin standard closely resembled the standard considered previously by Congress.

83. Interview with Victor Kimm, EPA director of the Office of Drinking Water, as reported in the *BNA Environment Reporter,* November 2, 1984, 1148; and interviews with EPA staff members, EPA headquarters, week of May 15, 1988.

84. Glenn L. Unterberger and John W. Lyon, "Municipal Enforcement under the Federal Clean Water Act and EPA's National Municipal Policy," *National Enforcement Journal* 1 (1986): 4; and interviews with EPA staff members, EPA headquarters, week of May 15, 1988.

85. Ibid.

86. EPA internal memorandum to regional counsels, from Glenn L. Unterberger, associate enforcement counsel for water, August 27, 1985; and EPA internal memorandum to Water Management Division directors, from James R. Elder, director, Office of Water Enforcement and Permits, September 22, 1987.

87. General Accounting Office, *Environmental, Economic and Political Issues Impede Potomac River Cleanup Efforts* (Washington, D.C.: Government Printing Office, January 6, 1982).

88. Unterberger memorandum.

89. Elder memorandum.

90. Suit also was filed against the cities of Detroit, Phoenix, and San Antonio on that date.

91. *U.S. v. El Paso,* Civ. No. E-P89 CA347, District Court of West Texas, 1990.

Chapter Three

1. For an informative political and historical perspective on the emergence of pesticide policy in the United States, see Christopher Bosso, *Pesticides and Politics: The Life Cycle of a Public Policy Issue* (Pittsburgh: University of Pittsburgh Press, 1987).

2. Federal Insecticide, Fungicide and Rodenticide Act, 7 U.S.C. section 135 et seq., as amended by PL 92-516, October 21, 1972; PL 94-140, November 28, 1975; PL 95-396, September 30, 1978; PL 96-539, December 17, 1980; PL 98-201, December 2, 1983; PL 98-620, November 8, 1984; PL 100-532, October 25, 1988; PL 101-624, November 28, 1990; and PL 102-237, December 13, 1991.

3. The court's decision was issued as *Monsanto v. Acting Administrator,* 564 F.Supp. 522 (1983).

4. The law firm, Covinton and Burling, requested the documents on behalf of an undisclosed client.

5. FIFRA section 136h(d)(1)(C).

6. FIFRA section 136h(g).

7. *Monsanto v. Gorsuch,* No. 79-0366-C(1), Eastern District of Missouri.

8. *Monsanto v. Acting Administrator,* 18 ERC at 2094 (1983). The judge consciously deviated from precedent in making his decision, acknowledging similar cases with different outcomes such as *Mobay Chemical Corp. v. Costle,* 517 F.Supp. 254 (1981), 682 F.2d 419 (1981), 103 S.Ct. 343 (1982); *Pennwalt Corp. v. Gorsuch,* 682 F.2d 419 (1982), aff'd *Mobay,* supra; *Chevron Chemical Co. v. Costle,* 499 F.Supp. 732, 499 F.Supp. 755, 641 F.2d 104, 452 U.S. 961 (1981); and *Petrolite Corp. v. EPA,* 519 F.Supp. 966 (1981).

9. *Monsanto v. Acting Administrator,* 18 ERC at 2095 (1983).

10. *BNA Environment Reporter,* April 22, 1983; and interviews with EPA staff members, EPA headquarters, week of May 15, 1988.

11. Brief of Jo Moore, Patrick J. Cafferty, and Rosanne Mayer, attorneys for the EPA, filed December 31, 1983, archived at EPA headquarters, Washington, D.C.

12. *BNA Environment Reporter,* April 22, 1983; the court in *National Agricultural Chemicals Association and Ciba-Geigy Corp. v. EPA,* 554 F.Supp. 1209 (1983), rejected an EPA rule that required applicants for federal pesticide registration to cite test data submitted by other firms.

13. *BNA Environment Reporter,* April 22, 1983, 2344.

14. Brief of Gary Dyer, W. Wayne Withers, and Kenneth Heineman, attorneys for Monsanto.

15. Abramson, EPA internal memorandum to Johnson, May 13, 1983.

16. 48 Fed. Reg. 34000 (1983).

17. The other decision was *National Agricultural Chemicals Association and Ciba-Geigy Corp. v. EPA,* 554 F.Supp. 1209 (1983).

18. *Ruckelshaus v. Monsanto,* 463 U.S. 1315 (1983).

19. Oral argument of Lawrence G. Wallace, Justice Department attorney representing the EPA, February 27, 1984.

20. Brief of Moore, Cafferty, and Mayer.

21. Oral argument of Raymond Randolph, Jr., attorney for Monsanto, February 27, 1984.

22. *Ruckelshaus v. Monsanto,* 467 U.S. 986 (1984).

23. Ibid. at 1015.

24. Ibid. at 1007.
25. 49 Fed. Reg. 30884 (1984).
26. For further information on the EPA's FIFRA policies concerning confidential business information, see U.S. Environmental Protection Agency, *FIFRA Confidential Business Information Security Manual* (Washington, D.C.: Government Printing Office, 1982); U.S. Environmental Protection Agency, *FIFRA Compliance/Enforcement Manual* (Washington, D.C.: Government Printing Office, 1983).
27. *BNA Environment Reporter,* July 5, 1983.
28. Section 3(c)(1)(D).
29. *Union Carbide Agricultural Products Co., Inc. v. Ruckelshaus,* 571 F.Supp. 117 (1983).
30. *Union Carbide v. Ruckelshaus,* ERC 2193 (1983).
31. *BNA Environment Reporter,* December 9, 1983, verified by interviews with EPA staff members, EPA headquarters, week of May 15, 1988.
32. Brief of Rudolph W. Giuliani, U.S. attorney for the Southern District of New York, Michael H. Dolinger, assistant U.S. attorney for New York, and Marcia Mulkey, EPA, March 20, 1984, archived at the District Court for the Southern District of New York. The attorneys also argued that the case was not ripe for review because "none of the appellees alleged or established that it had been injured by an actual arbitration under the statute."
33. *Ruckelshaus v. Monsanto,* 467 U.S. 986 (1984).
34. *Sathon, Inc. v. American Arbitration Association,* 20 ERC 2241 (1984).
35. *Union Carbide v. Ruckelshaus,* 21 ERC 1984 (1984).
36. Motion of Rex E. Lee, solicitor general, Rudolph W. Giuliani, U.S. attorney for the Southern District of New York, Michael H. Dolinger, assistant U.S. attorney for New York, and Marcia Mulkey, EPA, August 20, 1984, archived at the District Court for the Southern District of New York.
37. *Ruckelshaus v. Union Carbide,* 469 U.S. 876 (1984).
38. Within two months the Gulf and Great Plains Legal Foundation had filed a brief with the Court maintaining that cuts in private research and a halting of the production of new pesticide products were certain unless the Supreme Court helped pesticide firms protect their valuable data from competitors. The previous month, however, two pesticide producers had filed a brief arguing that without binding arbitration, small chemical companies would wither because of their inability to develop the data needed for EPA review.

39. *Thomas v. Union Carbide Agricultural Products Co.,* 473 U.S. at 590 (1985).
40. Ibid. at 593.
41. *BNA Environment Reporter,* July 12, 1985.
42. *Thomas v. Union Carbide* at 577 (1985).
43. *Thomas v. Union Carbide,* 473 U.S. 568 (1985).
44. *EDF v. EPA,* 489 F.2d 1247 (1973).
45. *EDF v. Finch,* 428 F.2d 1083 (1970); *EDF v. Hardin,* 325 F.Supp. 1401 (1970); *EDF v. Ruckelshaus,* 439 F.2d 584 (1971); *EDF v. EPA,* 465 F.2d 528 (1972); and *EDF v. EPA,* 489 F.2d 1247 (1973).
46. Rachel Carson, *Silent Spring* (Boston: Houghton Mifflin, 1962), 8.
47. *Yannacone v. Dennison,* 285 N.Y.S.2d 476 (1967).
48. For an excellent discussion of the history of the DDT issue, see Thomas R. Dunlap, *DDT: Scientists, Citizens, and Public Policy* (Princeton, N.J.: Princeton University Press, 1981).
49. *EDF v. Finch,* 428 F.2d 1083 (1970).
50. Dunlap, *DDT,* 209.
51. *EDF v. Hardin,* 325 F.Supp. 1401 (1970).
52. *EDF v. Ruckelshaus,* 439 F.2d 584 (1971).
53. Ibid. at 597.
54. Ibid. at 598.
55. FIFRA contains a detailed procedure for registrants who desire to challenge proposed cancellations. Pursuant to section 136d (d), any party to a public hearing may request that an advisory committee of scientific experts be selected by the National Academy of Sciences to review the proposed action. This option was utilized here.
56. *EDF v. Ruckelshaus,* Order No. 71-1256, December 9, 1971.
57. Environmental Protection Agency, *Consolidated DDT Hearing, Opinion of Examiner Sweeney* (Washington, D.C.: Environmental Protection Agency, 1972).
58. Environmental Protection Agency, *Consolidated DDT Hearing, Opinion and Order of the Administrator* (Washington, D.C.: Environmental Protection Agency, 1972).
59. The National Environmental Policy Act of 1970 (NEPA) requires that "to the fullest extent possible . . . all agencies of the Federal Government shall . . . include in every recommendation or report on proposals for legislation and other major Federal actions significantly affecting the quality of the human environment, a detailed statement by the responsible official on—(i) the environmental impact of the proposed action." (42 U.S.C. section 4322(2)(C) [1970]).
60. *EDF v. EPA,* 489 F.2d 1247 (1973).

61. "Toward a Noisier Spring: D.C. Circuit Upholds Cancellation of DDT Registrations," *Environmental Law Reporter,* January, 1974, 10013. It is interesting to note that several requests for emergency use of DDT followed the 1973 decision of the court of appeals. Requests from California (for use against the tree hole mosquito) and Louisiana (for use against the tobacco budworm) were denied by the EPA. Requests from Idaho, Washington, and Oregon, however, were approved (for use against the tussock moth and the pea leaf weevil).

62. Gladwin Hill, "Bureaucracy and EPA," *New York Times,* December 13, 1973; and interviews with EPA staff members, EPA headquarters, week of May 15, 1988.

63. This case eventually went to court as *EDF v. EPA,* 465 F.2d 528 (1972).

64. "EPA Delays Ban on Cancer-Producing Pesticide Dieldrin," *Environmental Law Reporter,* August, 1974, 10104. See also, Environmental Protection Agency, *In re: Aldrin/Dieldrin: Order of the Administrator* (Washington, D.C.: Government Printing Office, August 2, 1974).

65. Environmental Protection Agency, *Reasons Underlying Registration Decisions Concerning Products Containing DDT, 2,4,5-T, Aldrin and Dieldrin, before the Environmental Protection Agency* (Washington, D.C.: Government Printing Office, March 18, 1971).

66. *EDF v. EPA,* 465 F.2d 528 (1972). A report on aldrin and dieldrin, written by the EPA's scientific advisory committee, had been filed as oral arguments in *EDF v. EPA* were being heard.

67. See "Toward a Noisier Spring."

68. Ibid.

69. Ibid.

70. Letter from William D. Rogers to Russell Train, April 16, 1974, archived at EPA headquarters, Washington, D.C.

71. "EPA Campaign against Pesticide Dieldrin," *Washington Post,* July 28, 1974.

72. Train's statement mentioned five factors contributing to his decision: (1) Aldrin and dieldrin cause significant increases of tumors in mice and rats, even at low dietary levels; (2) measurable aldrin and dieldrin residues are present in 96 percent of meat, fish, and poultry, 88 percent of all garden fruits, and 83 percent of all dairy products sampled; (3) 99.5 percent of all U.S. citizens tested have aldrin or dieldrin in their fatty tissues; (4) the average human daily dietary intake of aldrin and dieldrin subjects U.S. citizens to an unacceptably high cancer risk; and (5) children, because of their high consumption of dairy products, take in more aldrin and dieldrin per pound of

body weight than any other group in the population. (As reprinted in *Environmental Law Reporter,* August, 1984), 10104.

73. To implement this part of the administrator's decision, the EPA issued an enforcement strategy entitled *Continuing State Registration of Products Containing Aldrin and Dieldrin for which Uses Have Been Suspended* (Washington, D.C.: Environmental Protection Agency, January 10, 1975).

74. The agency hearings ended on September 12, 1974; the hearing officer's report, *In re Shell Chemical* (archived at EPA headquarters, Washington, D.C.), was issued on October 1, 1974.

75. "Shell Battles to Save Dieldrin and to Weaken Federal Controls on Cancer Producing Chemicals," *Environmental Law Reporter,* October, 1974, 10164.

76. The cases were consolidated as *EDF v. EPA,* 7 ERC 1689 (1975).

77. The court noted that the EPA decision to allow the sale of pre-existing supplies of aldrin and dieldrin was "based on an assumption that no appreciable and realistically retrievable stocks existed at the time of the order." After the order was issued, however, the EPA became aware of the fact that approximately 5 percent of the total 1974 amount of the pesticides was still available for use in 1975. The issue of continued sale of pre-existing stocks of aldrin and dieldrin, therefore, was remanded to the EPA for further consideration based on new evidence that the amounts of the pesticides in existence greatly exceeded the EPA's original calculations.

78. Interviews with EPA staff members, EPA headquarters, week of May 15, 1988, and November 5, 1989.

79. *EDF v. EPA,* 548 F.2d 998 (1976); *Dow Chemical Co. v. Barbara Blum,* 469 F.Supp. 892 (1979); Phillip Shabecoff, "Chemical Barred as Pesticide but Safety Rules Are Blocked," *New York Times,* November 1, 1983; Phillip Shabecoff, "Emergency Order Bans Much-Used Pesticide," *New York Times,* November 8, 1986.

80. EPA press release, March 26, 1991, archived at EPA headquarters, Washington, D.C.

81. 58 Fed. Reg. 15014 (March 18, 1993).

82. *Chemicals and Food Crops,* Senate Committee on Environment and Public Works, Subcommittee on Toxic Substances, Environmental Oversight, Research and Development, 101st Cong., 1st sess., September 22, 1989.

83. *Inside EPA,* September 19, 1989.

84. *Les et al v. William K. Reilly, Administrator, Environmental Protection Agency,* 968 F.2d 985 (9th Cir. 1992).

85. *National Agricultural Chemicals Association v. Les,* 61 U.S.L.W. 3584 (February 22, 1993).

Chapter Four

1. *Natural Resources Defense Council v. Costle,* 10 ELR 20274 (1980). See also 11 ELR 20202 (1981).
2. The NRDC filed under 15 U.S.C. section 2619(b). The twelve-month period within which the EPA must act is mandated by 15 U.S.C. section 2603(e)(1)(B). 15 U.S.C. section 2603(e)(1)(A) requires the committee to give priority attention to such chemicals.
3. 15 U.S.C. section 2603(e)(1)(B).
4. For an intriguing explanation of the reasons for the slowness of the regulation process for toxic substances (with an emphasis on OSHA), see John M. Mendeloff, *The Dilemma of Toxic Substance Regulation* (Cambridge: MIT Press, 1988).
5. Letter from Dr. Warren Muir to the NRDC, April, 1979.
6. *NRDC v. Costle,* 14 ERC at 1864 (1979).
7. *NRDC v. Costle,* 11 ELR at 20202 (1981).
8. *NRDC v. Costle,* 11 ELR at 20203 (1981).
9. 15 U.S.C. section 2619(b)(1)(A). The waiver by a judge of a statutorily mandated sixty-day notice to the agency prior to filing a lawsuit later was deemed improper by the Supreme Court in the CERCLA case *Olaf A. Hallstrom v. Tillamook County,* 110 S.Ct. 304 (1989).
10. Interviews with EPA staff members, EPA headquarters, week of May 15, 1988, and November 9, 1989.
11. The agency proposed test rules for dichloromethane, nitrobenzene, and 1,1,1-trichloroethane. Decisions not to test were issued for benzidine dyes, dianisidine dyes, o-tolidine dyes, polychlorinated terphenyls, chlorinated naphthalenes, alkyl phthalates, and chlorinated paraffins. An advance notice of proposed rule making was issued for phenylenediamines on December 31, 1981. At this time the NRDC argued that the advance notice did not fulfill the requirement for the agency to initiate rule making. A subsequent court decision, however, supported the right of the agency to issue an advance notice in this instance. See *NRDC v. EPA,* 21 ERC 1625 (1984).
12. The agency said it would propose test rules or decide not to test antimony, antimony trioxide, antimony sulfide, aryl phosphate, cresols, and pyridine by the end of June. Determinations concerning xylenes, toluene, 4,4-methylenedianiline, hexachlorobutadiene,

acetonitrile, and alkyl epoxides, plus a decision on the environmental testing for acrylimide, were pledged by the end of 1982.

13. 47 Fed. Reg. 15706 (April 12, 1982).
14. *BNA Environment Reporter,* June 11, 1982.
15. *BNA Environment Reporter,* December 10, 1982.
16. Interviews with EPA staff members, EPA headquarters, week of May 15, 1988, and November 9, 1989.
17. Ibid.
18. *BNA Environment Reporter,* October 10, 1986, 937.
19. *BNA Environment Reporter,* December 10, 1982.
20. Affidavit of the EPA, filed with the U.S. District Court for the Southern District of New York, June 30, 1982, archived at the District Court for the Southern District of New York.
21. According to the affidavit, the EPA promised to issue test rule decisions in the third quarter of 1982 for acetonitrile, aryl phosphates, cresols, methyl ethyl ketone, and methyl isobutyl ketone, and would call for environmental testing on acrylimide. In the fourth quarter the agency planned to issue test rule decisions on antimony, antimony sulfide, antimony trioxide, hexachlorobutadiene, pyridine, toluene, and xylenes.
22. In September, 1981, the Chemical Manufacturers' Association's Phthalate Esters Special Program Panel volunteered to conduct testing on alkyl phthalates, the first voluntary testing negotiated by the EPA. At the same time, the Chlorinated Paraffins Consortium offered to test chlorinated paraffins instead of the agency issuing a test rule requiring examination of the substance. Interview with EPA staff members, EPA headquarters, week of May 15, 1988.
23. The agency announced that no additional testing would be required on toluene and xylenes. Voluntary testing agreements were accepted on antimony, antimony sulfide, and antimony trioxide; methyl ethyl ketone, methyl isobutyl ketone, and isophorone (47 Fed. Reg. 58025 [1982]); acrylimide; and acetonitrile. The agency decided not to require industry groups to conduct additional testing on hexachlorocyclopentadiene (47 Fed. Reg. 58023 [1982]) or hexachloro-1,3-butadiene (47 Fed. Reg. 58029 [1982]) because of their low exposure rates. The EPA also asked for comments on a tentative decision not to require industry groups to test pyridine (47 Fed. Reg. 58031 [1982]), which was reported as a "borderline" candidate.
24. According to the affidavit, the EPA would decide by June 30, 1983, whether to require industry testing of aryl phosphates, cresols, and

mesityl oxide. By December 31, 1983, the agency promised to complete test decisions on alkyl epoxides, chlorobenzenes, cyclohexanon, 1,2-dichloropropane, glycidol and derivatives, haloalkyl epoxides, hydroquinone, 4,4'-methylenedianiline, quinone, and aniline and bromo-, chloro-, and/or nitroanilines.

25. U.S. Environmental Protection Agency, *Fiscal Year 1984 EPA Budget Summary* (Washington, D.C.: Government Printing Office, 1983).

26. EPA, *1984 EPA Budget,* as summarized in *BNA Environment Reporter,* February 4, 1983, 1236.

27. Interviews with members of the EPA Budget staff, EPA headquarters; Congressional Budget Office; and Office of Management and Budget, week of May 15, 1988.

28. U.S. Environmental Protection Agency, *TSCA Annual Report to Congress* (Washington, D.C.: Government Printing Office, February 22, 1983).

29. EPA internal memorandum from Todhunter to Administrator Burford (Gorsuch), January 28, 1983, archived at EPA headquarters, Washington, D.C.

30. Proposed test rules on mesityl oxide and cresols, as well as a decision not to require testing on methylenedianiline, were signed June 23 and June 30 by Ruckelshaus. The EPA's affidavit to the court, dated June 30, 1983, promised to take action by December 13, 1983, on aryl phosphates; alkyl epoxides; aniline and bromo-, chloro-, and/or nitroanilines; chlorobenzenes; cyclohexanon; 1,2-dichloropropane; glycidol and its derivatives; haloalkyl epoxides; hydroquinone; and quinone. The affidavit is archived at the U.S. District Court for the Southern District of New York.

31. The EPA proposed testing on hydroquinone and quinone and issued advanced notices of proposed rule making covering aryl phosphates; aniline and chloro-, bromo-, and nitroanilines; and glycidol and its derivatives. The agency decided not to test cyclohexanon. Test rule decisions were completed on alkyl oxides and halogenated alkyl oxides. Rule decisions on the environmental effects of chlorobenzenes and 1,2-dichloropropane were published in the Federal Register in January, 1984.

32. *BNA Environment Reporter,* November 9, 1982, 936.

33. *BNA Environment Reporter,* February 18, 1983. The concerns of the NRDC were echoed by other environmental groups across the country. See, for example, *BNA Environment Reporter,* February 3, 1984, which discusses criticisms of the voluntary testing agreements by the League of Conservation Voters.

34. General Accounting Office, *EPA Implementation of Selected Aspects of the Toxic Substances Control Act* (Washington, D.C.: Government Printing Office, December 7, 1982).

35. Ibid.

36. *BNA Environment Reporter,* February 18, 1983.

37. *NRDC v. EPA,* 21 ERC 1625 (1984).

38. Pleadings of NRDC and AFL-CIO, filed with the U.S. District Court for the Southern District of New York, January, 1984, archived at the court.

39. Judge Duffy dismissed two counts concerning the use of advance notice of proposed rule making and the use of the two-phase process of rule making.

40. *BNA Environment Reporter,* September 14, 1984.

41. It is interesting to note that, in total, the EPA had accepted twenty-one voluntary testing agreements with industry groups. Duffy's first decision mentions sixteen of those chemicals. The final court-ordered schedule, however, concerns only eight chemicals. Under the schedule, the EPA agreed to decide whether to issue test rules on the following chemicals on which voluntary testing agreements had been accepted: benzyl butyl phthalate by October, 1985; chlorotoluene and 4-chlorobenzotrifluoride by October, 1985; fluoroalkenes by October, 1985; and formamide by March, 1986. On the final test rules that the court said were "unlawfully delayed," the EPA issued the following schedule: chloromethane—a program to review data "to yield withdrawal of proposed rule" was promised by June, 1985; chlorinated benzenes—a portion of the proposed rule was slated to be withdrawn by December, 1984, and a final rule was promised by June, 1986; 1,1,1-trichloroethane—a proposed rule was promised by July, 1985, and a final rule by March, 1986 (*NRDC v. EPA,* 21 ERC 1919 [1984]).

42. *NRDC v. EPA,* 21 ERC at 1920 (1984).

43. Interviews with EPA staff members, EPA headquarters, week of May 15, 1988.

44. *BNA Environment Reporter,* September 7, 1984, 588.

45. *BNA Environment Reporter,* September 14, 1984, 604.

46. EPA fears concerning a decrease in industry cooperation were unfounded. Preliminary test data on a chemical group and nine chemicals, including three included in the *NRDC* case, were submitted to the EPA by industry groups in the fourth quarter of 1984 (50 Fed. Reg. 5421). In the fourth quarter of 1985, test data on ten chemicals or chemical categories that were subjects of prior negotiated testing

agreements were voluntarily provided by chemical firms to the EPA (51 Fed. Reg. 6468).

47. *BNA Environment Reporter,* September 7, 1984, and September 14, 1984.
48. Ibid.
49. *BNA Environment Reporter,* October 19, 1984, 835.
50. In the meantime, the Chemical Manufacturers' Association (CMA) appealed Duffy's decision arguing, among other things, that the decision departed from "well-settled principles" of judicial review requiring the courts to defer to an agency's interpretation of its governing statute unless that interpretation is unreasonable or is directly prohibited by the statute. (Brief of CMA filed February, 1985, with the U.S. District Court of the Southern District of New York and archived with the court.)
51. Interviews with EPA staff members, EPA headquarters, week of May 15, 1988.
52. *BNA Environment Reporter,* August 23, 1985, 547.
53. 51 Fed. Reg. 23706 (1986).
54. 49 Fed. Reg. 50408 (December 28, 1984); 40 C.F.R. Part 773.
55. July, 1987.
56. The rule called for manufacturers and processors of 1,2,4-trichlorobenzene to conduct oncongenicity tests, while reproductive effects testing was required for monochlorobenzene, ortho- and para-dichlorobenzenes, and 1,2,4,5-tetrachlorobenzene.
57. 50 Fed. Reg. 19213 (1985); 50 Fed. Reg. 36446 (1985): Under the rule for benzyl butyl phthalate chemical makers were required to conduct acute and chronic toxicity tests in freshwater and saltwater organisms and a bioconcentration test in the eastern oyster and to test for the fate of benzyl butyl phthalate in undisturbed sediments; 50 Fed. Reg. 42216 (1985); 50 Fed. Reg. 51683 (1985) and consent order 52 Fed. Reg. 31445 (August 20, 1987); 51 Fed. Reg. 6929 (1986); and 52 Fed. Reg. 21516 (1987).
58. 53 Fed. Reg. 39786 (1988).
59. 51 Fed. Reg. 41331 (November 14, 1986).
60. *Inside EPA,* January 8, 1988. Some of the issues raised at the meeting included the type of initial exposure studies that should be done, as well as the types of mutagenicity, oncongenicity and dermal exposure studies that should be conducted.
61. Interviews with EPA staff members, EPA headquarters, week of November 9, 1989.

62. *Inside EPA,* January 8, 1988; verified by interviews with EPA staff members, EPA headquarters, week of November 9, 1989.
63. Interviews with EPA staff members, EPA headquarters, week of May 15, 1988, and November 9, 1989.
64. Ibid.
65. The Cadmus Group, *Testing Consent Order Policy Study, Phase I,* October 19, 1988; The Cadmus Group, *Testing Consent Order Policy Study, Phase II,* May 3, 1989.
66. Interviews with EPA staff members, EPA headquarters, week of May 15, 1988, and November 9, 1989, and subsequent telephone interviews.
67. 57 Fed. Reg. 31714 (July 17, 1992).
68. *BNA Chemical Regulation Reporter,* June 22, 1990; *BNA Chemical Regulation Reporter,* August 9, 1991; *BNA Environment Reporter,* July 24, 1992; *BNA Environment Reporter,* September 25, 1992.
69. 58 Fed. Reg. 1669 (March 30, 1993).
70. 15 U.S.C. sections 2605, 2607, and 2611.
71. 40 C.F.R. 761; 44 Fed. Reg. 31514 (May 31, 1979).
72. *Environmental Defense Fund v. EPA,* 15 ERC 1081 (1980).
73. 13 ERC at 1097. Also EPA internal memorandum from A. E. Conroy II, director of the Pesticides and Toxic Substances Enforcement Division, to regional enforcement directors and branch chiefs, November 11, 1980.
74. "EPA Proposal to Grant, Deny Exemptions from PCB Electrical Equipment Regulations," 48 Fed. Reg. 50486 (November 1, 1983).
75. The court's orders were issued on February 12, 1981 (preliminary stay); March 10, 1981 (46 Fed. Reg. 16090—"totally enclosed" stay); and April 13, 1981 (46 Fed. Reg. 27615–50 ppm stay).
76. The court's order was issued February 12, 1981.
77. 46 Fed. Reg. 16090 (March 10, 1981) and 46 Fed. Reg. 16096 (March 10, 1981).
78. *BNA Environment Reporter,* February 12, 1982, 1185 verified by interviews with EPA staff members, EPA headquarters, week of May 15, 1988.
79. *BNA Environment Reporter,* February 19, 1982, 1203.
80. Memorandum from A. E. Conroy II, director of the EPA Pesticides and Toxic Substances Enforcement Division, "PCB Interim Measures Program," August, 1981.
81. 47 Fed. Reg. 17426 (1982); 40 C.F.R. part 761. Specifically, the proposed regulation amended the existing PCB rule to authorize the use of "PCBs in capacitors and the use and servicing of PCBs in

electromagnets, circuit breakers, voltage regulators, reclosers, cables, switches/sectionalizers, and transformers other than railroad transformers." The EPA also proposed to amend other parts of the PCB rule to provide for the disposal and distribution in commerce of this electrical equipment.

82. 47 Fed. Reg. 37342 (1982); 40 C.F.R. 761.30[1]; 40 C.F.R. 761.30[a].

83. 49 Fed. Reg. 29625 (July 23, 1984); 40 C.F.R. part 761. The regulation defined a "totally enclosed" use of PCBs as "any manner that will ensure no exposure of human beings or the environment to any concentration of PCBs." The proposal also said that any exposure to PCBs may be significant "depending on such factors as the quantity of PCBs involved in the exposure, the likelihood of exposure to humans and the environment, and the effect of exposure."

For subsequent EPA action concerning "totally enclosed" PCBs, see 49 Fed. Reg. 44634 (November 8, 1984), 50 Fed. Reg. 29170 (July 17, 1985), and 51 Fed. Reg. 47241 (December 31, 1986).

84. 46 Fed. Reg. 27617 and 46 Fed. Reg. 27619 (1981).

85. April 9, 1982.

86. 47 Fed. Reg. 46980 (October 21, 1982); corrected at 48 Fed. Reg. 4467 (February 1, 1983). This rule permitted the "manufacture, processing, and distribution in commerce of PCBs without an exemption," provided that [1] the PCBs were released only in concentrations below the practical limits of quantitation for PCBs in air emission, water effluents, products, and process wastes and [2] the wastes from these manufacturing processes were controlled and disposed of in accordance with the methods of disposal specified in the rule.

87. The rule was proposed on December, 1983 (49 Fed. Reg. 28154 [1984]), and approved on June 27, 1984.

88. 48 Fed. Reg. 52402 (1983).

89. 49 Fed. Reg. 28154 (1984). A proposed amendment to the rule was published on July 8, 1987 (52 Fed. Reg. 25838), and a final rule was published on June 27, 1988 (53 Fed. Reg. 24206).

90. *EDF v. EPA,* 672 F.2d 42, 16 ERC 2149 (1982).

91. Section 19(d) of TSCA; 15 U.S.C. section 2618(d).

92. *Inside EPA,* July 14, 1989.

93. Ibid.

94. The decision of the Carter administration was due largely to findings of a Chemical Industry Institute of Toxicology study linking formaldehyde to nasal tumors in test animals. Interviews with EPA staff members, EPA headquarters, week of May 15, 1988.

95. Interviews with EPA staff members, EPA headquarters, week of May 15, 1988, and November 9, 1989.
96. Ibid.
97. *New York Times,* November 18, 1983.
98. *New York Times,* March 20, 1983.
99. The lawsuit was filed soon after a *Science* magazine article attacked EPA's "science policy" in deciding not to regulate formaldehyde. Elliot Marshall, "EPA's High-Risk Carcinogen Policy," *Science* 218 (November 26, 1982): 975–78.
100. Phillip Shabecoff, "EPA Will Consider Regulation of Formaldehyde," *New York Times,* May 19, 1984, 24.
101. *BNA Environment Reporter,* July 31, 1992, 799.
102. 57 Fed. Reg. 62573 (December 31, 1992).

Chapter Five

1. Section 112(b)(1); PL 549, 104 Stat. 2399, November 15, 1990.
2. 42 U.S.C. 7412(b)(1)(A) provided that "[t]he Administrator shall . . . publish (and shall from time to time thereafter revise) a list which includes each hazardous air pollutant for which he intends to establish an emission standard under this section." Radionuclides were the fifth substance regulated under section 7412 [112] after the act became law in 1970.
3. 44 Fed. Reg. 76738 (1979).
4. The Clean Air Act (42 U.S.C. 7401 et seq.) in its present form includes the Clean Air Act of 1963, PL 88-206, and amendments made by the Motor Vehicle Air Pollution Control Act, PL 89-272, October 20, 1965; the Clean Air Act Amendments of 1966, PL 89-675, October 15, 1966; the Air Quality Act of 1967, PL 90-148, November 21, 1967; the Clean Air Amendments of 1970, PL 91-604, December 31, 1970; the Comprehensive Health Manpower Training Act of 1971, PL 92-157, November 18, 1971; PL 93-15, April 9, 1973; the Energy Supply and Environmental Coordination Act of 1974, PL 93-319, June 22, 1974; Clean Air Act Amendments of 1977, PL 95-95, August 7, 1977; Safe Drinking Water Act of 1977, PL 95-190, November 16, 1977; Health Services Research, Health Statistics, and Health Care Technology Act of 1978, PL 95-623, November 9, 1978; PL 96-209, March 14, 1980; PL 96-300, July 2, 1980; PL 97-23, July 17, 1981; PL 97-375, December 21, 1982; PL 98-45, July 12, 1983; PL 98-213, December 8, 1983; and the Clean Air Act Amendments of 1990, PL 101-549, November 15, 1990.

5. 42 U.S.C. 7412(b)(1)(A). For an in-depth critique of section 7412, see John D. Graham, "The Failure of Agency-Forcing: The Regulation of Airborne Carcinogens under Section 112 of the Clean Air Act," 1985 *Duke Law Journal* (1985): 100–150. The 1990 Clean Air Act overhauled this statutory provision because the EPA regulated too few toxic air pollutants and because of the difficulties evidenced in this chapter's discussion of radionuclide regulation. The new Clean Air Act in part mimics the 1977 Clean Water Act amendments (see Chapter Two) in that it lists 189 toxic pollutants to be regulated through technology-based standards and, if necessary, additional health-based standards.

6. *Sierra Club v. Gorsuch,* 17 ERC 1748 (March 8, 1982).

7. *Sierra Club v. Gorsuch,* 551 F.Supp. 785 (1982).

8. Ibid. at 788.

9. 48 Fed. Reg. 15076 (1983).

10. Comments of Terrance McLaughlin, chief of the Environmental Standards Branch in the Office of Air, Noise and Radiation, as quoted in *BNA Environment Reporter,* April 1, 1983.

11. "E.P.A. Issues Proposed Standards for Reducing Radioactivity," *New York Times,* April 3, 1983), 20.

12. Ibid.

13. Section 7417(c) orders the administrator, "to the maximum extent practicable within the time provided, [to] consult with appropriate advisory committees, independent experts, and federal departments and agencies."

14. The Idaho Mining Association argued that the EPA regulations would prevent only one possible cancer death in 100 years at a cost of $200 million. *Sierra Club v. Ruckelshaus,* 21 ERC at 1826 (1984).

15. *BNA Environment Reporter,* June 17, 1983, 261; and July 27, 1984.

16. *BNA Environment Reporter,* February 10, 1984.

17. *BNA Environment Reporter,* March 9, 1984.

18. *BNA Environment Reporter,* July 27, 1984, 465. The SAB recommended that (1) procedures be set to delineate in a clearer fashion the risk assessment and management aspects of the standard development process; (2) a risk assessment document be prepared for each regulatory action being considered to provide a more detailed summary of the scientific literature; (3) a risk assessment document be prepared on the issue of airborne radioactivity and be used as a basis for future risk management decisions on radionuclide emissions; (4) a new standing committee be created to help the agency with the development of risk assessments for radiation regulations;

(5) procedures be developed for receiving public comment and for review by the SAB before proposed regulations are made public; and (6) communication between the Office of Radiation Programs and other EPA staff offices, as well as with the scientific community, be improved. In addition, the board made eighteen technical recommendations.

19. Related in an interview with the director of the SAB, Terry F. Yosie, as reported in *BNA Environment Reporter,* July 27, 1984.

20. Interview with Richard J. Guimond, director of the Office of Radiation's Criteria and Standards Division, as reported in *BNA Environment Reporter,* July 27, 1984.

21. Interview with Sjoblom, as reported in *BNA Environment Reporter,* July 27, 1984; verified by interview with EPA staff members, EPA headquarters, week of May 15, 1988.

22. Order of the District Court for the Northern District of California, September 17, 1984.

23. *Sierra Club v. Ruckelshaus,* 21 ERC at 1828 (1984).

24. *BNA Environment Reporter,* August 31, 1984.

25. Ibid at 689.

26. 49 Fed. Reg. 33695 (1984).

27. The request was made by Donald G. Scroggin, of Beveridge and Diamond Law Firm, Washington, D.C. The document is archived at EPA headquarters, Washington, D.C.

28. *BNA Environment Reporter,* October 19, 1984.

29. The EPA gave the following rationale for its policy change. First, radionuclide emissions from elemental phosphorus plants present a one in 1,000 lifetime risk of fatal cancer for persons living in the highest exposure areas. Next people living in high exposure areas near Department of Energy facilities face a lifetime risk of no more than 8 in 10,000. Last, for Nuclear Regulatory Commission facilities (and non–Department of Energy federal facilities), the lifetime risk of fatal cancer is no more than one in 10,000 in areas of high exposure.

30. Phillip Shabecoff, "Answering U.S. Court's Order, Agency Scraps Proposals on Emitted Materials," *New York Times,* October 24, 1984, A:17.

31. Ibid.

32. 49 Fed. Reg. 43906; 49 Fed. Reg. 43915; 49 Fed. Reg. 43916 (1984).

33. *EDF v. Ruckelshaus,* No. 84-1524.

34. *BNA Environment Reporter,* October 26, 1984, 1051.

35. Phillip Shabecoff, "Answering U.S. Court's Order, Agency Scraps Pro-

posals on Emitted Materials," *New York Times,* October 24, 1984, A:17.

36. Transcript of Hearing before William H. Orrick, District Judge, U.S. District Court of the Northern District of California, October 31, 1984, archived at the court.

37. "U.S. Judge Rules E.P.A. in Contempt," *New York Times,* December 12, 1984, A:27.

38. Ibid.

39. Transcript of Hearing before William H. Orrick, District Judge, U.S. District Court of the Northern District of California, November 21, 1984.

40. Ibid.

41. Judge Orrick also said that the SAB report criticizing the EPA radionuclide regulations "cannot be relied upon as justification for noncompliance with the order." *Sierra Club v. Ruckelshaus,* 602 F.Supp. at 903.

42. *Sierra Club v. Ruckelshaus,* 602 F.Supp. 892 (1984).

43. *BNA Environment Reporter,* December 14, 1985 and January 25, 1985.

44. *Sierra Club v. Thomas,* No. 84-2845.

45. *Sierra Club v. Thomas,* 469 U.S. 1309 (1985).

46. The regulations took effect February 6, 1985.

47. 50 Fed. Reg. 5190 (1985).

48. *BNA Environment Reporter,* January 25, 1985.

49. Waivers would be granted to DOE, NRC, and non-DOE federal facilities, the EPA announced, if the facility could show that no member of the public would receive a continuous dose exposure of more than 100 millirems per year or its equivalent and a noncontinuous effective dose exposure of 500 millirems per year or its equivalent, excluding natural and background procedures.

50. *BNA Environment Reporter,* January 25, 1985, 1531.

51. 50 Fed. Reg. 5190. The notice said that the EPA believed that the standards were unnecessary because emissions from the sources "are so low that the public health is already protected with an ample margin of safety."

52. *BNA Environment Reporter,* January 25, 1985, 1531.

53. 50 Fed. Reg. 7280 (1985). A public hearing on the regulations was held on February 27 and 28, 1985. Public comments were received until March 28.

54. 50 Fed. Reg. 15386 (1985). The regulations contained five significant differences from the proposed regulations. Alternatives to "bulk-

heading" were allowed. The EPA also changed provisions concerning applicability of the emission standard, added a more lenient schedule for bulkhead inspection and repair, and ordered an annual compliance certification.

55. *EDF v. EPA.*

56. Brief of Christopher Herman, EPA Office of General Counsel, December 19, 1985, archived at the Court of Appeals for the District of Columbia.

57. Memorandum of Idaho Mining Association, January 13, 1986, archived at the Court of Appeals for the District of Columbia.

58. Reply brief of EDF, NRDC, and Sierra Club, February 25, 1986, archived at the Court of Appeals for the District of Columbia.

59. *NRDC v. EPA,* 824 F.2d at 1164 (1987).

60. Ibid. at 1166, archived at the Court of Appeals for the District of Columbia.

61. Comments of Richard J. Guimond, director of the Office of Radiation Protection, as cited in *BNA Environment Reporter,* April 1, 1988.

62. The EPA increased its assessment of risk from exposure to radionuclides because of the new study. The Office of Radiation Protection had previously estimated that 280 cancer fatalities per million were caused by exposure to radionuclides. After the study, the agency changed the figure to 400 fatalities per million. The director of radiation protection, Richard J. Guimond, asked the SAB to review the agency's figure of 400 fatalities while the National Academy of Sciences reviewed the study of the Japanese atomic bomb survivors. Terrance McLaughlin, chief of the Office of Radiation Protection Environmental Standards Branch, said that because the new data indicated greater harm from radionuclides than had previously been thought, the radionuclides regulations would be affected. Guimond also indicated that a new method of analyzing the Japanese survivor data showed a lifetime risk of about 1,200 fatal cancers per million. Expressing frustration at a statement from the National Institute of Health that it could only "semiquantify" the overall uncertainty in the risk, Guimond expressed hope that more quantitative estimates of the uncertainty would be possible in the future. *BNA Environment Reporter,* April 1, 1988; and interviews with EPA staff members, EPA headquarters, week of May 15, 1988.

63. The new study examined twelve sources: facilities licensed by the Nuclear Regulatory Commission, Department of Energy (DOE) facilities, high-level nuclear waste, uranium fuel-cycle plants, elemental phosphorus plants, coal-fired boilers, underground uranium mines,

open-pit uranium mines, active mill-tailings, disposed mill-tailings, radon from DOE facilities, and phosphogypsum piles. *BNA Environment Reporter,* April 1, 1988; and interviews with EPA staff members, EPA headquarters, week of May 15, 1988.

64. 54 Fed. Reg. 9612 (March 7, 1989).

65. 54 Fed. Reg. 51654 (December 15, 1989).

66. 56 Fed. Reg. 6339 (February 15, 1991); 56 Fed. Reg. 10524 (March 12, 1991); 56 Fed. Reg. 18735 (April 24, 1991); 56 Fed. Reg. 37196 (August 5, 1991).

67. *Natural Resources Defense Council v. William K. Reilly, Administrator, Environmental Protection Agency,* 975 F.2d at 40 (1992).

68. 57 Fed. Reg. 54127 (November 16, 1992).

69. For an interesting perspective on "clientele capture" as applied to the Clean Air Act, see Paul Sabatier, "Social Movements and Regulatory Agencies: Toward a More Adequate—and Less Pessimistic—Theory of 'Clientele Capture,' " *Policy Sciences* 6 (September, 1975): 301–42.

70. Stuart Diamond, "Suit Charges E.P.A. Fails to Act on Pollutants," *New York Times,* January 22, 1986.

71. *NRDC v. EPA,* 489 F.2d 390 (1974).

72. *NRDC v. EPA,* 529 F.2d 755 (1976).

73. *NRDC et al v. EPA,* 838 F.2d at 1254 (1988).

74. 58 Fed. Reg. 15422 (March 23, 1993); 58 Fed. Reg. 8245 (February 12, 1993); 58 Fed. Reg. 4902 (January 19, 1993); and *BNA Environment Reporter,* October 30, 1992, 1678.

Chapter Six

1. Westat, Inc., for the EPA, *National Survey of Hazardous Waste Generators and Treatment, Storage and Disposal Facilities Regulated under RCRA in 1981* (Washington, D.C.: Government Printing Office, April, 1984).

2. Allen A. Boraiko, "Storing Up Trouble—Hazardous Waste," *National Geographic* (March, 1984): 325.

3. Office of Technology Assessment, *Superfund Strategy* (Washington, D.C.: Government Printing Office, 1985). See also, General Accounting Office, *Cleaning Up Hazardous Wastes: An Overview of Superfund Reauthorization Issues* (Washington, D.C.: Government Printing Office, 1985).

4. Steven Ferrey, "The Toxic Time Bomb: Municipal Liability for the Cleanup of Hazardous Waste," *George Washington Law Review* 57 (1988): 197.

5. The Resource Conservation and Recovery Act, PL 94-580, October 21, 1976, as amended by the Quiet Communities Act of 1978, PL 95-609; the Solid Waste Disposal Act of 1980, PL 96-482; the Used Oil Recycling Act of 1980, PL 96-463; the Comprehensive Environmental Response, Compensation and Liability Act of 1980, PL 96-510; PL 97-272, September 30, 1982; PL 98-45, July 12, 1983; the 1984 Hazardous and Solid Waste Amendments, PL 98-616, November 9, 1984; PL 99-160, November 25, 1985; PL 99-339, June 19, 1986; and PL 99-499, October 17, 1986.

6. Underground storage tanks are defined as tanks "used to contain an accumulation of regulated substances" with 10 percent or more of their volume beneath the ground. 42 U.S.C. section 6991. Underground storage tanks are regulated pursuant to RCRA Subchapter IX, sections 6991, 6991a–i.

7. The suit was filed on May 30, 1985; see *EDF v. Thomas,* 627 F.Supp. 566 (D.C. D.C. 1986).

8. 3 C.F.R. 127 (1982).

9. The EPA is an executive agency for the purposes of EO 12291, section 1(d). The purpose of EO 12291, according to its preamble, is "to reduce the burdens of existing and future regulations, increase agency accountability for regulatory actions, provide for presidential oversight of the regulatory process, minimize duplication and conflict of regulations, and insure well-reasoned regulations." In addition to providing for OMB review of regulations, EO 12291 orders a detailed cost-benefit analysis for all "major" rules, defined as rules with an annual effect on the economy of $100 million or more.

10. 3 C.F.R. 323 (1985).

11. OMB Bulletin 86-4 (December 23, 1985) defines "significant regulatory actions" as including considerations as to whether to initiate a rule making and actions to develop guidelines, policy proposals, or similar documents that may influence rule making at a later date. The OMB is authorized under section 3 of EO 12498 to review each agency's regulatory agenda to see if it is consistent "with the Administration's policies and priorities." Approved regulatory actions are then incorporated into the OMB's annual "Regulatory Program." Agencies may not deviate from the "Regulatory Program" without the approval of the OMB.

12. Interview with OMB staff members, Washington, D.C., week of May 15, 1988.

13. *EDF v. Thomas,* 627 F.Supp. at 568 (1986).

14. Ibid.

15. Ibid.
16. Ibid.
17. Ibid.
18. *BNA Environment Reporter,* May 17, 1985.
19. *EDF v. Thomas,* 627 F.Supp. at 568 (1986).
20. Ibid.
21. 50 Fed. Reg. 26444 (1985).
22. *EDF v. Thomas,* No. 85-1747; Pleadings at ELR Pend. Lit. 65863, May 30, 1985; 65872, July 29, 1985; and 65892, December 2, 1985.
23. *BNA Environment Reporter,* July 26, 1985.
24. Ibid.
25. *BNA Environment Reporter,* November 11, 1985.
26. *EDF v. Thomas,* 627 F.Supp. at 571 (1986); and interviews with EPA staff members, EPA headquarters, week of May 15, 1988.
27. The Reagan administration had just issued its "Regulatory Program of the United States Government," August 8, 1985, in which it proclaimed that environmental regulations "must avoid whenever possible disrupting the efficient operation of the market." The report further warned that environmental regulations must be based on analyses of risks that are "real and significant, rather than hypothetical and remote." (Full text published in *BNA Environment Reporter,* August 16, 1985.)
28. The subcommittee alleged that the OMB unlawfully pressured the EPA into stopping its plans to regulate asbestos and referring asbestos to other federal agencies for regulation. In addition, the subcommittee charged that the OMB had interfered in internal EPA policies and administration by ordering the removal of a Utah mining waste site from the National Priorities List for CERCLA cleanup action; by pressuring the EPA to consider cost-benefit analyses of health-based air pollution standards when Congress had directed that such analyses not be considered; by directing the EPA to eliminate a section of a proposed rule meant to protect water quality, citing only philosophical differences with the rule; and forcing the EPA to revoke gasoline lead phasedown rules. See *OMB Review of EPA Regulations: Hearing before a Subcommittee on Oversight and Investigations of the House Committee on Energy and Commerce,* 99th Cong., 2d sess., 1986.
29. *Oversight of the Office of Management and Budget Regulatory Review and Planning Process: Hearing before a Subcommittee on Intergovernmental Relations of the Senate Committee on Governmental Affairs,* 99th Cong., 2d sess., January 28, 1986, 11–12.

30. Ibid. at 66.
31. Ibid. at 74.
32. Ibid.
33. Ibid.
34. *EDF v. Thomas,* 627 F.Supp. at 570 (1986).
35. Ibid.
36. Ibid.
37. Ibid. at 571.
38. Interviews with members of EPA budget staff, EPA headquarters, week of May 15, 1988.
39. 52 Fed. Reg. 12662 (1987). For supplemental information, see also 52 Fed. Reg. 19895 (May 28, 1987); 52 Fed. Reg. 48638 (December 23, 1987); and 53 Fed. Reg. 10403 (March 31, 1988).
40. Interviews with EPA staff members, EPA headquarters, week of May 15, 1988.
41. 53 Fed. Reg. 37082 and 37212 (September 23, 1988); 53 Fed. Reg. 43322 (October 24, 1988); 53 Fed. Reg. 51273 (December 21, 1988).
42. Philip Shabecoff, "Budget Office Limited on Delays," *New York Times,* January 30, 1986), B:9.
43. Ibid.
44. Ibid.
45. Interviews with OMB staff members, Washington, D.C., week of May 15, 1988.
46. Interviews with EPA staff members, EPA headquarters, week of May 15, 1988.
47. *Inside EPA,* August 11, 1989.
48. Oral arguments were heard by the U.S. Court of Appeals for the District of Columbia on February 3, 1993, in the case of *Ohio v. EPA,* C.A. DC. No. 86-1096.
49. *BNA Environment Reporter,* February 19, 1993, 2720.
50. The plant, consisting of approximately 260 buildings, had been built in the 1940s as part of the Manhattan Project. According to Barbara A. Finamore, attorney for the NRDC, the plant had not changed its ways of handling wastes since the plant was first opened. *Legal Environmental Assistance Foundation v. Hodel,* 586 F.Supp. at 1165 (1984), and *BNA Environment Reporter,* March 23, 1984.
51. *The Extent and Impact of Mercury Releases and Other Pollutants at the Department of Energy's Oak Ridge Complex at Oak Ridge, Tennessee,* House Comm. on Science and Technology, 98th Cong., 1st sess., 1983, H. Rept. 558.
52. *BNA Environment Reporter,* March 23, 1984.

53. Ibid.
54. *LEAF v. Hodel,* 586 F.Supp. 1163 (1984); Barbara A. Finamore, "Regulating Hazardous and Mixed Waste at Department of Energy Nuclear Weapons Facilities: Reversing Decades of Environmental Neglect," *Harvard Environmental Law Review* 9 (1985): 83.
55. Letter from Stephen H. Greenleigh, assistant general counsel for environment for the Department of Energy, to James A. Rogers, associate general counsel for the Environmental Protection Agency, November 14, 1980.
56. Memorandum from A. James Barnes, EPA acting general counsel, to Pasquale A. Alberico, acting director of the EPA's Office of Federal Activities, June 22, 1983.
57. Interviews with EPA staff members, EPA headquarters, week of May 15, 1988. See also Finamore, "Regulating Hazardous and Mixed Waste." Memorandum archived at EPA headquarters, Washington, D.C.
58. EO 12088: "Federal Compliance with Pollution Control Standards," October 13, 1978. The January 4, 1984, EPA memorandum is archived at EPA headquarters, Washington, D.C.
59. EO 12146: "Management of Federal Legal Resources."
60. The memorandum of understanding was signed by Donald Paul Hodel, secretary of the Department of Energy, and William Ruckelshaus, administrator of the Environmental Protection Agency.
61. "Agency Disputing Law's Jurisdiction," *New York Times,* March 15, 1984, A:28.
62. Ibid.
63. Brief of Dean K. Dunsmore, U.S. Department of Justice, archived at the U.S. District Court for the Eastern District of Tennessee. The Justice Department's position in the case was in sharp contrast to an opinion issued in an internal agency memorandum a month before. On February 9, 1983, Theodore B. Olson, assistant attorney general for legal counsel, wrote a memorandum to F. Henry Habicht III, assistant attorney general for land and natural resources, concluding that "DOE's Atomic Energy Act facilities are generally subject to the requirements of RCRA, including compliance with applicable standards, regulations and permitting requirements and are generally subject to the enforcement mechanisms established by RCRA." Olson qualified his opinion, however, by writing that "particular RCRA regulations or requirements may not be applicable to some of the facilities when they would be inconsistent with the requirements of the Atomic Energy Act."

64. Ibid.
65. *LEAF v. Hodel,* 586 F.Supp. at 1165 (1984).
66. Ibid.
67. Ibid.
68. Letter from Barbara A. Finamore of NRDC, Jane L. Bloom of NRDC, and Gary A. Davis of LEAF, to William Ruckelshaus, EPA administrator, June 14, 1985, archived at EPA headquarters, Washington, D.C.
69. Environmental Protection Agency, press release, August 1, 1984.
70. Since the regulations in question are also applicable to facilities regulated by the Nuclear Regulatory Commission, NRC representatives also participated in the EPA-DOE task force meetings. *BNA Environment Reporter,* August 10, 1984.
71. EPA draft regulations, December 21, 1984, 1.
72. Ibid., 2–4.
73. Ibid., 3–4.
74. General Accounting Office, *Department of Energy Acting to Control Hazardous Wastes at Its Savannah River Nuclear Facilities,* Report No. GAO/RCED-85-23 (Washington, D.C.: Government Printing Office, 1985).
75. General Accounting Office, *Hazardous Waste: Federal Civil Agencies Slow to Comply With Regulatory Requirements,* Report No. GAO/RCED-86-76 (Washington, D.C.: Government Printing Office, 1986).
76. *BNA Environment Reporter,* April 19, 1991.
77. 52 Fed. Reg. 24504 (1987).
78. Memorandum from J. Winston Porter, assistant administrator, Office of Solid Waste and Emergency Response, to regional administrators, January 25, 1988.
79. Memorandum from J. Winston Porter, assistant administrator, Office of Solid Waste and Emergency Response, to regional administrators, March 24, 1988.
80. 102 PL 386; 1992 H.R. 2194; 106 Stat. 1550.
81. *United States Department of Energy v. Ohio,* 112 S.Ct. 1627 (1992).
82. *BNA Environment Reporter,* March 19, 1993, 3019.
83. Keith Schneider, "A Nuclear Cleanup's Staggering Cost," *New York Times,* June 19, 1989, A:12.
84. *BNA Chemical Regulation Reporter,* February 2, 1990.
85. *Inside EPA,* August 11, 1989.
86. *Conservation Law Foundation of New England et al. v. William K. Reilly,* 743 F.Supp. 933 (1990).

87. *Conservation Law Foundation of New England et al. v. William K. Reilly,* 950 F.2d 38 (1991).
88. *BNA Environment Reporter,* January 24, 1992.
89. *BNA Environment Reporter,* December 6, 1991.
90. Comprehensive Environmental Response, Compensation and Liability Act, 94 Stat. 2767, 42 U.S.C. sections 9601 et seq., PL 96-510, December 11, 1980; as amended by PL 96-561, December 22, 1980; PL 97-216, July 18, 1982; PL 97-272, September 30, 1982; PL 98-45, July 12, 1983; PL 98-80, August 23, 1983; PL 98-369, July 18, 1984; PL 98-371, July 18, 1984; PL 98-396, August 22, 1984; and PL 99-499, October 17, 1986; PL 101-508, November 5, 1990; PL 101-584, November 15, 1990; PL 102-426, October 19, 1992; and PL 102-484, October 23, 1992.
91. The National Contingency Plan was actually established by the 1972 amendments to the Federal Water Pollution Control Act. It was intended to provide a comprehensive framework for cleaning up spills of oil and hazardous substances into waterways. When CERCLA was passed in 1980, a provision was added mandating the development of a revised NCP that would address onshore spills of toxic substances and releases from hazardous waste disposal sites.
92. *BNA Environment Reporter,* March 19, 1982.
93. Ibid.
94. *Environmental Defense Fund v. Gorsuch,* 12 ELR 20376 (1982).
95. *BNA Environment Reporter,* March 19, 1982, 1475.
96. Ibid.
97. Ibid.
98. Interview with Khristine Hall, attorney for the Environmental Defense Fund, as reported in *BNA Environment Reporter,* March 19, 1982, 1475.
99. Phillip Shabecoff, "U.S. Plan Offered for Cleaning up Toxic Dump Sites," *New York Times,* March 13, 1982: 1.
100. *BNA Environment Reporter,* March 19, 1982.
101. Ibid.
102. *BNA Environment Reporter,* March 26, 1992, 1533.
103. *EDF v. Gorsuch [II],* 17 ERC 1173 (1982).
104. 47 Fed. Reg. 13174 (1982).
105. *BNA Environment Reporter,* May 14, 1982.
106. The appeal was filed on April 7, 1982 and is archived with U.S. Court of Appeals for the District of Columbia.
107. Affidavit of William Hedeman Jr., director of the EPA's Office of Emergency and Remedial Response, filed with the U.S. District

Court for the District of Columbia, May 7, 1982, archived at the court.

108. *BNA Environment Reporter,* June 4, 1982.

109. *EDF v. Gorsuch [II],* 17 ERC 1173 (1982).

110. *BNA Environment Reporter,* July 9, 1982.

111. *BNA Environment Reporter,* November 5, 1982.

112. Ibid.

113. *BNA Environment Reporter,* October 22, 1982.

114. *BNA Environment Reporter,* November 26, 1982.

115. *Environmental Defense Fund v. EPA,* C.A. DC. No. 82-2234; *New Jersey v. EPA,* C.A. DC. No. 84-2238.

116. 50 Fed. Reg. 5862 (1985).

117. *BNA Environment Reporter,* February 1, 1985.

118. *BNA Environment Reporter,* November 29, 1985.

119. PL 99-499, October 17, 1986.

120. *BNA Environment Reporter,* September 30, 1988.

121. *BNA Environment Reporter,* February 9, 1990.

122. 55 Fed. Reg. 8666 (March 8, 1990).

123. *Ohio v. EPA,* C.A. DC. No. 86-1096. Oral arguments were heard on February 3, 1993, by the U.S. Court of Appeals for the District of Columbia.

124. *Cohen v. EPA,* 19 ERC 1377 (1983).

125. Ibid.

126. Ibid.

127. EPA internal memorandum from Gene Lucero, director of the Office of Waste Programs Enforcement, and Kirk Sniff, associate enforcement counsel for waste in the Office of Enforcement and Compliance Monitoring, to regional offices, January 16, 1984.

128. Phillip D. Reed, "CERCLA 1985: A Litigation Update," *Environmental Law Reporter,* December, 1985, 10395.

129. Barnett M. Lawrence, "Preenforcement Review under CERCLA: Potentially Responsible Parties Seek an Early Day in Court," *Environmental Law Reporter,* April, 1986.

130. Editor's note in Reed, "CERCLA 1985," 10395. See also Alfred R. Light, "A Defense Counsel's Perspective on Superfund," *Environmental Law Reporter,* July, 1985.

131. See, for example, Environmental Protection Agency, *A Management Review of the Superfund Program* (Washington, D.C.: Government Printing Office, May, 1989). A similar report was issued by the Rand Institute for Civil Justice in September, 1989.

132. *BNA Environment Reporter,* February 19, 1993, 2720.
133. Ibid.

Chapter Seven

1. See J. Woodford Howard, Jr., "Adjudication Considered as a Process of Conflict Resolution: A Variation on Separation of Powers," *Journal of Public Law* 18, 2 (1969): 339–70; Ralph Cavanaugh and Austin Sarat, "Thinking about Courts: Toward and beyond a Jurisprudence of Judicial Competence," *Law and Society Review* 14, 2 (1980): 371–420; Martin M. Shapiro, *The Supreme Court and Administrative Agencies* (New York: Free Press, 1968); Daniel J. Fiorino, "Judicial-Administrative Interaction in Regulatory Policy Making: The Case of the Federal Power Commission," *Administrative Law Review* 28, 1 (1976): 41–88; J. Brian Sheehan, *The Boston Integration Dispute: Social Change and Legal Maneuvers* (New York: Columbia University Press, 1984); Phillip J. Cooper, "Conflict or Constructive Tension: The Changing Relationship of Judges and Administrators," *Public Administration Review* 45, special issue (November, 1985): 643–52; Phillip J. Cooper, *Hard Judicial Choices* (Oxford: Oxford University Press, 1988); Theodore Becker and Malcom Feeley, eds., *The Impact of Supreme Court Decisions* (Oxford: Oxford University Press, 1973); Lawrence Baum, "Implementation of Judicial Decisions," *American Politics Quarterly* 4, 1 (January, 1976): 86–114; Donald W. Crowley, "Selection Tests and Equal Opportunity: The Court and the EEOC," *Administration and Society* 17, 3 (November, 1985): 361–84; Susan Gluck Mezey, "Policymaking by the Federal Judiciary: The Effects of Judicial Review on the Social Security Disability Program," *Policy Studies Journal* 14, 3 (March, 1986): 343–62; Yong S. Lee, "Civil Liability of State and Local Governments: Myth and Reality," *Public Administration Review* 47, 2 (March/April, 1987): 160–70; M. Kay Harris and Dudley P. Spiller, Jr., *After Decision: Implementation of Judicial Decrees in Correctional Settings* (Washington, D.C.: Government Printing Office, 1976); Judith Resnik, "Managerial Judges," *Harvard Law Review* 96 (1982): 376; Steven Flanders, "Blind Umpires—A Response to Professor Resnik," *Hastings Law Journal* 35 (1984): 505; E. Donald Elliot, "Managerial Judging and the Evolution of Procedure," *University of Chicago Law Review* 53 (1986): 306; Edward H. Cooper and reply by Judge Robert Keeton, "Mass and Repetitive Litigation in the Federal Courts," *South Carolina Law Review* 38 (1987): 489; Jeremy Rabkin, *Judicial Compulsions* (New York: Basic Books,

1989); Richard Neely, *Why Courts Don't Work* (New York: McGraw-Hill, 1982); Robert A. Katzman, "Judicial Intervention and Organization Theory: Changing Bureaucratic Behavior and Policy," *Yale Law Journal* 89 (1980): 512–37; William V. Luneberg, "Petitioning Federal Agencies for Rulemaking: An Overview of Administrative and Judicial Practice and Some Recommendations for Improvement," *Wisconsin Law Review* 1988 (1988): 1; Richard J. Pierce, Jr., "The Role of the Judiciary in Implementing an Agency Theory of Government," *New York University Law Review* 64 (1989): 1226; Tim J. Filer, "The Scope of Judicial Review of Agency Actions in Washington Revisited—Doctrine, Analysis, and Proposed Revisions," *Washington Law Review* 60 (1985): 636; Peter L. Strauss, "One Hundred Fifty Cases per Year: Some Implications of the Supreme Court's Limited Resources for Judicial Review of Agency Action," *Columbia Law Review* 87 (1987): 1093–1136; Peter H. A. Lehner, "Judicial Review of Administrative Inaction," *Columbia Law Review* 83 (1983): 626–89; Gerald N. Rosenberg, *The Hollow Hope: Can Courts Bring about Social Change?* (Chicago: University of Chicago Press, 1991).

2. Lettie M. Wenner, *The Environmental Decade in Court* (Bloomington: Indiana University Press, 1982).

3. Christopher J. Bosso, *Pesticides and Politics: The Life Cycle of a Public Policy Issue* (Pittsburgh: University of Pittsburgh Press, 1987); Frank Graham, Jr., *Since Silent Spring* (Boston: Houghton Mifflin, 1970); Thomas R. Dunlap, *DDT: Scientists, Citizens, and Public Policy* (Princeton, N.J.: Princeton University Press, 1981).

4. David Doniger, *The Law and Policy of Toxic Substances Control: A Case Study of Vinyl Chloride* (Washington, D.C.: Resources for the Future, 1978).

5. See, for example, Jacqualee Story, "Administrative Agency Inaction: Misapplication of the Finality Doctrine," *Washington Law Review* 59 (1984): 982; Thomas O. McGarity, "Judicial Enforcement of NEPA-Inspired Promises," *Environmental Law* 20 (1990): 569–609; and Robert E. Steinberg, "OMB Review of Environmental Regulations: Limitations on the Courts and Congress," *Yale Law and Policy Review* 4 (1986): 404–25.

6. R. Shep Melnick, *Regulation and the Courts: The Case of the Clean Air Act* (Washington, D.C.: Brookings Institution, 1983), 343.

7. It should be noted that some cases may be placed in more than one category.

8. Interviews with EPA staff members, EPA headquarters, week of May 15, 1988, and November 9, 1989.

9. *Natural Resources Defense Council and American Public Health Association v. Gorsuch;* there was no final court decision in this case since the EPA reversed its actions soon after the filing of the lawsuit.
10. *Shell Oil v. EPA.*
11. See *United States v. Northeastern Pharmaceutical & Chemical Co.,* 579 F.Supp. 823 (1984) and *U.S. v. Chem-Dyne Co.,* 572 F.Supp. 802 (1983).
12. For a discussion of court decisions confirming and strengthening government policy in the area of civil rights policy, see Charles S. Bullock and Charles M. Lamb, *Implementation of Civil Rights Policy* (Monterey, Calif.: Brooks, Cole, 1984).
13. *Illinois et al. v. Costle,* 530 F.Supp. 337 (1979).
14. For an excellent discussion of the ongoing, affirmative decree, see Abram Chayes, "The Role of the Judge in Public Law Litigation," *Harvard Law Review* 89, 7 (1976): 1281–1316.
15. For excellent discussions of detailed judicial supervision, see Gerald E. Frug, "The Judicial Power of the Purse," *University of Pennsylvania Law Review* 126 (1978): 715; Donald L. Horowitz, "Decreeing Organizational Change: Judicial Supervision of Public Institutions," *Duke Law Journal* 1983 (1983): 1265; Chayes, "The Role of the Judge."
16. *NRDC et al. v. EPA,* 21 ERC 1624 (1984).
17. For additional discussions of active, aggressive judges, see Melnick, *Regulation and the Courts;* Gerald E. Frug, "The Judicial Power of the Purse," *University of Pennsylvania Law Review* 126 (1978): 715; David Rosenbloom, *Public Administration and Law* (New York: Marcel Dekker, 1983).
18. Melnick found this same phenomena under the Clean Air Act in his study, *Regulation and the Courts.*
19. *NRDC v. Costle,* 10 ELR 20274 (1980). See also 11 ELR 20202 (1981).
20. For a general discussion of the implementation of court decrees, see Charles A. Johnson and Bradley C. Canon, *Judicial Policies: Implementation and Impact* (Washington, D.C.: Congressional Quarterly, Inc., 1984).
21. Some of these administrative consequences of court actions were noted by Melnick in his study of the Clean Air Act. Examples include the diversion and expansion of the EPA's Clean Air Act staff (pages 379–80), the increased power of the legal staff (page 380), and the reduction in the ability of EPA administrators to set agency priorities (page 381). It is interesting to note, however, that Melnick downplays the potential positives in these developments and concentrates on the negatives.

22. Horowitz, "Decreeing Organizational Change"; George E. Hale, "Federal Courts and the State Budgetary Process," *Administration and Society* 11, 3 (1979): 357–68; Jeffrey D. Straussman, "Courts and Public Purse Strings: Have Portraits of Budgeting Missed Something?" *Public Administration Review* 46, 4 (1986): 345–51; W. S. Allerton, "An Administrator Responds," in *Paper Victories and Hard Realities*, ed. V. Bradley and G. Clarke (Washington, D.C.: Georgetown University Health Policy Center, 1976); Louis Fisher, *Presidential Spending Power* (Princeton: Princeton University Press, 1975).

23. The one exception is the Flannery Decision pertaining to the Clean Water Act, discussed in Chapter Two.

24. Interview with former EPA budget director, EPA headquarters, week of May 15, 1988.

25. Interviews with EPA staff members, EPA headquarters, week of May 15, 1988, and November 9, 1989.

26. Hale, "Federal Courts and the State Budgetary Process."

27. Ibid.

28. Ibid.

29. Ibid.

30. Ibid.

31. Interviews with members of the Office of Management and Budget staff, Washington, D.C., week of May 15, 1988.

32. Interviews with members of the Congressional Budget Office staff, Washington, D.C., week of May 15, 1988.

33. This finding agrees in part with Nathan Glazer's conclusions as discussed in "Should Judges Administer Social Services?" *Public Interest* 50 (1978): 64–80.

34. Interviews with EPA staff members, EPA headquarters, week of May 15, 1988.

35. *Monsanto v. Acting Administrator,* 564 F.Supp. 522 (1983). The case was later reversed by the Supreme Court in *Ruckelshaus v. Monsanto,* 463 U.S. 1315 (1983).

36. Interviews with EPA staff members, EPA headquarters, week of May 15, 1988, and November 9, 1989. The case was eventually reversed on appeal.

37. Interviews with EPA staff members, EPA headquarters, week of May 15, 1988, and November 9, 1989.

38. Glazer, "Should Judges Administer Social Services?"; Jeffrey Pfeffer and Gerald R. Salancik, *The External Control of Organizations* (New York: Harper and Row, 1978).

39. James D. Thompson, *Organizations in Action* (New York: McGraw-Hill, 1967).

40. Ibid. The case was the Clean Water Act "Flannery Decision."

41. Interviews with EPA staff members, EPA headquarters, week of May 15, 1988, and November 9, 1989. The case was *Cohen v. EPA,* 19 ERC 1377 (1983). Whether these findings are positive or negative depends on one's perspective. Melnick, for example, considers an increase in the power of individual programmatic offices a negative, since it may insulate bureaucrats from the will of elected officials.

42. *LEAF v. Hodel,* 586 F.Supp. 1165 (1984); General Accounting Office *Department of Energy Acting to Control Hazardous Wastes at Its Savannah River Nuclear Facilities,* Report No. GAO/RCED-85-23 (Washington, D.C.: Government Printing Office, 1985).

43. See Environmental and Energy Study Institute and the Environmental Law Institute, *Statutory Deadlines in Environmental Legislation: Necessary but Need Improvement* (Washington, D.C.: Environmental Law Institute, September, 1985).

44. Donald L. Horowitz, *The Courts and Social Policy* (Washington, D.C.: Brookings Institution, 1977); idem, "The Courts as Guardians of the Public Interest," *Public Administration Review* 37, 1 (1977): 148–54; idem, "Decreeing Organizational Change."

45. *Sierra Club v. Ruckelshaus,* 602 F.Supp. 892 (1984); interviews with EPA staff members, EPA headquarters, week of May 15, 1988, and November 9, 1989.

46. For a discussion of the representative democracy problem in general, see Rosenbloom, *Public Administration and Law.*

47. See dissenting opinion of Judge Wilkey in *Citizens for a Better Environment v. Gorsuch,* 718 F.2d 1117 (1983).

48. The case was the Flannery Decision, pertaining to Clean Water Act, *NRDC v. Train,* 8 ERC 2120 (1976).

49. "Environmentalists are not the only entities filing under citizen suit provisions. One study found that in a two-year period (January, 1979, to January, 1981), nineteen cases were brought under citizen suit provisions and decided in the federal courts. Of these, twelve were brought by environmental groups, four by industries, and three by state and local governments. See Ross Sandler, "Citizen Suit Litigation," *Environment* 23, 2 (March, 1981): 38–39.

50. William E. Kovacic, "The Reagan Judiciary and Environmental Policy: The Impact of Appointments to the Federal Courts of Appeals," *Boston College Environmental Affairs Law Review* 18 (1991): 669–713.

51. Patricia M. Wald, "Some Thoughts on Judging as Gleaned from One Hundred Years of the *Harvard Law Review* and Other Great Books," *Harvard Law Review* 100 (1987): 895.

52. For a balanced examination of the pros and cons of environmental mediation, see Douglas J. Amy, *The Politics of Environmental Mediation* (New York: Columbia University Press, 1987).

Bibliography

Books and Articles

Ackerman, Bruce A., and William T. Hassler. *Clean Coal/Dirty Air.* New Haven: Yale University Press, 1981.

Allerton, W. S. "An Administrator Responds." In *Paper Victories and Hard Realities,* ed. V. Bradley and G. Clarke. Washington, D.C.: Georgetown University Health Policy Center, 1976.

Amy, Douglas J. *The Politics of Environmental Mediation.* New York: Columbia University Press, 1987.

Arbuckle, J. Gordon, Timothy A. Vanderver, Jr., and Russell V. Randle. "Water Pollution Control." *Environmental Law Handbook.* Rockville, Md.: Government Institutes, Inc., 1991.

Baum, Lawrence. "Implementation of Judicial Decisions." *American Politics Quarterly* 4, 1 (1976): 86–114.

Bazelon, David L. "The Impact of Courts on Public Administration." *Indiana Law Journal* 52 (1977): 101.

Becker, Theodore, and Malcom Feeley, eds. *The Impact of Supreme Court Decisions.* Oxford: Oxford University Press, 1973.

Boraiko, Allen A. "Storing Up Trouble—Hazardous Waste." *National Geographic* (March, 1984): 325–52.

Bosso, Christopher J. *Pesticides and Politics: The Life Cycle of a Public Policy Issue.* Pittsburgh: University of Pittsburgh Press, 1987.

Bozeman, Barry. "Retrospective Technology Assessment." Unpublished paper, 1985.

Bullock, Charles S., and Charles M. Lamb. *Implementation of Civil Rights Policy.* Monterey, Calif.: Brooks, Cole, 1984.

Campbell, Donald T. "Degrees of Freedom and the Case Study." *Comparative Political Studies* 8 (1975): 178–93.

Carson, Rachel. *Silent Spring.* Boston: Houghton Mifflin, 1962.

Cavanaugh, Ralph, and Austin Sarat. "Thinking about Courts: Toward and beyond a Jurisprudence of Judicial Competence." *Law and Society Review* 14, 2 (1980): 371–420.

Chayes, Abram. "The Role of the Judge in Public Law Litigation." *Harvard Law Review* 89, 7 (1976): 1281–1316.

Chilton, Bradley S., and Susett M. Talarico. "Politics and Constitutional Interpretation in Prison Reform Litigation: The Case of *Guthrie v. Evans.*" In *Courts, Corrections and the Constitution*, ed. John J. Dilulio, Jr. New York: Oxford University Press, 1990.

Claveloux, Ronald L. "The Conflict between Executive Privilege and Congressional Oversight: The Gorsuch Controversy." *Duke Law Journal* (1983): 1333.

Cooper, Edward H. "Mass and Repetitive Litigation in the Federal Courts." *South Carolina Law Review* 38 (1987): 489.

Cooper, Phillip J. "Conflict or Constructive Tension: The Changing Relationship of Judges and Administrators." *Public Administration Review* 45, special issue (November, 1985): 643–52.

———. *Hard Judicial Choices*. Oxford: Oxford University Press, 1988.

———. *Public Law and Public Administration*. Englewood Cliffs, N.J.: Prentice Hall, 1988.

Cramton, Roger. "Judicial Lawmaking and Administration in the Leviathan State." *Public Administration Review* 36, 5 (1976): 551–55.

Crowley, Donald W. "Selection Tests and Equal Opportunity: The Court and the EEOC." *Administration and Society* 17, 3 (November, 1985): 361–84.

Davies, J. Clarence, and Barbara Davies. *The Politics of Pollution*. Indianapolis: Bobbs-Merrill, 1975.

Diamond, Edwin. "What Business Thinks." *Fortune* 81, 2 (1970): 118–72.

Diver, Colin. "The Judge as Political Powerbroker: Superintending Structural Change in Public Institutions," *Virginia Law Review* 65 (1979): 43–106.

Dolbeare, Kenneth M., and Phillip E. Hammond. *The School Prayer Decisions*. Chicago: University of Chicago Press, 1971.

Doniger, David. *The Law and Policy of Toxic Substance Control: A Case Study of Vinyl Chloride*. Washington, D.C.: Resources for the Future, 1978.

Dunlap, Thomas R. *DDT: Scientists, Citizens, and Public Policy*. Princeton, N.J.: Princeton University Press, 1981.

Eckstein, Harry. "Case Study and Theory in Political Science." In *Political Science: Scope and Theory*, ed. Fred I. Greenstein and Nelson W. Polsby. Reading, Mass.: Addison-Wesley, 1975.

Editor's Note in Phillip D. Reed, "CERCLA 1985: A Litigation Update," *Environmental Law Reporter* 15 (December, 1985).

Elliot, E. Donald. "Managerial Judging and the Evolution of Procedure." *University of Chicago Law Review* 53 (1986): 306.

Environmental and Energy Study Institute and the Environmental Law Institute. *Statutory Deadlines in Environmental Legislation: Necessary but Need Improvement.* Washington, D.C.: Environmental Law Institute, September, 1985.

Epstein, Lee, and C. K. Rowland. "Debunking the Myth of Interest Group Invincibility in the Courts." *American Political Science Review* 85 (March, 1991): 205–17.

Ferrey, Steven. "The Toxic Time Bomb: Municipal Liability for the Cleanup of Hazardous Waste." *George Washington Law Review* 57 (1988): 197–277.

Filer, Tim J. "The Scope of Judicial Review of Agency Actions in Washington Revisited—Doctrine, Analysis, and Proposed Revisions." *Washington Law Review* 60 (1985): 636.

Finamore, Barbara A. "Regulating Hazardous and Mixed Waste at Department of Energy Nuclear Weapons Facilities: Reversing Decades of Environmental Neglect." *Harvard Environmental Law Review* 9 (1985): 83.

Fiorino, Daniel J. "Judicial-Administrative Interaction in Regulatory Policy Making: The Case of the Federal Power Commission." *Administrative Law Review* 28, 1 (1976): 41–88.

Fisher, Louis. *Presidential Spending Power.* Princeton: Princeton University Press, 1975.

Fiss, Owen M. "The Bureaucratization of the Judiciary." *Yale Law Journal* 92 (1983): 1442–68.

———. "The Supreme Court, 1978 Term—Forward: The Forms of Justice." *Harvard Law Review* 93 (1979): 1.

Flanders, Steven. "Blind Umpires—A Response to Professor Resnik." *Hastings Law Journal* 35 (1984): 505.

Frug, Gerald E. "The Judicial Power of the Purse." *University of Pennsylvania Law Review* 126 (1978): 715.

Galanter, Marc. "Why the Haves Come Out Ahead: Speculations on the Limits of Legal Change." *Law and Society Review* 9 (1974): 95.

Glazer, Nathan. "Should Judges Administer Social Services?" *Public Interest* 50 (1978): 64–80.

Glick, Henry Robert. "Policy-Making and State Supreme Courts: The Judiciary as an Interest Group." *Law and Society Review* 5, 2 (1970): 271–91.

Graham, Frank, Jr. *Since Silent Spring*. Boston: Houghton Mifflin, 1970.

Graham, John D. "The Failure of Agency-Forcing: The Regulation of Airborne Carcinogens under Section 112 of the Clean Air Act." *Duke Law Journal* 1985 (1985): 100–150.

Hale, George E. "Federal Courts and the State Budgetary Process." *Administration and Society* 11, 3 (1979): 357–68.

Hall, Khristine L. "The Control of Toxic Pollutants under the Federal Water Pollution Control Act Amendments of 1972." *Iowa Law Review* 63 (1978): 616.

Harriman, Linda, and Jeffrey D. Straussman. "Do Judges Determine Budget Decisions? Federal Court Decisions in Prison Reform and State Spending for Corrections." *Public Administration Review* 43, 4 (1983): 343–51.

Harris, M. Kay, and Dudley P. Spiller, Jr. *After Decision: Implementation of Judicial Decrees in Correctional Settings*. Washington, D.C.: Government Printing Office, 1976.

Harris, Richard A., and Sidney M. Milkis. *The Politics of Regulatory Change: A Tale of Two Agencies*. New York: Oxford University Press, 1989.

Harwood, Gerald (Judge). "Hearings before an EPA Administrative Law Judge." *Environmental Law Reporter* 17 (November, 1987): 10441.

Hirschhorn, James M. "Where the Money Is: Remedies to Finance Compliance with Strict Structural Injunctions." *Michigan Law Review* 82 (1984): 1815.

Horowitz, Donald L. *The Courts and Social Policy*. Washington, D.C.: Brookings Institution, 1977.

———. "The Courts as Guardians of the Public Interest." *Public Administration Review* 37, 1 (1977): 148–54.

———. "Decreeing Organizational Change: Judicial Supervision of Public Institutions." *Duke Law Journal* (1983): 1265.

Howard, J. Woodford, Jr. "Adjudication Considered as a Process of Conflict Resolution: A Variation on Separation of Powers." *Journal of Public Law* 18, 2 (1969): 339–70.

Hueber, Graham. "Americans Report High Levels of Environmental Concern, Activity." *Gallup Poll Monthly* 307 (April, 1991): 6–12.

Johnson, Charles A. "Judicial Decisions and Organizational Change." *Administration and Society* 11, 1 (1979): 27–51.

———. "Judicial Decisions and Organization Change: Some Theoretical and Empirical Notes on State Court Decisions and State Administrative Agencies." *Law and Society Review* 14, 1 (1979): 27–56.

Johnson, Charles A., and Bradley C. Canon. *Judicial Policies: Implemen-*

tation and Impact. Washington, D.C.: Congressional Quarterly, Inc., 1984.

Johnson, R. M. *The Dynamics of Compliance.* Evanston, Ill.: Northwestern University Press, 1967.

Katzman, Robert A. "Judicial Intervention and Organization Theory: Changing Bureaucratic Behavior and Policy." *Yale Law Journal* 89 (1980): 512–37.

Kennedy School of Government. *William Ruckelshaus and the Environmental Protection Agency.* Case # C16-74-0270. Boston: Harvard University, 1974.

Kovacic, William E. "The Reagan Judiciary and Environmental Policy: The Impact of Appointments to the Federal Courts of Appeals." *Boston College Environmental Affairs Law Review* 18 (1991): 669–713.

Landy, Marc K., Marc J. Roberts, and Stephen R. Thomas. *The EPA: Asking the Wrong Questions.* New York: Oxford University Press, 1990.

Lawrence, Barnett M. "Preenforcement Review under CERCLA: Potentially Responsible Parties Seek an Early Day in Court." *Environmental Law Reporter* 16 (April, 1986): 10093.

Lee, Yong S. "Civil Liability of State and Local Governments: Myth and Reality." *Public Administration Review* 47, 2 (March/April, 1987): 160–70.

Lehner, Peter H. A. "Judicial Review of Administrative Inaction." *Columbia Law Review* 83 (1983): 626.

Light, Alfred R. "A Defense Counsel's Perspective on Superfund." *Environmental Law Reporter* 15 (July, 1985): 10203.

Lijphart, Arend. "Comparative Politics and the Comparative Method." *American Political Science Review* 65 (1971): 682–93.

Luneberg, William V. "Petitioning Federal Agencies for Rulemaking: An Overview of Administrative and Judicial Practice and Some Recommendations for Improvement." *Wisconsin Law Review* 1988 (1988): 1.

McGarity, Thomas O. "Judicial Enforcement of NEPA-Inspired Promises." *Environmental Law* 20 (1990): 569–609.

Marcus, Alfred A. *Promise and Performance: Choosing and Implementing an Environmental Policy.* Westport, Conn.: Greenwood Press, 1980.

———. "What Does Reorganization Accomplish? The Case of the Environmental Protection Agency." Ph.D. diss., Department of Government, Harvard University, August, 1977.

Marshall, Elliot. "EPA's High-Risk Carcinogen Policy." *Science* 218 (November 26, 1982): 975–78.

Melnick, R. Shep. "The Politics of Partnership." *Public Administration Review* 45 (1985): 653–60.

———. *Regulation and the Courts: The Case of the Clean Air Act.* Washington, D.C.: Brookings Institution, 1983.

Mendeloff, John M. *The Dilemma of Toxic Substance Regulation.* Cambridge: MIT Press, 1988.

Mezey, Susan Gluck. "Policymaking by the Federal Judiciary: The Effects of Judicial Review on the Social Security Disability Program." *Policy Studies Journal* 14, 3 (1986): 343–62.

Moss, Kathryn. "The Catalytic Effect of a Federal Court Decision on a State Legislature." *Law and Society Review* 19, 1 (1983): 147–57.

Murphy, Walter K. "Chief Justice Taft and the Lower Court Bureaucracy: A Study in Judicial Administration." *Journal of Politics* 24, 3 (1962): 453–76.

Neely, Richard. *Why Courts Don't Work.* New York: McGraw-Hill, 1982.

O'Leary, Rosemary, and Charles Wise. "Public Managers, Judges and Legislators: Redefining the 'New Partnership.' " *Public Administration Review* 52, 4 (1991): 316–27.

Pfeffer, Jeffrey, and Gerald R. Salancik. *The External Control of Organizations.* New York: Harper and Row, 1978.

Pierce, Richard J., Jr. "The Role of the Judiciary in Implementing an Agency Theory of Government." *New York University Law Review* 64 (1989): 1226.

Polkinghorn, Brian. "The Influence of Regulatory Negotiation on EPA as an Institution." Draft Ph.D. diss., Department of Social Science, Maxwell School of Citizenship and Public Affairs, Syracuse University, April, 1993.

Rabkin, Jeremy. *Judicial Compulsions.* New York: Basic Books, 1989.

Reed, Phillip D. "CERCLA 1985: A Litigation Update." *Environmental Law Reporter* 15 (December, 1985) 10395.

Resnik, Judith. "Managerial Judges." *Harvard Law Review* 96 (1982): 376.

Rosenberg, Gerald N. *The Hollow Hope: Can Courts Bring about Social Change?* Chicago: University of Chicago Press, 1991.

Rosenbloom, David. *Public Administration and Law.* New York: Marcel Dekker, 1983.

Rothman, David J., and Sheila M. Rothman. *The Willowbrook Wars.* New York: Harper and Row, 1984.

Sabatier, Paul. "Social Movements and Regulatory Agencies: Toward a More Adequate—and Less Pessimistic—Theory of Clientele Capture." *Policy Sciences* 6 (September, 1975): 301–42.

Sandler, Ross. "Citizen Suit Litigation." *Environment* 23, 2 (March, 1981): 38–39.

Sax, Joseph L. *Defending the Environment.* New York: Alfred A. Knopf, 1971.

Scheingold, Stuart A. *The Politics of Rights: Lawyers, Public Policy, and Political Change.* New Haven: Yale University Press, 1974.

Shapiro, Martin M. *The Supreme Court and Administrative Agencies.* New York: Free Press, 1968.

———. *Who Guards the Guardians? Judicial Control of Administration.* Athens: University of Georgia Press, 1988.

Sheehan, J. Brian. *The Boston Integration Dispute: Social Change and Legal Maneuvers.* New York: Columbia University Press, 1984.

Steinberg, Robert E. "OMB Review of Environmental Regulations: Limitations on the Courts and Congress." *Yale Law and Policy Review* 4 (1986): 404–25.

Story, Jacqualee. "Administrative Agency Inaction: Misapplication of the Finality Doctrine." *Washington Law Review* 59 (1984): 982.

Strauss, Peter L. "One Hundred Fifty Cases per Year: Some Implications of the Supreme Court's Limited Resources for Judicial Review of Agency Action." *Columbia Law Review* 87 (1987): 1093–1136.

Straussman, Jeffrey D. "Courts and Public Purse Strings: Have Portraits of Budgeting Missed Something?" *Public Administration Review* 46, 4 (1986): 345–51.

Taggert, William A. "Redefining the Power of the Federal Judiciary: The Impact of Court-Ordered Prison Reform on State Expenditures for Corrections." *Law and Society Review* 23, 2 (1989): 241–71.

Thompson, James D. *Organizations in Action.* New York: McGraw-Hill, 1967.

Unterberger, Glenn L., and John W. Lyon. "Municipal Enforcement under the Federal Clean Water Act and EPA's National Municipal Policy." *National Enforcement Journal* 1 (1986): 4.

Wald, Patricia M. "Some Thoughts on Judging Gleaned from One Hundred Years of the *Harvard Law Review* and Other Great Books," *Harvard Law Review* 100 (1987): 895.

Weinstein, Jack B. "The Effect of Austerity on Institutional Litigation," *Law and Human Behavior* 6 (1982): 145.

Wenner, Lettie M. *The Environmental Decade in Court.* Bloomington: Indiana University Press, 1982.

Wildavsky, Aaron. *The New Politics of the Budgetary Process.* Glenview, Ill.: Scott, Foresman, 1988.

Wood, Robert C. "Professionals at Bay: Managing Boston's Public

Schools." *Journal of Policy Analysis and Management* 1, 4 (1982): 454–68.

————. *Remedial Law: When Courts become Administrators.* Amherst: University of Massachusetts Press, 1990.

Wyche, Bradford W. "The Regulation of Toxic Pollutants under the Clean Water Act: EPA's Ten Year Rulemaking Nears Completion." *Natural Resources Lawyer* 15 (1983): 511.

Yannacone, Victor J. "Sue the Bastards." In *Earth Day: The Beginning,* ed. Staff of Environmental Action. New York: Bantam, 1970.

Yarbrough, Tinsley. "The Judge as Manager: The Case of Judge Frank Johnson." *Journal of Policy Analysis and Management* 1, 3 (1982): 386–400.

————. "The Political World of Federal Judges as Managers." *Public Administration Review* 45 (1985): 660–66.

Yin, Robert K. "The Case Study as Serious Research Strategy." *Knowledge* 3 (1981): 97–114.

————. "The Case Study Crisis: Some Answers." *Administrative Science Quarterly* 26 (March, 1981): 58–65.

————. *Case Study Research: Design and Methods.* Newbury Park, Calif.: Sage Publications, 1989.

————. "Studying Phenomenon and Context across Sites." *American Behavioral Scientist* 26 (1982): 84–100.

Yin, Robert K., and Karen A. Heald. "Using the Case Survey Method to Analyze Policy Studies." *Administrative Science Quarterly* 20 (1975): 371–81.

Newspapers and Newsletters

Air and Water News, July 26, 1971.

BNA Chemical Regulation Reporter, February 2, 1990; June 22, 1990; August 9, 1991.

BNA Environment Reporter, May 7, 1976; June 4, 1976; June 11, 1976; February 12, 1982; February 19, 1982; March 19, 1982; May 14, 1982; June 4, 1982; June 11, 1982; July 9, 1982; October 22, 1982; November 5, 1982; November 12, 1982; November 19, 1982; November 26, 1982; December 10, 1982; February 4, 1983; February 18, 1983; April 1, 1983; April 22, 1983; June 17, 1983; July 5, 1983; December 9, 1983; February 3, 1984; February 10, 1984; March 9, 1984; March 23, 1984; July 27, 1984; August 10, 1984; August 31, 1984; September 7, 1984; September 14, 1984; October 19, 1984; November 2, 1984; January 11, 1985; January 25, 1985; February 1, 1985; May 17, 1985;

July 12, 1985; July 26, 1985; August 16, 1985; August 23, 1985; November 11, 1985; November 29, 1985; December 14, 1985; October 10, 1986; June 19, 1987; April 1, 1988; September 30, 1988; February 2, 1990; February 9, 1990; April 19, 1991; December 6, 1991; January 24, 1992; July 24, 1992; July 31, 1992; September 25, 1992; October 30, 1992; February 19, 1993; March 5, 1993; March 19, 1993.

Environmental Law Reporter, January, 1974; August, 1974; October, 1974; August, 1984.

Inside EPA, January 10, 1986; January 8, 1988; July 14, 1989; August 11, 1989; September 19, 1989; November 10, 1989.

New York Times, July 12, 1970; November 7, 1970; September 2, 1971; September 13, 1971; December 13, 1973; April 23, 1981; March 13, 1982; March 20, 1983; April 3, 1983; November 1, 1983; November 18, 1983; March 15, 1984; May 19, 1984; October 24, 1984; December 12, 1984; January 22, 1986; January 30, 1986; November 8, 1986; June 19, 1989; December 23, 1990.

Washington Post, July 28, 1974; July 31, 1989.

Court Cases

Note: A complete listing of all court cases reviewed for this study may be obtained by writing the author at Department of Public Administration, Maxwell School of Citizenship and Public Affairs, Syracuse University, Syracuse, NY 13244-1090.

Artesian Water Co. v. the Government of New Castle County, 605 F.Supp. 1348 (D.C. DE. 1985).

Cadillac Fairview/California Inc. v. Dow Chemical Co., 21 ERC 1108, 21 ERC 1584 (C.D. CA. 1984).

Chevron Chemical Co. v. Costle, 499 F.Supp. 732, 499 F.Supp. 755, 641 F.2d 104, 452 U.S. 961 (1981).

Citizens for a Better Environment v. Gorsuch, 718 F.2d 1117 (D.C. Cir. 1983).

Cohen v. EPA, 19 ERC 1377 (1983).

Conservation Law Foundation of New England et al. v. William K. Reilly, 743 F.Supp. 933 (D.C. MA. 1990).

Conservation Law Foundation of New England et al. v. William K. Reilly, 950 F.2d 38 (1st Cir. 1991).

Dow Chemical Co. v. Barbara Blum, 469 F.Supp. 892 (E.D. MI. 1979).

Eagle-Pitcher Industries v. EPA, 759 F.2d 905, 759 F.2d 922 (DC. Cir. 1985).

Environmental Defense Fund, Inc. v. Douglas M. Costle, Administrator, Environmental Protection Agency, 578 F.2d 337 (DC. Cir. 1978).

Environmental Defense Fund, Inc. et al. v. Douglas M. Costle, Administrator, United States Environmental Protection Agency, et al., 636 F.2d 1229 14 ERC 2161 (DC. Cir. 1980).

Environmental Defense Fund v. Environmental Protection Agency, C.A. DC. No. 82-2234.

Environmental Defense Fund v. Environmental Protection Agency, 465 F.2d 528 (DC. Cir. 1972).

Environmental Defense Fund v. Environmental Protection Agency, 7 ERC 1688 (DC. Cir. 1975).

Environmental Defense Fund, Inc. v. Environmental Protection Agency, 636 F.2d 1267, 15 ERC 1081 (DC. Cir. 1980).

Environmental Defense Fund, Inc. v. Environmental Protection Agency, 672 F.2d 42 16 ERC 2149 (DC. Cir. 1982).

Environmental Defense Fund, Inc. et al. v. Environmental Protection Agency and William D. Ruckelshaus, Administrator et al., 489 F.2d 1247 (DC. Cir. 1973).

Environmental Defense Fund et al. v. Environmental Protection Agency and Russel Train, administrator, 548 F.2d 998 (DC. Cir. 1976).

Environmental Defense Fund v. Finch, 428 F.2d 1083 (1970).

Environmental Defense Fund, Inc. v. Anne M. Gorsuch, 12 ELR 20376 (DC. Cir. 1982).

Environmental Defense Fund, Inc. v. Anne M. Gorsuch, 17 ERC 1173 (DC. Cir. 1982).

Environmental Defense Fund v. Hardin, 325 F.Supp. 1401 (D.C. DC. 1970).

Environmental Defense Fund, Inc. v. Ruckelshaus, 439 F.2d 584 (DC. Cir. 1971).

Environmental Defense Fund et al. v. Lee M. Thomas, Administrator, United States Environmental Protection Agency, et al., 627 F.Supp. 566 (D.C. DC. 1986).

Environmental Defense Fund et al. v. Lee M. Thomas, Administrator, Environmental Protection Agency, 657 F.Supp. 302 (D.C. DC. 1987).

Olaf A. Hallstrom v. Tillamook County, 110 S.Ct. 304 (1989).

Illinois v. Costle/Gorsuch, 530 F.Supp. 337 (D.C. DC. 1979).

In re: T. P. Long Chemical Co., 45 Bankr. 278 (N.D. OH. 1985).

J. V. Peters and Co., Inc. et al. v. Administrator, 767 F.2d 263 (6th Cir. 1985).

Legal Environmental Assistance Foundation, Inc. et al. v. Donald Hodel, Secretary, United States Department of Energy, et al., 586 F.Supp. 1163 (E.D. TN. 1984).

Les et al. v. William K. Reilly, Administrator, Environmental Protection Agency, 968 F.2d 985 (9th Cir. 1992).

Lone Pine Steering Committee v. EPA, 600 F.Supp. 1487, 777 F.2d 822 (3d Cir. 1985), cert denied 106 S.Ct. 1970 (1986).

Mobay Chemical Corp. v. Douglas M. Costle, Administrator, United States Environmental Protection Agency, 517 F.Supp. 252 (W.D. PA. 1981), 682 F.2d 419 (1981), 103 S.Ct. 343 (1982).

Monsanto v. Acting Administrator, 18 ERC 2081 (E.D. MO. 1983).

Monsanto v. Gorsuch, E.D. MO. No. 79-0366-C(1).

Mumford Cove et al. v. Town of Groton et al., 786 F.2d 530 (2d Cir. 1985).

National Agricultural Chemicals Association v. Les, 61 U.S.L.W. 3584 (1993).

National Agricultural Chemicals Association and Ciba-Geigby Corp. v. EPA, 554 F.Supp. 1209 (D.C. DC. 1983).

National Wildlife Federation v. Environmental Protection Agency, No. 83-1333 (D. CO. 1984).

Natural Resources Defense Council et al. v. Administrator, Environmental Protection Agency, et al., 595 F.Supp. 65 (D.C. DC. 1984).

Natural Resources Defense Council et al. v. Douglas M. Costle, Administrator, Environmental Protection Agency, et al., 561 F.2d 904 (DC. Cir. 1977).

Natural Resources Defense Council v. Costle, 12 ERC 1181 (D.C. DC. 1978).

Natural Resources Defense Council v. Costle, 12 ERC 1833 (D.C. DC. 1979).

Natural Resources Defense Council, Inc. v. Douglas Costle, as Administrator, Environmental Protection Agency, 14 ERC 1858 (S.D. NY. 1979).

Natural Resources Defense Council v. Costle, 10 ELR 20274 (S.D. NY. 1980).

Natural Resources Defense Council v. Costle, 636 F.2d 1229 (C.A. DC. 1980).

Natural Resources Defense Council v. Costle, 11 ELR 20202 (S.D. NY. 1981).

Natural Resources Defense Council, Inc. et al. v. United States Environmental Protection Agency, 489 F.2d 390 (5th Cir. 1974); rev'd *Train v. Natural Resources Defense Council, Inc.,* 421 U.S. 60 (1975).

Natural Resources Defense Council, Inc. et al. v. Environmental Protection Agency, 529 F.2d 755 (5th Cir. 1976).

Natural Resources Defense Council, Inc. et al. v. United States Environmental Protection Agency et al., 824 F.2d 1258 (1st Cir. 1987).

Natural Resources Defense Council et al. v. Environmental Protection Agency, William Ruckelshaus, Administrator, 21 ERC 1625, 595 F.Supp. 1255 (S.D. NY. 1984).

Natural Resources Defense Council et al. v. Environmental Protection Agency and William Ruckelshaus, Administrator, 21 ERC 1919 (S.D. NY. 1984).

Natural Resources Defense Council v. Gorsuch, 12 ELR 20371 (D.C. DC. 1982).

Natural Resources Defense Council v. Gorsuch, 17 ERC 2013 (DC. Cir. 1982).

Natural Resources Defense Council, Inc. v. Lee M. Thomas, Administrator, Environmental Protection Agency, et al., 801 F.2d 457 (DC. Cir. 1986).

Natural Resources Defense Council, Inc. et al. v. Lee M. Thomas, Administrator, United States Environmental Protection Agency, et al., 838 F.2d 1224 (DC. Cir. 1988).

Natural Resources Defense Council, Inc. v. Russell E. Train et al., 6 ERC 1702 (D.C. DC. 1974).

Natural Resources Defense Council, Inc. et al. v. Russell E. Train, Administrator, Environmental Protection Agency, 519 F.2d 287, 8 ERC 1233 (DC. Cir. 1975).

Natural Resources Defense Council, Inc. et al. v. Russell E. Train et al., 8 ERC 2120 (D.C. DC. 1976).

New Jersey v. Environmental Protection Agency, C.A. DC. No. 84-2238.

Ohio v. EPA, C.A. DC. No. 86-1096.

Pennwalt Corp. v. Gorsuch, 682 F.2d 419 (3d Cir. 1982), cert. den. *Ruckelshaus, Administrator, United States Environmental Protection Agency v. Monsanto Co.,* 463 U.S. 1315 (1983).

Petrolite Corp. v. Environmental Protection Agency, 519 F.Supp. 966 (D.C. DC. 1981).

Ruckelshaus v. Monsanto, 463 U.S. 1315 (1983).

Ruckelshaus, Administrator, United States Environmental Protection Agency v. Monsanto Co., 467 U.S. 986 (1984).

Ruckelshaus, Administrator, United States Environmental Protection Agency v. Union Carbide Agricultural Products Co., Inc. et al., 469 U.S. 876 (1984).

Sathon, Inc. v. American Arbitration Association, 20 ERC 2241 (N.D. IL. 1984).

Sierra Club v. Anne M. Gorsuch, Administrator, Environmental Protection Agency, et al., 672 F.2d 33, 17 ERC 1748 (DC. Cir. 1982).

Sierra Club et al. v. Anne Gorsuch, Administrator, United States Environmental Protection Agency, et al., 551 F.Supp. 785 (N.D. CA. 1982).

Sierra Club v. William D. Ruckelshaus, Administrator, and United States Environmental Protection Agency et al., 602 F.Supp. 892 (N.D. CA. 1984).

Sierra Club v. Ruckelshaus, 21 ERC 1826 (N.D. CA. 1984).

Sierra Club v. William D. Ruckelshaus, Administrator, and United States Environmental Protection Agency, 21 ERC 2153 (N.D. CA. 1984).

Sierra Club v. Lee M. Thomas, Administrator, Environmental Protection Agency, 469 U.S. 1309 (1985).

State Water Control Board v. Train, 424 F.Supp. 146 (E.D. VA. 1976).

Thomas v. Union Carbide Agricultural Products Co., Inc., 473 U.S. 568, 105 S.Ct. 3325, 22 ERC 2033 (1985).

Township of Franklin Sewerage Authority v. Middlesex County Utilities Authority, 787 F.2d 117 (3d Cir. 1986).

Union Carbide Agricultural Products Co., Inc. et al., v. Natural Resources Defense Council et al., 467 U.S. 1219 (1984).

Union Carbide Agricultural Products Co., Inc. et al. v. William D. Ruckelshaus, as Administrator of the United States Environmental Protection Agency, et al., 571 F.Supp. 117 (S.D. NY. 1983).

Union Carbide Agricultural Products Co., Inc. et al. v. William D. Ruckelshaus, as Administrator of the United States Environmental Protection Agency, et al., 19 ERC 2193 (S.D. NY. 1983).

Union Carbide Agricultural Products Co., Inc. et al. v. William D. Ruckelshaus, Administrator, United States Environmental Protection Agency, et al., 21 ERC 1984 (S.D. NY. 1984).

United States v. A&F Materials Co., Inc., 578 F.Supp. 1249, 582 F.Supp. 842 (S.D. IL. 1984).

United States v. Argent Co., 21 ERC 1353, 21 ERC 1353, 21 ERC 1356 (D.C. NM. 1984).

United States v. Bear Marine Services, 509 F.Supp. 710 (E.D. LA. 1980); reversed on other grounds, 696 F.2d 1117 (1st Cir. 1983).

United States v. Carolawn, 14 ELR 20698 (D. SC. 1984).

United States v. Cauffman, 21 ERC 2167 (C.D. CA. 1984).

United States v. Chem-Dyne Co., 572 F.Supp. 802 (S.D. OH. 1983).

United States v. City of Detroit, 476 F.Supp. 512 (E.D. MI. 1979).

United States v. City of Moore, Slip. Op. No. 84 C 618 (W.D. OK. 1984).

United States of America v. Conservation Chemical Co., et al., 619 F.Supp. 162 (W.D. MO. 1985).

United States v. Dickerson et al., 640 F.Supp. 228 (D. MD. 1986).

United States v. El Paso, Civ. No. E-P89 CA. 347 (D.C. W.TX. 1990).

United States v. Hardage, 18 ERC 1685 (W.D. OK. 1982).

United States v. Lebeouf Bros. Towing Co., 621 F.2d 787 (5th Cir. 1980); cert. denied, 452 U.S. 906 (1981).

United States v. Maryland Bank and Trust, 632 F.Supp. 573 (D.C. MD. 1986).

United States v. Metropolitan District Commission, 23 ERC 1350 (D. MA. 1985).

United States v. Miami Drum Services, Inc., 25 ERC 1469 (S.D. FL. 1986).

United States v. Mirable, 14 ELR 20992 (E.D. PA. 1985).

United States v. M/V Big Sam, 681 F.2d 432 (5th Cir. 1982).

United States of America v. Northeastern Pharmaceutical and Chemical Co., Inc. et al., 579 F.Supp. 823 (W.D. MO. 1984); Affirmed in part, reversed in part and remanded (1986).

United States v. Northernaire Plating Co., 670 F.Supp. 742 (W.D. MI. 1987).

United States v. Ottati & Goss, 23 ERC 1733 (D. NH. 1984).

United States v. Price, 577 F.Supp. 1103 (D. NJ. 1983).

United States v. Reilly Tar, 546 F.Supp. 1100 (D. MN. 1982).

United States v. Seymour Recycling Corp., 618 F.Supp. 1 (S.D. IN. 1984).

United States of America et al. v. South Carolina Recycling and Disposal, Inc. et al., 653 F.Supp. 984 (D. SC. 1984).

United States v. Standard, 49 Bankr. 623 (D. CO. 1985).

United States v. Tex-Tow, 589 F.2d 1310 (7th Cir. 1978).

United States v. Tyson, 25 ERC 1897 (E.D. PA. 1986).

United States v. Vertack Chemical Corp., 489 F.Supp. 870 (E.D. AR. 1980).

United States v. Ward, 618 F.Supp. 884 (E.D. NC. 1985).

United States v. Waste Ind., 734 F.2d 159 (4th Cir. 1984).

United States v. Western Processing, 751 F.Supp. 902 (W.D. WA. 1990).

United States Department of Energy v. Ohio, 112 S.Ct. 1627 (1992).

Wheaton Industries v. EPA, 781 F.2d 354 (1986).

Yannacone et al. v. Dennison et al., 285 N.Y.S.2d 476 (1967).

Statutes

The Administrative Procedure Act, 5 U.S.C. 551 et seq., 60 Stat. 237 (1946); amended by 80 Stat. 378 (1966); 81 Stat. 54 (1967); 88 Stat. 1561 (1974); 90 Stat. 1241, 2721 (1976); and 92 Stat. 183, 1225 (1978).

Asbestos Hazard Emergency Response Act (Title III of the Toxic Substances Control Act), 20 U.S.C. 4011 et seq., PL 99-579, 1986.

The Clean Air Act, 42 U.S.C. 7401 et seq., PL 88-206; as amended by the Motor Vehicle Air Pollution Control Act, PL 89-272, October 20, 1965; the Clean Air Act Amendments of 1966, PL 89-675, October 15, 1966; the Air Quality Act of 1967, PL 90-148, November 21, 1967; the Clean Air Amendments of 1970, PL 91-604, December 31, 1970; the Comprehensive Health Manpower Training Act of 1971, PL 92-157, November 18, 1971; PL 93-15, April 9, 1973; the Energy Supply and

Environmental Coordination Act of 1974, PL 93-319, June 22, 1974; Clean Air Act Amendments of 1977, PL 95-95, August 7, 1977; Safe Drinking Water Act of 1977, PL 95-190, November 16, 1977; Health Services Research, Health Statistics, and Health Care Technology Act of 1978, PL 95-623, November 9, 1978; PL 96-209, March 14, 1980; PL 96-300, July 2, 1980; PL 97-23, July 17, 1981; PL 97-375, December 21, 1982; PL 98-45, July 12, 1983; PL 98-213, December 8, 1983; and PL 101-549, November 15, 1990.

The Clean Water Act, PL 92-500, October 18, 1972; amended by PL 93-207, December 28, 1973; PL 93-243, January 2, 1974; PL 93-592, January 2, 1975; PL 93-238, March 23, 1976; PL 94-273, April 21, 1976; PL 94-558, October 19, 1976; PL 95-217, December 28, 1977; PL 95-576, November 2, 1978; PL 96-148, December 16, 1979; PL 96-478 and PL 96-483, October 21, 1980; PL 96-561, December 22, 1980; PL 97-35, April 2, 1982; PL 97-216, July 18, 1982; PL 97-272, September 30, 1982; PL 97-440, January 8, 1983; PL 98-45, July 12, 1983; PL 98-623, November 8, 1984; PL 99-396, August 27, 1986; PL 100-4, February 4, 1987; PL 101-340, July 31, 1990.

The Comprehensive Environmental Response, Compensation and Liability Act, 94 Stat. 2767, 42 U.S.C. 9601 et seq., PL 96-510, December 11, 1980; as amended by PL 96-561, December 22, 1980; PL 97-216, July 18, 1982; PL 97-272, September 30, 1982; PL 98-45, July 12, 1983; PL 98-80, August 23, 1983; PL 98-369, July 18, 1984; PL 98-371, July 18, 1984; PL 98-396, August 22, 1984; PL 99-499, October 17, 1986; PL 101-508, November 5, 1990; PL 101-584, November 15, 1990; PL 102-426, October 19, 1992; and PL 102-484, October 23, 1992.

The Emergency Planning and Community Right-to-Know Act (Title III of the Superfund Amendments and Reauthorization Act of 1986), 42 U.S.C. 11001 et seq., PL 99-499, October 17, 1986.

The Federal Facilities Compliance Act, 106 Stat. 1550; PL 386, October 6, 1992.

The Federal Insecticide, Fungicide and Rodenticide Act, 7 U.S.C. section 135 et seq.; as amended by PL 92-516, October 21, 1972; PL 94-140, November 28, 1975; PL 95-396, September 30, 1978; PL 96-539, December 17, 1980; PL 98-201, December 2, 1983; PL 98-620, November 8, 1984; PL 100-532, October 25, 1988; PL 101-624, November 28, 1990; and PL 102-237; December 13, 1991.

The National Environmental Policy Act, 42 U.S.C. 432 et seq.; as amended by PL 94-52, July 3, 1975; and PL 994-83, August 9, 1975.

The Resource Conservation and Recovery Act, PL 94-580, October 21, 1976; as amended by the Quiet Communities Act of 1978, PL 95-609;

234 *Bibliography*

the Solid Waste Disposal Act of 1980, PL 96-482; the Used Oil Recycling Act of 1980, PL 96-463; the Comprehensive Environmental Response, Compensation and Liability Act of 1980, PL 96-510; PL 97-272, September 30, 1982; PL 98-45, July 12, 1983; the 1984 Hazardous and Solid Waste Amendments, PL 98-616, November 9, 1984; PL 99-160, November 25, 1985; PL 99-339, June 19, 1986; and PL 99-499, October 17, 1986.

The Safe Drinking Water Act, PL 93-523, December 16, 1974; as amended by PL 94-317, June 23, 1976; PL 94-484, October 12, 1976; PL 95-190, November 16, 1977; PL 96-63, September 6, 1979; PL 96-502, December 5, 1980; PL 98-620, November 8, 1984; and PL 99-339, June 19, 1986.

The Toxic Substances Control Act, PL 94-469, October 11, 1976; amended by PL 97-129, December 29, 1981; PL 98-80, August 23, 1983; PL 98-620, November 8, 1984; and PL 99-519, October 22, 1986; PL 100-551, October 28, 1988; PL 100-368, July 18, 1988; PL 101-637, November 28, 1990; and PL 102-550, October 28, 1992.

Public Documents

EPA Reports and Documents

Environmental Protection Agency. *Case Studies of Successful Actions Taken under the National Municipal Policy (Draft).* Washington, D.C.: Environmental Protection Agency, 1985.

———. *Consolidated DDT Hearing, Opinion of Examiner Sweeney.* Washington, D.C.: Environmental Protection Agency, 1972.

———. *Consolidated DDT Hearing, Opinion and Order of the Administrator.* Washington, D.C.: Environmental Protection Agency, 1972.

———. *Continuing State Registration of Products Containing Aldrin and Dieldrin for which Uses Have Been Suspended.* Washington, D.C.: Environmental Protection Agency, January 10, 1975.

———. *FIFRA Compliance/Enforcement Manual.* Washington, D.C.: Government Printing Office, 1983.

———. *FIFRA Confidential Business Information Security Manual.* Washington, D.C.: Government Printing Office, 1982.

———. *Fiscal Year 1984, EPA Budget Summary.* Washington, D.C.: Government Printing Office, 1983.

———. *In re: Aldrin/Dieldrin: Order of the Administrator.* Washington, D.C.: Environmental Protection Agency, August 2, 1974.

———. *In re: Shell Chemical: Report of the Hearing Examiner.* Washington, D.C.: Environmental Protection Agency, 1974.

————. *A Management Review of the Superfund Program.* Washington, D.C.: Environmental Protection Agency, May, 1989.

————. *PCB Interim Measures Program.* Washington, D.C.: Environmental Protection Agency, August, 1981.

————. *Press Release,* March 26, 1991.

————. *Reasons Underlying the Registration Decisions Concerning Products Containing DDT, 2,4,5-T, Aldrin and Dieldrin, before the Environmental Protection Agency.* Washington, D.C.: Government Printing Office, March, 1971.

————. *TSCA Annual Report to Congress.* Washington, D.C.: Environmental Protection Agency, 1983.

Westat, Inc., for the U.S. Environmental Protection Agency, *National Survey of Hazardous Waste Generators and Treatment, Storage and Disposal Facilities Regulated under RCRA in 1981.* Washington, D.C.: Government Printing Office, April, 1984.

Federal Register

38 Fed. Reg. 24344 (1973); 40 Fed. Reg. 11990 (1975); 40 Fed. Reg. 59566 (1975); 41 Fed. Reg. 23577 (1976); 41 Fed. Reg. 28402 (1976); 44 Fed. Reg. 31514 (1979); 44 Fed. Reg. 42246 (1979); 44 Fed. Reg. 68624 (1979); 44 Fed. Reg. 76738 (1979); 45 Fed. Reg. 168 (1980); 45 Fed. Reg. 15542 (1980); 45 Fed. Reg. 33066 (1980); 45 Fed. Reg. 33156 (1980); 46 Fed. Reg. 16090 (1981); 46 Fed. Reg. 16096 (1981); 46 Fed. Reg. 27615 (1981); 46 Fed. Reg. 27617 (1981); 46 Fed. Reg. 27619 (1981); 46 Fed. Reg. 38318 (1981); 46 Fed. Reg. 58345 (1981); 47 Fed. Reg. 5864 (1982); 47 Fed. Reg. 8304 (1982); 47 Fed. Reg. 8307 (1982); 47 Fed. Reg. 9350 (1982); 47 Fed. Reg. 9352 (1982); 47 Fed. Reg. 9356 (1982); 47 Fed. Reg. 13174 (1982); 47 Fed. Reg. 15706 (1982); 47 Fed. Reg. 15720 (1982); 47 Fed. Reg. 17426 (1982); 47 Fed. Reg. 27516 (1982); 47 Fed. Reg. 32274 (1982); 47 Fed. Reg. 37342 (1982); 47 Fed. Reg. 46980 (1982); 47 Fed. Reg. 58023 (1982); 47 Fed. Reg. 58025 (1982); 47 Fed. Reg. 58029 (1982); 47 Fed. Reg. 58031 (1982); 48 Fed. Reg. 2775 (1983); 48 Fed. Reg. 4467 (1983); 48 Fed. Reg. 15076 (1983); 48 Fed. Reg. 34000 (1983); 48 Fed. Reg. 45502 (1983); 48 Fed. Reg. 47892 (1983); 48 Fed. Reg. 50486 (1983); 48 Fed. Reg. 52402 (1983); 48 Fed. Reg. 52507 (1983); 49 Fed. Reg. 3832 (1984); 49 Fed. Reg. 16388 (1984); 49 Fed. Reg. 20138 (1984); 49 Fed. Reg. 20238 (1984); 49 Fed. Reg. 21870 (1984); 49 Fed. Reg. 24330 (1984); 49 Fed. Reg. 28154 (1984); 49 Fed. Reg. 29625 (1984); 49 Fed. Reg. 30884 (1984); 49 Fed. Reg. 33695 (1984); 49 Fed. Reg. 42165 (1984); 49 Fed. Reg. 43906 (1984); 49 Fed. Reg. 43915 (1984); 49 Fed. Reg. 43916 (1984); 49 Fed. Reg. 44634 (1984); 49 Fed. Reg. 44878 (1984); 49 Fed. Reg.

45292 (1984); 49 Fed. Reg. 45502 (1984); 49 Fed. Reg. 50408 (1984); 50 Fed. Reg. 974 (1985); 50 Fed. Reg. 5190 (1985); 50 Fed. Reg. 5421 (1985); 50 Fed. Reg. 5862 (1985); 50 Fed. Reg. 7268 (1985); 50 Fed. Reg. 7280 (1985); 50 Fed. Reg. 15386 (1985); 50 Fed. Reg. 19312 (1985); 50 Fed. Reg. 20164 (1985); 50 Fed. Reg. 20166 (1985); 50 Fed. Reg. 26444 (1985); 50 Fed. Reg. 27892 (1985); 50 Fed. Reg. 29170 (1985); 50 Fed. Reg. 36446 (1985); 50 Fed. Reg. 42216 (1985); 50 Fed. Reg. 47142 (1985); 50 Fed. Reg. 47156 (1985); 50 Fed. Reg. 51683 (1985); 51 Fed. Reg. 6468 (1986); 51 Fed. Reg. 6929 (1986); 51 Fed. Reg. 11396 (1986); 51 Fed. Reg. 23706 (1986); 51 Fed. Reg. 41331 (1986); 51 Fed. Reg. 47241 (1986); 52 Fed. Reg. 12662 (1987); 52 Fed. Reg. 19895 (1987); 52 Fed. Reg. 21516 (1987); 52 Fed. Reg. 24504 (1987); 52 Fed. Reg. 25838 (1987); 52 Fed. Reg. 31445 (1987); 52 Fed. Reg. 42522 (1987); 52 Fed. Reg. 48638 (1987); 53 Fed. Reg. 10403 (1988); 53 Fed. Reg. 24206 (1988); 53 Fed. Reg. 37082 (1988); 53 Fed. Reg. 37212 (1988); 53 Fed. Reg. 39786 (1988); 53 Fed. Reg. 43322 (1988); 53 Fed. Reg. 51273 (1988); 54 Fed. Reg. 9612 (1989); 54 Fed. Reg. 51654 (1989); 55 Fed. Reg. 8666 (1990); 56 Fed. Reg. 6339 (1991); 56 Fed. Reg. 10524 (1991); 56 Fed. Reg. 17980 (1991); 56 Fed. Reg. 18735 (1991); 56 Fed. Reg. 37196 (1991); 57 Fed. Reg. 31714 (1992); 57 Fed. Reg. 54127 (1992); 57 Fed. Reg. 60848 (1992); 57 Fed. Reg. 62573 (1992); 58 Fed. Reg. 1667 (1993); 58 Fed. Reg. 4902 (1993); 58 Fed. Reg. 8245 (1993); 58 Fed. Reg. 15014 (1993); 58 Fed. Reg. 15422 (1993).

Congressional Hearings

Chemicals and Food, Senate Committee on Environment and Public Works, Subcommittee on Toxic Substances, Environmental Oversight, Research and Development, 101st Cong., 1st sess., September 22, 1989.

Costle, Douglas. "Statement of Douglas Costle." *Implementation of the Federal Water Pollution Control Act: Hearings before the Subcommittee on Oversight and Review of the House Committee on Public Works and Transportation,* 97th Cong., 2d sess., 1980.

The Extent and Impact of Mercury Releases and Other Pollutants at the Department of Energy's Oak Ridge Complex at Oak Ridge, Tennessee, House Committee on Science and Technology, 98th Cong., 1st sess., 1983, H. Rept. 558.

Implementation of the Clean Water Act (A Case Study of Lawmaking by Rulemakers), House Public Works and Transportation Subcommittee on Investigation and Oversight, 97th Cong., 2d sess., December 5, 1982.

OMB Review of EPA Regulations: Hearing before a Subcommittee on Oversight and Investigations of the House Committee on Energy and Commerce, 99th Cong., 2d sess., 1986.

Oversight of the Office of Management and Budget Regulatory Review and Planning Process: Hearing before a Subcommittee on Intergovernmental Relations of the Senate Committee on Governmental Affairs, 99th Cong., 2d sess., January 28, 1986.

Reauthorization of Superfund, House Public Works and Transportation Subcommittee on Water Resources, 99th Cong., 1st sess., 1985.

Miscellaneous

The Cadmus Group. *Testing Consent Order Policy Study, Phase I,* October 19, 1988.

—————. *Testing Consent Order Policy Study, Phase II,* May 3, 1989.

123 *Cong. Rec.* S. 19647–48 (daily ed. December 15, 1977).

126 *Cong. Rec.* H. 11787 (December 3, 1980).

126 *Cong. Rec.* S. 14964, H. 11787, H. 11799 (November 24, 1980).

Council on Environmental Quality. *Second Annual Report of the Council on Environmental Quality.* Washington, D.C.: Government Printing Office, August, 1971.

Executive Office of the President, Office of Management and Budget. Bulletin 86-4. Washington, D.C.: Government Printing Office, 1985.

—————. *Regulatory Program of the United States Government, April 1, 1986–March 31, 1987.* Washington, D.C.: Government Printing Office, 1986.

Executive Order 12088.

Executive Order 12146.

Executive Order 12291.

Executive Order 12498.

General Accounting Office. *Cleaning Up Hazardous Wastes: An Overview of Superfund Reauthorization Issues.* Washington, D.C.: Government Printing Office, 1985.

—————. *Department of Energy Acting to Control Hazardous Wastes at Its Savannah River Nuclear Facilities.* Report No. GAO/RCED-85-23. Washington, D.C.: Government Printing Office, 1985.

—————. *Environmental, Economic and Political Issues Impede Potomac River Cleanup Efforts.* Washington, D.C.: Government Printing Office, January 6, 1982.

—————. *EPA Implementation of Selected Aspects of the Toxic Substances Control Act.* Washington, D.C.: Government Printing Office, December 7, 1982.

—————. *Hazardous Waste: Federal Civil Agencies Slow to Comply with*

Regulatory Requirements. Report No. GAO/RCED-86-76. Washington, D.C.: Government Printing Office, 1986.

———. *Hazardous Waste: Responsible Party Clean Up Efforts Require Improved Oversight.* Washington, D.C.: Government Printing Office, 1986.

National Academy of Sciences. *Drinking Water and Health: Report to Congress.* Washington, D.C.: National Academy of Sciences, June 20, 1977.

National Cancer Institute, Division of Cancer Cause and Prevention. *Report on the Carcinogenesis Bioassay of Chloroform.* Washington, D.C.: National Cancer Institute, March 1, 1976.

Office of Federal Register. *The United States Government Manual.* Washington, D.C.: Government Printing Office, 1991–1992.

Office of Technology Assessment. *Are We Cleaning Up? Ten Superfund Case Studies.* Washington, D.C.: Government Printing Office, 1988.

———. *Superfund Strategy.* Washington, D.C.: Government Printing Office, 1985.

S. Rept. 95-370 at 56. Reprinted in *U.S. Code Cong. & Ad. News* (1977): 4380.

Letters and Memoranda

Abramson, Stanley H., EPA associate general counsel for pesticides and toxic substances. Memorandum to Edwin L. Johnson, director of the EPA Office of Pesticide Programs, May 13, 1983, archived at EPA headquarters, Washington, D.C.

Barnes, A. James, EPA acting general counsel. Memorandum to Pasquale A. Alberico, acting director, EPA Office of Federal Activities, June 22, 1983, archived at EPA headquarters, Washington, D.C.

Cannon, Jonathan Z., EPA acting assistant administrator, EPA Office of Solid Waste and Emergency Response, and Richard E. Sanderson, director of the EPA Office of Federal Activities, to Leo Duffy, DOE special assistant to the secretary for coordination of DOE waste management, July 14, 1989, archived at EPA headquarters, Washington, D.C.

Cannon, Joseph A., EPA acting associate administrator for policy and resource management. Memorandum to EPA Administrator Anne M. Gorsuch, December 18, 1982, archived at EPA headquarters, Washington, D.C.

————, Assistant Administrator, EPA Office of Air and Radiation. Memorandum to director, Air and Waste Management Divisions, Regions II–IV, VI–VIII, X and director, Air Management Divisions, Regions I, V, IX, May 15, 1984, archived at EPA headquarters, Washington, D.C.

Conroy, A. E., II, director, EPA Pesticides and Toxic Substances Enforcement Division. Memorandum, "PCB Interim Measures Program," August, 1981, archived at EPA headquarters, Washington, D.C.

————, director, EPA Pesticides and Toxic Substances Enforcement Division. Memorandum to regional enforcement directors and branch chiefs, November 11, 1980, archived at EPA headquarters, Washington, D.C.

Elder, James R., director, EPA Office of Water Enforcement & Permits. Memorandum to Water Management Division directors, September 22, 1987, archived at EPA headquarters, Washington, D.C.

EPA General Counsel's Office. Memorandum, "Model Administrative Order on Consent for Private Party Conduct of RI/FS," January 31, 1985, archived at EPA headquarters, Washington, D.C.

Finamore, Barbara A., attorney, Natural Resources Defense Council; Jane L. Bloom, attorney, Natural Resources Defense Council; and Gary A. Davis, attorney, Legal Environmental Assistance Foundation. Letter to William Ruckelshaus, EPA administrator, June 14, 1985, archived at EPA headquarters, Washington, D.C.

Ginsberg, Douglas, administrator for information and regulatory affairs, Executive Office of the President, Office of Management and Budget. Letter to the administrator of the Environmental Protection Agency, April 26, 1985, archived at EPA headquarters, Washington, D.C.

Ginsberg, Eric, EPA Office of Air Quality Planning and Standards. Memorandum, November 19, 1984, archived at EPA headquarters, Washington, D.C.

Greenleigh, Stephen H., assistant general counsel for environment, Department of Energy. Letter to James A. Rogers, EPA associate general counsel, November 14, 1980, archived at EPA headquarters, Washington, D.C.

Hodel, Donald Paul, secretary of the Department of Energy, and William Ruckelshaus, administrator of the EPA. "Memorandum of Understanding on Responsibilities for Hazardous and Radioactive Mixed Waste Management," February 22, 1984, archived at EPA headquarters, Washington, D.C.

Lucero, Gene A., director, EPA Office of Waste Programs Enforcement. Memorandum, "Delegation of Authority to Issue Demand Letters," March 8, 1984, archived at EPA headquarters, Washington, D.C.

————, director, EPA Office of Waste Programs Enforcement. Memorandum, "Procedures for Issuing Notice Letters," October 12, 1984, archived at EPA headquarters, Washington, D.C.

————, director, EPA Office of Waste Programs Enforcement, and Kirk Sniff, associate enforcement counsel for waste, EPA Office of Enforcement and Compliance Monitoring. Memorandum to EPA regional offices, January 16, 1984, archived at EPA headquarters, Washington, D.C.

————, EPA director, Office of Waste Programs Enforcement, and Kirk F. Sniff, associate enforcement counsel for waste. Memorandum, "Releasing Identities of Potentially Responsible Parties in Response to FOIA Requests," January 26, 1984, archived at EPA headquarters, Washington, D.C.

Muir, Warren (Dr.), EPA. Letter to Natural Resources Defense Council, April, 1979, archived at EPA headquarters, Washington, D.C.

Olson, Theodore B., assistant attorney general for legal counsel, Department of Justice. Memorandum to F. Henry Habicht III, assistant attorney general for land and natural resources, Department of Justice, February 9, 1983, archived at U.S. Department of Justice, Washington, D.C.

Porter, J. Winston, assistant administrator, EPA Office of Solid Waste and Emergency Response. Memorandum to regional administrators, January 25, 1988, archived at EPA headquarters, Washington, D.C.

————, assistant administrator, EPA Office of Solid Waste and Emergency Response. Memorandum to regional administrators, March 24, 1988, archived at EPA headquarters, Washington, D.C.

Rogers, William D., attorney, Shell Oil Company. Letter to Russell Train, EPA administrator, April 16, 1974, archived at EPA headquarters, Washington, D.C.

Sniff, Kirk F., EPA acting associate enforcement counsel for waste. Memorandum to regional counsels, August 3, 1983, archived at EPA headquarters, Washington, D.C.

Todhunter, John A., EPA assistant administrator for pesticides and toxic substances. Memorandum to Anne M. Burford, EPA administrator, January, 1983, archived at EPA headquarters, Washington, D.C.

Unterberger, Glenn L., EPA associate enforcement counsel for water. Memorandum to regional counsels, August 27, 1985, archived at EPA headquarters, Washington, D.C.

General Index

Index of Cases